DATE DUE			
Jul 7'82			

A Guidebook for Teaching
LITERATURE

A Guidebook for Teaching LITERATURE

RAYMOND J. RODRIGUES
University of Utah

DENNIS BADACZEWSKI
Northern Michigan University

Allyn and Bacon, Inc.   **Boston • London • Sydney**

This book is part of A GUIDEBOOK FOR TEACHING Series

Library of Congress Cataloging in Publication Data

Rodrigues, Raymond J., 1938–
  A guidebook for teaching literature.

  Includes bibliographies.
  1. Literature—Study and teaching (Secondary)
I. Badaczewski, Dennis, 1943–   joint author.
II. Title.
PN59.R58   807'.12   77-18918
ISBN 0-205-06068-4

10 9 8 7 6 5 4 3   85 84 83 82 81 80

About the authors

Raymond J. Rodrigues received his M.A. from Rutgers University and his Ph.D. from the University of New Mexico. Co-author of six anthologies of high school literature, Dr. Rodrigues also lists among his professional accomplishments: past president of the Southern Nevada Teachers of English, president of the Utah Council of Teachers of English, Associate Professor at the University of Utah, and member of the National Council of Teachers of English Committee on Classroom Practices in the Teaching of English and the Commission of the English Language.

Dennis Badaczewski received his M.A. from Eastern Michigan University and his Ed.D. from the University of Kansas. A consultant for over thirty school districts, Dr. Badaczewski has written for several journals including *English Education, Education Digest,* and *Classroom Practices in Teaching English.* He has held the positions of Associate Professor of Education and Coordinator of Secondary Education at Wright State University and is currently Associate Professor of Education at Northern Michigan University.

Gene Stanford (Consulting Editor) received his Ph.D. and his M.A. from the University of Colorado. Among his numerous professional affiliations are: Associate Professor of Education and Director of Teacher Education Programs at Utica College of Syracuse University, member of the National Council of Teachers of English, and member of the International Council on Education for Teaching. Dr. Stanford is the author of several books, among them, *A GUIDEBOOK FOR TEACHING COMPOSITION, A GUIDEBOOK FOR TEACHING CREATIVE WRITING, A GUIDEBOOK FOR TEACHING ABOUT THE ENGLISH LANGUAGE,* and *HUMAN INTERACTION IN EDUCATION,* all published by Allyn and Bacon, Inc.

Contents

Preface

How can I make the study of literature more interesting? Can the basic skills of reading, writing, listening, speaking, and thinking be taught while students are studying literature? Where can I find a collection of activities relating to literature from which I can select those most appropriate for my classes? What can I do to make my literature classes better?—In this book we attempt to answer these questions.

We believe the following:

1. All classes are not alike.

2. Ultimately, only teachers can decide which specific activities are best for their classes.

3. What works best for one teacher or class may not succeed with another teacher or class.

4. Students must be involved personally with literature.

5. The teacher must not be the sole arbiter of literary taste.

6. True involvement with literature results from approaching it from many different perspectives.

7. Many different activities can achieve the same ends, just as one activity can lead to many ends.

Therefore, we have provided new and traditional activities, grouped into general categories, aimed at developing the student's personal response to literature in ways that improve the other language skills. In addition, we have included lists of other resources to supplement this book.

Chapter 1 considers the main options available to the teacher. Drama activities appear next, for we believe that creative drama must be a central feature of the English classroom. The other chapters are grouped by genre, as well as "non-literary" literature—those forms that influence our thinking. In the final chapter, we suggest ways to plan a literature program, prepare for potential censorship issues, and conduct informal in-class research.

Recent changes in teaching literature include more media studies, expanded ways to respond to literature, skills training that integrates all aspects of language, an increased concern for human values, and an increase in female and ethnic authors in anthologies. If literature is to speak to us and to our students, we must be actively involved with it. Such involvement takes many forms: drama activities, games, writing, discussions, individual speeches, and creative efforts such as film production or drawing.

If this is the good fight, this involvement with life through literature, let us not give it up though the pressures be great to do so. Question the person who accuses us of not teaching the basics when we are actively bringing students into contact with literature. Question our own behavior when we allow ourselves to consider the literature itself to be more important than the interaction between the reader and literature. And, be forever willing to try new approaches.

The decisions that teachers must make have to be carried out in the classroom, not in this book. Toward that end, this book hopefully will serve as a valuable source for ideas and materials. If so, then the teaching of literature will have been served.

We wish particularly to thank Gene Stanford, Utica College, for his support and direction during the production of this book. In addition, although we cannot possibly list them all, we confess our debt to our students, those both in the secondary schools and in our methods classes, and to our colleagues whose writings and ideas have helped shape our writing and ideas. Special thanks go to our families for their tolerance.

Finally, some word about the division of labors of the authors. Raymond Rodrigues was primarily responsible for the discussion and activities in chapters 1–3 and 5–8, as well as the resources for chapter 3. Dennis Badaczewski was primarily responsible for the discussion and activities in chapter 4 and the resources in chapters 1, 2, and 4–8.

Raymond J. Rodrigues
Dennis Badaczewski

1

Getting Started: Organizing for Literature Study

Literature study has been the traditional mainstay of English teaching in the public schools since the late nineteenth century. The literature curriculum in those days emphasized literary history, biographies of authors, and literary criticism; and such works as *Silas Marner* and *Julius Caesar* were studied by all students. Since that time, literature teaching has not changed so much as it has grown in depth and scope. In 1917, the National Council of Teachers of English and National Education Association "Committee of Seventeen" concluded that the English class was to prepare students for life, not simply for college; but, at the same time, the committee considered the study of classical literature essential for the student. In 1935 the idea of the "Experience Curriculum" was introduced, emphasizing the social value of the English class and the importance of students' experiences to that class. Teachers began to teach literature in arrangements by patterns, themes, and ideas.

In 1958, the Basic Issues Conference of the National Council of Teachers of English, the Modern Language Association, the American Studies Association, and the College English Association specified the tripartite nature of English studies: literature, language, and composition. The Conference also helped stress the importance of English curriculum being sequential and cumulative. In 1966, the Anglo-American Seminar on the Teaching of English (more commonly known as the Dartmouth Conference) enabled teachers from England and the United States to compare notes. One primary conclusion of the conference was that English classes should help students grow as individuals and that the strong emphasis in U.S. schools upon literary analysis did not always enable such growth to occur. In the decade following that conference, diversity became characteristic of English classes. Drama activities, games, inductive learning, and an untold number of specialized classes organized around some literary scheme or skills orientation (typified by the mini-course, most commonly a course of one marking period's duration) proliferated in the schools. One could hardly tell whether any two secondary English departments ever taught the same thing. Then, in the mid-1970s, teachers began to question the value of what they had been teaching for the past ten years.

1

PURPOSES OF THIS BOOK

What choices are available to the English teacher in teaching literature? Where should the beginning teacher begin? If the experienced teacher is considering a change in curricular structure, what options are available? These are a few of the key questions this book hopes to answer. One of the basic underlying premises of the book is that it is impossible to generalize about the best approach for any given class: That is the teacher's decision, for only the teacher knows the characteristics of a given class and the particular needs of the students. The purposes of this book are to provide basic introductions to each of the options available to the teacher, to specify potential objectives students may meet through the study within each option, to provide a variety of teaching strategies for the teacher, to suggest ways of evaluating student growth within the limits of the particular option, and to suggest both print and nonprint materials available for both the students and the teacher.

OBJECTIVES FOR THE TEACHER

After reading this chapter, the teacher should be able to:
1. Specify a rationale for teaching literature.
2. Identify ways to group literature for teaching.
3. Select methods of individualizing student learning.

RATIONALES FOR TEACHING LITERATURE

As with so many other aspects of the language arts program, specifying what should be taught in any particular class is something this book cannot pretend to do. However, English teachers should at least be able to justify their teaching of literature, the selections they employ, and the methods they adopt. Teaching literature simply because that is what English teachers do is not justification enough.

Cultural Heritage

One reason for teaching literature is to enable students to be aware of their cultural heritage. As a result, schools have established such courses as American literature or English literature or some variation of these. Two approaches are used most often: the chronological and the thematic. The chronological approach is perhaps more systematic than the thematic and may be related to historical events and movements as well as to philosophical developments. The thematic approach may enable students to perceive universals throughout historical periods and to develop a sense of today's indebtedness to the past or differences from its thinking and attitudes. The cultural-heritage approach also may be overly selective and culturally biased, ignoring some of the various ethnic backgrounds of the students. Does the class curriculum include the African, Asian, or American Indian heritages? In general, the greatest weakness of the cultural-heritage approach is that it often fails to involve the students with the literature.

Rhetorical Modeling

A second reason for teaching literature is to use the literature for rhetorical modeling or language development. Students are encouraged to develop an awareness of style and to improve their flexibility in employing language by having more linguistic tools to use. Some teachers have been extremely successful in using this approach with selected students. The primary weakness is that many students are not sophisticated readers and are therefore unable to detect nuances of style or any stylistic shifts except the most obvious ones. Rather than assume that students will automatically learn to write and speak better after studying literature, teachers should structure exercises that direct students to rhetorical techniques in the literature they read and enable them to practice such techniques. Most writers change their style when their purpose changes and when they are overtly aware of the influence their word and syntactic choices will have upon the reader. Undoubtedly, the more individuals read, the greater the possibility that they may be aware of stylistic effects. But oral and written composition exercises, not merely reading and discussing the literature, must be employed to improve students' rhetorical skills.

Individual Development

A third justification for studying literature is to stimulate ideas. Therefore, the activities listed in this book are primarily designed to involve students as active learners. Fourth, literature study will help individuals achieve a sense of self-identity and clarify their values. This is an important outcome, one that will grow out of involvement with the literature, the very personal act of relating literature to oneself. And fifth, literature study provides readers with vicarious experiences they may not, and sometimes should not, otherwise acquire. In the hands of a skillful teacher, all aims may be accomplished with at least some success. Furthermore, these reasons are applicable in any structural situation.

Invalid Assumptions

Still, there are teacher assumptions about literature teaching that have little or no validity. One is that all students will react the same way to a given literary selection. The same teacher who maintains that all individuals are different often fails to see the implications of that statement for the language arts class. Thus, we sometimes find the same classes reading the same text at the same time and being expected to respond in identical ways to any particular work. Student reading levels, interests, values, and motivations vary so widely that requiring all students to read the same work at the same time and rate will not provide equal results except on a factual level. However, when the teacher wants to emphasize a particular writing technique or to use literature as a model for skills training, this approach may be the most efficient.

Another assumption with little validity is that all individuals must be exposed to specific works—the "classics" approach. Therefore, even though the United States does not have a national curriculum and even though parents and teachers will fight to maintain the right of the local community to decide what is of worth educationally for its students, we still find almost all students reading not just Shakespeare, but very specific works of his: *Hamlet, Macbeth, Julius Caesar,* or a combination of these are typical fare in most high schools throughout the nation. Do teachers question their being taught at all, or do they simply assume that since they have "always" been taught they should continue to be? The "classics" approach is directly related to the cultural-heritage approach, and it suffers the same drawbacks.

Cautions and Weak Approaches

Teachers must relate the literature teaching to the students' interests and goals as well as to the teacher's reasons for including literature in the curriculum at all. Can a teacher presume to be developing evaluative criteria for judging literature (and the media) in the students if he cannot justify the selection of any particular literature?

Stressing factual information only causes students to view literature as an obstacle— something to be "learned" rather than experienced. By asking students to interpret litera- ture, to relate the literature to their lives, and to allow their own imaginations to range widely into areas even vaguely suggested by the literature, the teacher enables students to perceive literature as meaningful to them as individuals, not as an artifact of the educational monolith. The Dartmouth Conference made many of us aware of the many ways in which students may respond to literature. For a more in-depth study of literature response models, read:

> Dixon, John. *Growth Through English.* Reading, England: National Association for the Teach- ing of English, 1967.

> Moffett, James. *A Student-Centered Language Arts Curriculum: Grades K–13.* Boston: Houghton Mifflin, 1968.
> Moffett describes a sequential, integrated program which involves students with language and literature in an active fashion.

> Purves, Alan C. *The Elements of Writing about a Literary Work: A Study of Response to Literature.* Champaign, Ill.: NCTE, 1968.
> This study may help the teacher realize all the possible variables which may influence the students. This is an important study for its consideration of reading habits, patterns of interest, and student differences. See also: *Literature Education in Ten Countries* by Purves. New York: Wiley, 1973.

Another weakness in teaching literature is the concentration upon analytic terms at the expense of the literature itself. In this approach, students learn poetry, for instance, to memorize such terms as simile, metaphor, rhyme scheme, or onomatopoeia. This is not to say that knowing such terms may not help the student to discuss literature, but too often learning the terms becomes the sole end of the poetry study. The knowledge of literary terms ought to result from a need-to-know situation. Such a situation may be developed in a creative-writing experience. Students who have attempted to write poems or short stories are much more aware of the techniques available to an author and how well the author succeeds with such techniques than are students who must memorize words they have no need for. Is it more worthwhile to know that Shakespeare personifies time in his sonnets or to consider his attitudes toward time and how meaningful those attitudes are to the reader?

In addition, using literary techniques creatively must not be limited to those students who are the most mature readers or the best memorizers. Kenneth Koch, in his book *Wishes, Lies, and Dreams,* provides substantial evidence that elementary students can manipulate literary techniques with great facility.[1] His techniques can easily be adapted for use in the secondary classroom. For more specific examples of techniques such as Koch suggests, see Chapter 5, "Teaching Poetry."

Methods to study literature are many, and surely enterprising teachers will employ a variety in their classrooms: class discussions, group discussions, one-to-one discussions, role playing, dramatization of scenes, media presentations, interest or value surveys, creative writing, literary reviews, oral interpretations, and so on. Variety is a spice and, more to the point, provides the student with glimpses of literature from widely divergent points of reference.

Students will respond to literature if they can experience literature in new and varied ways. Not all students will respond in the same manner, nor should the teacher expect them to. Variety in the techniques employed by the teacher should stimulate not only the students, but also the teacher, thus creating a cycle that is positive and cumulative.

DECIDING HOW TO GROUP THE LITERATURE FOR TEACHING

Each particular way of grouping literature enables students to gain special insights into literature and into themselves that other ways of grouping may not promote as well. Therefore, it is not very worthwhile to argue whether any one approach is the best approach, for each has its good and bad aspects. Seven of the most common ways of organizing literature for study are:

1. organization by genre
2. organization by chronology
3. organization by theme
4. organization by topic
5. organization for rhetorical awareness
6. study of a single text in depth
7. organization by correlation

Organization by Genre

Literature has historically been grouped by genre for a number of reasons. First, it is a natural way of organizing literature, for it enables literature to be studied according to the particular conventions of the genre. Second, the history of literature supports the generic organization in that different genres developed at different times and for special reasons, some relating to the mechanical process of reproducing the literature and some relating to

---

1. Kenneth Koch, *Wishes, Lies, and Dreams* (New York: Chelsea House, 1970).

the particular demands of the literature-consuming public. Third, the concept of treating genres as distinct types has been promoted by book publishers, who found that they could appeal to particular groups of readers by organizing works according to genre.

For the teacher, the advantages of teaching by genre include the following:

1. The study of genres facilitates the process of literary analysis in that the same criteria can be applied to all works within the genre.

2. The teacher can increase students' motivation to read literature by eliminating genres that happen to be less appealing to students at the moment.

3. The students can improve evaluative judgments by comparing and contrasting genres.

Several disadvantages result from classifying literature by genre. For instance, students may begin to view literature study as the study of literary characteristics rather than of the consideration of ideas, aesthetic enjoyment, or ways of gaining greater insight into oneself and others. In addition, the special insight a poem may give as a result of metaphoric manipulation of language may never be revealed if the student concentrates upon prose alone. The same may be said about all the genres. Topics and themes of identical nature are to be found in all genres. Teachers should enable students to realize how each particular genre adds a special dimension to the perception of a subject or theme.

If the teacher's purpose is to teach the unique characteristics of a given genre in order to encourage students to read more within the genre or to develop the students' abilities to evaluate and value that genre, then the development of genre studies is justified.

Organization by Chronology

One of the basic reasons given for education in any society is that it preserves and passes on culture. In that respect, the study of literature based upon a chronological pattern is essential at some time during the education of the individual. Through studying literature chronologically, the student can become more aware of the heritage which has somehow brought us to the point where we are today.

For the teacher, the advantages of teaching literature chronologically include the following:

1. The development of literary technique can be explained.

2. The heritage of the student is laid out in an orderly fashion.

3. The influences of history—including the history of language as well as of politics—can be related to the literature of the time, and vice versa.

4. The potential for involving all of the humanities exists, for music and other art forms can be correlated with the literature.

The disadvantages of teaching literature chronologically include:

1. Earlier literature is much harder for students to read than most contemporary

literature. One way around this problem is to have students start with the modern age in their chronological study, but they still have to read the older literature at some point.

2. Teachers often feel a compulsion to "get through" the literature. ("Here it is spring and I'm only starting the Victorian era.") As a result, they rush through the selections with little consideration for the value of studying a work in depth or branching out on tangents that may excite and involve the students.

3. Often the literature that is selected ignores the input of minority groups to the nation as a whole. Because the work of minorities was often ignored in the past, only the literature and viewpoints of the dominant groups are available to us.

4. The longer the period of time covered in the chronological course, the less depth and breadth can be given to any particular period of time.

If the teacher wants students to develop a sense of literary history and thus be more aware of heritage, and if the teacher realizes that the student's sense of literary history may be skewed by the circumstances of both class time and historical selection, then the chronological approach would be of potential worth.

Organization by Theme

By far the most popular way of organizing literature study in recent years has been the thematic organization. A direct outgrowth of study by theme is the mini-course, typically a well-developed unit that may be organized in any of the ways we are talking about but that most often is thematic in basic format.

Among the advantages of organization by theme are the following:

1. Themes are found in all types of literature. The teachers can mix poems, short stories, novels, plays, essays, and all the other genres in a way that stresses the basic concern of many different authors for the same themes. The opportunities for comparing many different approaches to the same theme are very great and challenging.

2. The teacher can select themes that will appeal to the students. Sometimes students are so concerned with their own personal problems that they fail to see the relevance of literary study. But the problems of youth have been the problems of humanity for generations, and a careful selection of literature, both classical and modern, will reveal that to students.

3. Because so-called ancient literature (the nineteenth century for many students) has been concerned with problems that apply to today, that literature becomes meaningful to students today, and therefore students approach the literature seriously and do not reject it as irrelevant ancient history.

4. Because themes appeal to the students if the themes are selected with that relevance in mind, students can be encouraged to read further on their own, and thus the curriculum has more potential for individualizing.

The disadvantages of organization by theme include:

1. When works are put into a unit based upon one theme, students may leave that unit believing that only one theme is present in any given work. This would be a great disservice to the literary work and to the author. The teacher should thus not be afraid to allow discussions of particular works within given thematic units to take whatever apt course they may in class.

2. Finding published materials that fit a theme the teacher or students may want to study can often be difficult. While publishers produce numerous anthologies based upon themes, those themes may not be appropriate for a given class at all times. Therefore, the teacher will either have to select classroom anthologies with an eye to wide application or work hard at gathering the appropriate materials.

3. If students are constantly exposed to thematic studies of literature, they may not develop evaluative criteria for particular genres or have a historical awareness of their literary heritage. An alert teacher can keep students in touch with those aspects as literature is studied by theme, but doing so systematically is difficult and may work against the interest generated by the specific nature of the theme.

Before deciding to teach literature by theme, the teacher must weigh the advantages of developing high student interest against the disadvantages of not treating aspects of literature traditionally covered in English classes.

However, a well-balanced secondary curriculum can prevent such disadvantages from happening. After all, no one English class is the total curriculum of a school.

Organization by Topic

Topical organization is very similar to thematic organization in that a great many diverse selections can be gathered under one heading. The topical organization differs from the thematic organization in its breadth of coverage. A topic is broader than a theme, encompassing many selections in a format that may be more loose than the thematic approach

The advantages of teaching by topical organization include:

1. Rather than having to be certain that the selections relate closely, as one would have to do in the thematic organization, the teacher can select particular works simply because they illustrate the topic, not because they are necessarily comparable. For instance, a topic could deal with "war" or "satire" or "modern man" or even with something as vague as "ways of communicating." In essence, a topic is a label that is broad enough to encompass much literature.

2. Topics can be adjusted fairly easily and rapidly to match the sometimes ephemeral interests of students. Current events may spark a particular interest in students and thus eliminate the need to motivate interest in the subject. Fads may also lend themselves to such self-motivation.

3. Like the thematic approach, topics enable students and teachers to compare and contrast works of widely varying nature.

4. Topics can be studied even when the students of a particular class and school and community are interested in something that no one else may be interested in. For instance, a historical pageant in a given town or a local tradition can easily become an umbrella topic for the study of literature.

The disadvantages of teaching according to topic are similar to those for teaching thematically. Particular weaknesses of the topical approach include:

1. The structure is often so loose that comparisons of the works for the purposes of studying authors' crafts or the relationships of ideas may not be easy to make.

2. The few anthologies published with topics as the organizing structure offer little additional information and few structured exercises that will develop students' abilities and appreciation. The editors may not be able to predict why the teacher has chosen a particular topic.

3. The unique value of a given selection may be subverted in an attempt to consider it as another element of the topic. Teachers must not lose sight of the intrinsic value of any given selection.

In general, the topical arrangement may be so appealing to teachers that they select it without any further consideration of the reasons for teaching literature. In an attempt to find material that will motivate students, teachers may be willing to ignore more important, long-range reasons for studying literature. Nevertheless, having a group of students highly motivated by a topic of current interest may be the first step toward involving them more deeply with literature.

Organization for Rhetorical Awareness

In contrast to the thematic approach, organizing literature study for developing rhetorical awareness is one of the least-used approaches. Wayne C. Booth, in *Toward a New Rhetoric*, noted that rhetoric encompasses the possible arguments about a given subject, awareness of the intended audience, and the voice or stance of the writer.[2] Since a student needs to develop the encoding skills of speaking and writing, and since the tendency to treat works of literature as literature and not as models of communication skills is common in schools, employing literature for rhetorical awareness is highly productive.

The advantages of the rhetorical-awareness approach include:

1. Literature, writing, and speaking are closely tied to one another. Through the study of literature, the student develops communication skills.

2. The student is in contact with appropriate models of communication that the student can then employ in writing. Instead of treating writing as a separate activity, the teacher presents to the students an integrated approach.

3. As rhetoric is reflected in the literature, students become more aware of the tech-

---

2. Wayne C. Booth, *Toward a New Rhetoric* (Champaign, Ill.: NCTE, 1963).

niques authors employ to communicate their message, to influence a particular audience, and to "pretend" to be a particular character when they write.

The difficulties of teaching literature for rhetorical awareness may be summarized by the word "difficulty."

1. Finding models that are most appropriate for the given intellectual level and needs of the students is time-consuming, often frustrating work. Literature anthologies are seldom organized for rhetorical study, and those that are may be of a higher reading level than students can handle.

2. An additional difficulty is that the unit must be highly structured or the skills illustrated by a given literary selection may be missed.

3. The humanistic value of literary study may be sacrificed in an attempt to teach writing skills. Themes, feelings, exploratory applications, and individual inclinations may be ignored or passed over rapidly.

4. Finally, the teacher must be certain that all of the students can profit from the study of the particular rhetorical devices. Some students may be more mature than others, and the less mature students may not comprehend why the literature is being read or may develop an unneeded dislike for literature.

It would seem, then, that studying literature for its rhetorical modeling would be a sound approach, for it combines both receptive and productive training. Nevertheless, if the teacher is concerned with motivating students and wants students to leave school viewing literature as something enjoyable, both intellectually and aesthetically, then it might be best to sacrifice the rhetorical study of literature to the need to develop the students' affective skills. Perhaps that is why this organizational format has typically been reserved for more advanced students, and even then as an elective.

Study of a Single Text in Depth

Studying a single text is clearly not an approach that may be used for an entire year, but the "great-books" approach is one way of studying single texts for a year. Typically, though, teachers select this method for single instances scattered rather sparingly throughout the year. The study of Shakespeare, for instance, exemplifies the single-text study in depth. We ought not to look at this approach as involving only one selection, however, for conceivably other works may be brought into play by the teacher to draw contrasts, to extend particular aspects of the work under consideration, and to add depth to understanding.

Among the advantages a teacher ought to consider before deciding whether to choose the single-text approach are these:

1. Students do not have to rush through their reading trying to get as much out of the way as soon as possible. This approach demands that students consider carefully the text as they read. Many other activities will fill out the time besides the reading itself.

2. The variety of classroom activities available to the teacher and students can make

this form of literature study extremely appealing to students in many ways. For example, guest speakers can be brought in; films relating to the work can be shown; individual projects in reading, speaking, and writing can develop from the study; and any aspect of the work can be studied in detail.

3. The multiplicity of awareness and skills that potentially can result from such study should intrigue and challenge the most conscientious teacher. Rhetorical modeling, historical awareness, humanistic considerations, involvement with the humanities, and all the elements of literary appreciation are possible.

4. Individual students can approach the work from angles that appeal to them most. Individualization is very possible.

The disadvantages of studying a single text in depth may be easily overcome, but they should not be ignored when deciding whether to employ this strategy.

1. Perhaps the greatest possible danger of studying one text in depth is that students may lose interest in, become bored with, and actually learn to hate, the work in question. Therefore, both timing and the exact amount of depth needed—depth that does not involve all aspects of the work or all the possible explorations—may be advisable considerations.

2. If all the students are always doing the same thing with the work, then individualization is lost and opportunities for greater understanding may not result.

3. Spending all of the class time with the text itself may be self-defeating, for the study may become tedious for both teacher and student.

The in-depth study of a single work, chosen after careful consideration on the teacher's part and planned with variety as a key factor, offers a great deal to students and may be quite rewarding for the teacher. The study of a single text, poorly planned, too highly structured, and extended beyond the staying power of the students, can end up being a disaster

Organization by Correlation

Correlating literature with another subject is growing in prominence despite the objections of many English teachers who are disturbed by the idea of subjugating literature to another discipline. The proponents of correlation claim that the organization strengthens rather than subjugates all the subjects involved.

The greatest impetus for correlation has grown out of the core curriculum in junior high school. In most core programs, the same teacher conducts a double period for both language arts and social studies. Large units or topics are chosen from the realm of social studies, and the literature is related to the unit or topic. A ninth-grade unit on "Problems of Black Americans" might include *Black Like Me, Blues for Mr. Charlie, Native Son*, and *The Autobiography of Malcolm X.*

On the senior high level, English has typically been correlated with history. In this type of arrangement, the English part of the course is usually taught chronologically, as most history courses are. When history is taught by units, the literature, as in the core program, is related to the unit topic. The degree of correlation varies. In some instances, the same teacher has a group of students for both English and history. In other schools, English and history are team-taught. More loosely organized systems have separate classes, but the teachers plan together or keep each other informed about where they are.

A newer approach to correlation is the humanities program. Several schools have melded literature, social studies, art, and music into a unified, interdisciplinary program. The National Endowment for the Humanities (NEH), through grants, consultants, materials, or moral support, has provided much of the impetus for this concept. The NEH offers summer scholarships for teachers interested in teaching in humanities programs. It also publishes relatively inexpensive print and nonprint materials suitable for classroom use.

The advantages of correlation are many. The primary advantage for the student is that the student can begin to comprehend the interrelationship of events and actions. Walt Whitman becomes a writer who experienced and responded to the Civil War, not merely a person who wrote poetry. By correlating English and social studies or history classes, both classes are reinforced. Students reading *The Red Badge of Courage* in English while studying the Civil War in American history will probably gain a better understanding of both. In humanities programs, students are able to see the interrelationship of all artistic endeavors. According to this point of view, the art, the music, and the literature of a particular period cannot be divorced from the social and historical background of the works. An incidental advantage is the opportunity to work with other teachers in a professional, cooperative setting.

Objections to correlation come from three directions. First, English can become the handmaiden of social studies or history. Often literary selections must be chosen to fit a particular social theme or historical event. Second, especially for humanities programs, the cost of correlation may be more than a given school district is willing to pay. Assistance from the NEH and the recent introduction of inexpensive materials by publishers may help alleviate this problem. The final disadvantage is related to team teaching and cooperative planning. If some team members are unwilling to assume their full share of planning and teaching or others try to dominate those areas, the students will lose. However, it may stimulate students to see their teachers disagreeing about interpretation in an inquiring, intellectually stimulating manner and may encourage them to realize that, yes, there may be more than one correct viewpoint. Then, the development of thinking skills can only benefit.

DECIDING HOW TO INDIVIDUALIZE

Many beginning teachers believe that individualized instruction is better than nonindividualized instruction. However, once they are faced with an actual class, they allow certain other concerns to override their stated belief in individualized instruction. For example, they are concerned with control and discipline; they believe or they know that they must cover a specified body of content; they learn that not all students are highly motivated; and they are overwhelmed by the quantity of work required to teach a class.

Actually, *individualized* instruction does not mean that individual exercises must be specially prepared for each student. Nor does individualization always have to go on in a classroom. To illustrate the many different levels of individualizing, Robert C. Small, Jr.

and Alan M. McLeod, writing in *English Education*, developed fifteen different levels of individualization in English.[3]

1. *Great Wisdom by General Lecture*   The student is perceived as an empty bottle into whom knowledge must be poured quickly and, if necessary, by force.

   - *Examples:*   Teacher lecture on the life of E. A. Poe as an introduction to his works. Teacher analysis of an essay as an example of a "good" composition. Teacher lecture on the parts of speech as an illustration of how language functions.

   - *Degree of Individualization:*   Zero except as the teacher stops to answer student questions (see 4 below).

2. *Great Wisdom by General Activities*   Still an empty bottle needing contents, the student is induced to accept a predetermined content through classroom activities which are based on the belief that people learn by doing rather than by listening. What is done, however, is the conception of the teacher alone.

   - *Examples:*   Class completion of a crossword puzzle based on *Silas Marner*. Writing and distribution of a newspaper giving the characters and events of *Julius Caesar*. Class dramatization of scenes from *A Tale of Two Cities*.

   - *Degree of Individualization:*   Minimal for the majority unless the class has unusual commonality of interests and abilities and those conform to the activities the teacher designs.

3. *Use of General Adolescent Characteristics*   The particular students are seen as embodiments of most or all of the characteristics of "the American Adolescent." Materials and activities are chosen because research supports the belief that they will appeal to the generalized student.

   - *Examples:*   Study by the entire class of a teenage mystery novel. Playing of word baseball using automotive terms as the vocabulary. Examining the requirements of various occupations.

   - *Degree of Individualization:*   Some, since materials and approaches are based on the nature of adolescents, but limited by the fact that many students will not fit the generalized mold and that learning must take place in a class setting.

4. *Attention to Individual Concerns*   Although materials and activities are designed for the class as a whole, students' individual problems, knowledge, interests, etc. are given attention by the teacher insofar as she can determine them and find time for them.

   - *Examples:*   Repeating an explanation when a student requests it. Encouraging a student to report to the class on a subject of special interest to him. Having conferences after school with a student who needs special tutoring.

---

3. Robert C. Small, Jr. and Alan M. McLeod, "Promoting Individualization in English," *English Education* 5 (1974), 84–89. Copyright © 1974 by the National Council of Teachers of English. Reprinted by permission of the publisher and the authors.

- *Degree of Individualization:* Usually minimal because the pressure of time and numbers and the class setting limit a teacher's ability to individualize in this unplanned way.

5. *Assigned Group Work: No Choice*   Students are divided into small groups (5 or 6 students) to work on a common project assigned by the teacher.

   - *Examples:* Development of a biographical portrait of Hester Prynne. Reading and discussion by students of each other's compositions. Preparation of a dictionary of sports terms.

   - *Degree of Individualization:* Minimal unless the teacher has unusual insight into each student's interests and abilities.

6. *Programmed Instruction*   The student is expected to learn a certain set body of knowledge and in the same way as all other students, but the rate of his learning is individualized.

   - *Examples:* SRA Reading Laboratories. Paul Robert's *English Syntax* or Blumenthal's *English 2600.* Computer Assisted Instruction.

   - *Degree of Individualization:* Moderate if rate is the main problem students are having with the content of the course; otherwise minimal.

7. *Assigned Group Work: Choice*   Students divide themselves into small groups by choosing which of the projects developed by the teacher each wishes to pursue.

   - *Examples:* A choice of developing a biographical portrait of Hester Prynne, building a model scaffold, or writing a short story about what happens to Pearl when the story ends. Reading and discussion by students of each other's compositions. A choice of preparing a dictionary of sports terms, recording local idiomatic expressions, or comparing the jargon of different occupations such as truck drivers, waitresses, cooks, etc.

   - *Degree of Individualization:* Moderate, but limited by the forced choice among a few projects and the need to work in a group setting.

8. *Assigned Individual Work*   The student is assigned homework and classwork for his individual completion (see also number 12).

   - *Examples:* Writing of a composition on a topic of his choice or keeping a personal journal. Completing fifteen sentences dealing with infinitives. Preparing an oral report on the American Indian as background to *The Light in the Forest* or *When the Legends Die.*

   - *Degree of Individualization:* Moderate if the assignments are made with care; otherwise minimal.

9. *Contracting*   The student is presented with several items to fulfill during a unit. Acceptable performance on what he selects determines his grade. For example, items for an "A". The contract criteria are determined by the teacher rather than the student. (Student determination of contract items is discussed in number 12 below.)

   - *Degree of Individualization:* Moderate in that the student has choice and can in part bend the assignment toward his capability and interest, but limited in that the student's choices are controlled by the teacher's original decisions.

10. *Elective Units: Limited*   Each student is given an opportunity to select from a list those units he wishes to study, selection being limited to a certain number from each of several categories of units.

  • *Examples:* Selection of at least one language, one composition, and two literature semesters and completion of the rest of high school career with any of the remaining units.

  • *Degree of Individualization:* May be considerable depending on the nature, number, and variety of units available, but limited by the requirement of choice from categories, the teachers' willingness and ability to offer suitable units, and the need to work in a class setting.

11. *Elective Units: Unlimited*   Same as above except that students are free to select any unit which interests them.

  • *Examples:* Selection of a unit on the literature of sports from ten units offered. Selection of a course in individualized reading. Selection of a course in creative writing. Selection of a course in theories of English syntax.

  • *Degree of Individualization:* Considerable, but limited by the teachers' willingness to offer units of interest to students, by a possible lack of attention to the students' capacities, and by the need to work in a class setting.

12. *Free Group Work*   Students are divided into small groups and work on a common project which they decide upon, possibly within some broad area. The students as a group, or even individually, might construct a contract obligating them to do certain things. The teacher might make suggested modifications, but the group or individual would still basically determine the contract.

  • *Examples:* Decision by a group of boys to examine the picture of baseball in sports literature. Decision by a group of five students to tape examples of various American dialects.

  • *Degree of Individualization:* Large; limited only by compromises within the group.

13. *Free Individual Work: Restricted Field*   The student selects an individual project in English, prepares a proposal, submits it for approval, and completes the project. The student may work within a class or be enrolled in independent study.

  • *Examples:* An examination of the view of life expressed in the plays of selected theater-of-the-absurd playwrights. A semester-long, individualized reading program.

  • *Degree of Individualization:* Nearly complete; but limited by the need to do some kind of project in a certain school subject such as English.

14. *Free Individual Work: Unrestricted Field*   The student selects an individual project on anything of interest to him, prepares a proposal, submits it for approval, and completes the project.

- *Examples:* Building a rocket engine. Writing a play. Painting a portrait of the principal.

- *Degree of Individualization:* Nearly complete; limited only by the need to do some kind of project.

15. *Unrestricted, Unguided* The student does whatever he wants, however he wants, and whenever he wants; or he does nothing at all.

- *Examples:* Attending any class that suits the student's whim, spending one day a week at museums, working in the local hospital, etc. Polishing a piece of bark for the entire year. Spending all day, every day, in the science laboratory.

- *Degree of Individualization:* Complete; limited only by the danger that the student may accomplish nothing which he wants to accomplish because of a lack of direction.

The following books, while limited in number, should give the teacher some firm direction in developing individualized programs:

Boston, R. E. *How to Write and Use Performance Objectives to Individualize Instruction,* vols. 1–4. Englewood Cliffs, N.J.: Educational Technology Publications, 1972.
 For those teachers who are increasingly being held accountable for results in their classrooms, this book is an important addition to their library.

Doll, R. C., ed. *Individualizing Instruction,* 1964 Yearbook. Washington, D.C.: NEA, 1964.
 This series of essays lays out a number of varied approaches to the subject.

Dunn, R., and Dunn, K. *Educator's Self-Teaching Guide to Individualized Instructional Programs.* West Nyack, N.Y.: Parker, 1975.
 Defining, designing, supervising, and evaluating individual learning programs are clearly explained here.

Gallagher, J. J. *Teaching the Gifted Child.* Boston: Allyn & Bacon, 1975.
 The characteristics of gifted students, identifying them, and planning for their education are clearly specified by Gallagher.

Kaplan, S. N., et al. *Change for Children; Ideas and Activities for Individualizing Learning.* Pacific Palisades, Calif.: Goodyear Publishing Co., 1973.
 The book contains good, practical ideas which can be adapted by the teacher.

Wilson, J. A. R., ed. *Diagnosis of Learning Difficulties.* New York: McGraw-Hill, 1973.
 This is an area that many teachers must take into account. The advice herein is sound.

English Journal 64 (4), April 1975.
 Most of this issue is devoted to specific practices in the English classroom.

The activities contained in this book vary widely in their degrees of individualization. Teachers planning to use them should select those that offer the amount of individualization needed to provide students with the most effective learning experiences.

A statement that occurs several times in this book is a variation of the following: Only the teacher can know the students in an actual classroom; only the teacher, often with the overt suggestions of the students, can select the activities that will benefit the students most. So let the literature class be a place where variety, involvement, and excitement reign and where time-wasting rote learning is confined to the lower depths.

Exhilaration is the Breeze
That lifts us from the Ground
And leaves us in another place
Whose statement is not found—

Returns us not, but after time
We soberly descend
A little newer for the term
Upon Enchanted Ground—
Emily Dickinson[4]

A SELECTED BIBLIOGRAPHY FOR THE TEACHER OF LITERATURE

The following list, while not all-inclusive, is selected to provide the English teacher with a broad view of the profession. Each of the authors offers a different way of viewing the process of teaching literature, and each book can add to the store of ideas of the teacher.

Print

Bergman, Floyd L. *The English Teacher's Activities Handbook.* Boston: Allyn & Bacon, 1976.
This book consists entirely of 1,001 activities to use in class, 250 of which are devoted to literature. All activities are cross-referenced in the index.

Bleich, David. *Readings and Feelings/Response to Literature.* Urbana, Ill.: NCTE, 1975.
Subjective response to literature is explored. In particular, includes discussion of student responses to *Vanity Fair*, Robert Frost's poetry, and Katherine Mansfield's and D. H. Lawrence's short stories.

Burton, Dwight L. *Literature Study in the High Schools.* 3d ed. New York: Holt, Rinehart & Winston, 1970.
Burton discusses the development of literature curriculum, the study of genres, writing, and literature of interest to adolescents.

Carlsen, G. Robert. *Books and the Teenage Reader.* New York: Bantam Books, 1971.

Annotated bibliographies of materials suitable for the adolescent reader and discussions of such materials provide the teacher with information for selection of literature for the curriculum.

Crosby, Muriel, ed. *Reading Ladders for Human Development.* 4th ed. Washington, D.C.: American Council on Education, 1964.
Basically an extensive annotated list of books for students to read, the book begins with worthwhile suggestions on the teaching of literature.

Danziger, M. K., and Johnson, W. S. *An Introduction to Literary Criticism.* Boston: D. C. Heath, 1961.
This work summarizes definitions of literature, explanations of technical terms, analytic techniques, traditions and conventions, and evaluative criteria. Essays by prominent critics add to the work.

Dodds, Barbara. *Negro Literature for High School Students.* Champaign, Ill.: NCTE, 1968.
Dodds surveys the work of major black authors, includes biographies, and comments on the value and reading level of specific selections.

Donelson, Kenneth, ed. "Adolescent Literature, Adolescent Reading and the English Class." *Arizona English Bulletin* 14, 1972.
Practical articles about teaching, critiques of specific works, and good bibliographies help the teacher develop curricula for this very popular area.

---

4. Copyright 1914, 1942 by Martha Dickinson Bianchi. From *The Complete Poems of Emily Dickinson*, edited by Thomas H. Johnson, by permission of Little, Brown and Co. Reprinted by permission of the publishers and the Trustees of Amherst College from *The Poems of Emily Dickinson*, Harvard University Press, Copyright © 1951, 1955 by the President and Fellows of Harvard College.

____. "Popular Culture and the Teaching of English." *Arizona English Bulletin* 17, 1975.

The area of literature is vastly expanded in this very practical publication: comics, science fiction, ballads, detective stories, graffiti, old radio shows, and much, much more.

Dunning, Stephen, and Howes, Alan B. *Literature for Adolescents.* Glenview, Ill.: Scott, Foresman, 1975.

Dunning and Howes treat the study of short stories, novels, plays, and poetry through basic principles and specific examples of the genre. In addition, they discuss the relationship of reading and writing to the literature program.

Fader, Daniel, and McNeil, Elton. *Hooked on Books: Program and Proof.* New York: Putman & Sons, 1968.

This book is now virtually a classic—concerned with motivating students to read by exposing them to a great variety of materials.

Fagan, Edward R. *Field: A Process for Teaching Literature.* University Park, Pa: Pennsylvania State Univ. Press, 1964.

Fagan applies James C. Maxwell's field theory to the teaching of literature. He emphasizes the need to consider the "levels of perspective students bring to the classroom in their experiences with symbols."

Guerin, Wilfred L.; Labor, Earl G.; Morgan, Lee; and Willingham, John R. *A Handbook of Critical Approaches to Literature.* New York: Harper & Row, 1966.

This handbook summarizes such critical approaches as the formalistic, psychological, archetypal, exponential, historical, moral, and linguistic.

Hipple, Theodore W. *Teaching English in Secondary Schools.* New York: Macmillan, 1973.

The chapters on literature study are concerned with planning, purposes, structure, evaluation, values, and several specific problems. One chapter treats the literature of blacks. An annotated list of books for the English teacher is valuable.

Hoetker, James. *Dramatics and the Teaching of Literature.* Champaign, Ill.: NCTE, 1969.

Hoetker explains how creative dramatics provides a new way to develop the critical skills of students and their aesthetic appreciations.

Jenkinson, Edward B., and Daghlian, Philip B., eds. *Teaching Literature in Grades Ten through Twelve.* Bloomington, Ind.: Indiana Univ. Press, 1968.

The book treats teaching poetry, short stories, dramas, and novels in grades ten, eleven, and twelve. It is essentially a series of justified lessons.

Judy, Stephen N. *Explorations in the Teaching of Secondary English.* New York: Dodd, Mead, 1974.

The subtitle proclaims this a "source book for experimental teaching." Two chapters specifically treat literature, but all the activities stress involvement of the students with their studies.

Loban, Walter; Ryan, Margaret; and Squire, James R. *Teaching Language and Literature.* 2d ed. New York: Harcourt, Brace & World, 1969.

Chapters 10, 11, and 12 treat literature, with units on Macbeth and humanities, good comments on evaluation, and a plan for teaching poetry inductively. The bibliography is quite extensive.

McGuire, Richard L. *Passionate Attention.* New York: Norton, 1973.

The author discusses criticism from a practical perspective, not criticism from a theoretical perspective: not "Is the work good or bad?" but "Why and how does it do what it does?"

O'Neal, Robert, ed. *Teacher's Guide to World Literature for the High School.* Champaign, Ill.: NCTE, 1966.

This is an extensively annotated review of over 200 works by authors from around the world. It should expand the depth of the literature taught in our classes through suggestions for thematic units and authors' biographies.

Parker, Robert P., Jr., and Daly, Maxine E. *Teaching English in the Secondary School.* New York: The Free Press, 1973.

While the primary emphasis of the book is not literature study, it does treat literature in a realistic way. The authors are clearly experienced with inner-city problems and relate the teaching of literature to those problems.

Perrine, Laurence. *Literature: Structure, Sound, and Sense.* 2d ed. New York: Harcourt Brace Jovanovich, 1974.

Containing critical discussion of the elements of short stories, poetry, and drama, followed by clear examples, the text enables the teacher to relate specific aspects of literature study to the teaching of specific works.

Pilgrim, Geneva H., and McAllister, Marianna K. *Books, Young People, and Reading Guidance.* 2d ed. New York: Harper & Row, 1968.

The authors relate the interests, needs, and development of young readers to specific activities in guiding adolescents through books.

Purves, Alan C. *How Porcupines Make Love.* Lexington, Mass.: Xerox College Publishing, 1972.
A good selection of ideas for the teacher willing to be innovative.

Reeves, Ruth. *Ideas for Teaching English.* Urbana, Ill.: NCTE, 1966.
The junior high and middle school teacher will find a number of good suggestions for teaching literature in this looseleaf binder.

Rosenblatt, Louise. *Literature as Exploration.* New York: Noble & Noble, 1968.
Rosenblatt explains how to make literature relate to the personal experiences of students. The book is essential reading for the teacher who hopes to develop student response to literature.

Simmons, John S.; Shafer, Robert E.; and West, Gail B. *Decisions about the Teaching of English.* Boston: Allyn & Bacon, 1976.
Chapters 4 and 5 deal with literature specifically. The authors emphasize readiness, reinforcement, the teaching of themes and genres, and specific suggestions for teaching.

Slatoff, Walter J. *With Respect to Readers.* Ithaca, N.Y.: Cornell Univ. Press, 1970.
Slatoff argues against detached criticism and for human involvement with literature. The author and reader are viewed as struggling to meet each other.

Squire, James R., ed. *Response to Literature.* Champaign, Ill.: NCTE, 1968.
This series of essays explains some of the basic principles that grew out of the Dartmouth Conference.

____. *The Teaching of English.* The Seventy-sixth Yearbook of the Society for the Study of Education. Chicago: Univ. of Chicago Press, 1977.
This collection of essays by leaders in the field of English education provides a scholarly, comprehensive introduction to the many aspects of and developments in the field. It should be in every English teacher's library.

Stanford, Gene, and Smith, Marie. *A Guide to Teaching High School Composition.* Boston: Allyn & Bacon, 1977.
Provides teachers with many specific ideas and resources, including performance objectives, mini-lectures, independent projects, and work sheets that can be duplicated for the class.

Wellek, René, and Warren, Austin. *Theory of Literature.* New York: Harcourt, Brace & World, 1956.
An approach to literary criticism, the book discusses both internal and external concepts that may be related to literature study.

Workman, Brook. *Teaching the Decades: A Humanities Approach to American Civilization.* Urbana, Ill.: NCTE, 1975.
A course of inquiry into the nature of U.S. culture. The author includes lesson plans, handouts, term project ideas, ways of extending the curriculum, and an extensive bibliography.

Books By and About Women. Arno Press.
A free 114-page catalogue of books, both old and new, by and about women. An invaluable resource.

Multi-Ethnicity in American Publishing.
A newsletter containing book reviews, editorials, teaching suggestions, and news of interest. To get on mailing list write: Dr. Laverne Gonzalez, English Department, Purdue University, West Lafayette, IN 47907.

1001 Cinematic Voyages. Films, Inc.
A *free* guide written by and for high school teachers. The topics include novels into films and plays into films.

Scriptographic Study Booklets. Channing L. Bete Co.
Clear, concise study booklets that start with a basic definition of the topic and then present key facts about it in step-by-step progression. Charts and line drawings are included. While meant for student use, they could also be used on an opaque projector. Topics include the novel, biographies, essays, drama, mythology, poetry, short stories, and Shakespeare. Excellent beginning guides.

12,000 Students and Their English Teachers. Urbana, Ill.: NCTE, 1968.
This volume contains a number of specific units on literature as well as on language and composition. It is designed for grades 9 to 12.

Nonprint

The American Experience in Literature: The Romantic Age. Encyclopaedia Britannica Educational Corp.
Series of five filmstrips on Poe, Hawthorne, Melville, Thoreau, and Emerson. The programs are seventeen minutes each and available for preview. Very well done.

The Devil in American Literature Series. Cassettes Unlimited.

A series of five filmstrips, cassettes, and quizzes on a popular theme in American literature. Individual titles are: *The Devil Lives Through Witchcraft, The Faust Legend: A Bargain with the Devil, The Devil Arrives on the* Mayflower, *The Devil Comes to Salem Village,* and *The Devil Lives in American Literature.* Available as a set or individually. Excellent for use in a mini-course or unit.

Forms of Literature Series. Guidance Associates.

Six sound filmstrip programs consisting of two filmstrips and two cassettes or tapes each. The programs are: *Drama/Tragedy, Drama/Comedy, Poetry, The Novel, The Short Story,* and *Biography/Autobiography.* Expensive but will be well used. Can be used for genre studies or as an introduction to any of the forms. Available for preview.

Literature Is Alive and Well Series. Cassettes Unlimited.

Series of twelve cassettes, a half hour each, that introduce each major literary genre. Titles are: *Introduction to Prose Fiction, Prose Fiction and Its Forms, The Lottery, The Bear, Introduction to Drama, The Visual Aspects of Drama, Oedipus Rex, Death of a Salesman, Introduction to Poetry, Sights and Sounds of Poetry, Sir Patrick Spence, The Love Song of J. Alfred Prufrock.* Available individually or as a set. Inexpensive.

Themes in Literature Series. Guidance Associates.

Four sound filmstrip programs consisting of two filmstrips and two cassettes or records each. The four themes are love, courage, conscience and the law, and search for self. Excellent for use in mini-courses or as thematic units. Available for preview.

12 Great American Authors Series. Guidance Associates.

Ten sound filmstrip programs consisting of two filmstrips and two cassettes or records each. Programs are: *Edgar Allan Poe; The Private World of Emily Dickinson; Concord: A Nation's Conscience; American Gothic: Hawthorne/Melville; Walt Whitman: An American Original; The World of Mark Twain; The Vision of Stephen Crane; Jack London: A Life of Adventure; Streets, Prairies and Valleys, The Life of Carl Sandburg; Ernest Hemingway the Man.* Superbly done program on American literature. Available for preview.

We Are Indians: American Indian Literature. Guidance Associates.

Illustrates the eloquence of great tribal leaders in depicting life before contact with whites, and the impact of white values and culture on Indian values. A natural for use in native American units. Available for preview.

What Is Satire? Guidance Associates.

Sound filmstrip program consisting of two filmstrips and two cassettes or records. Explores the goals of satire and satiric devices: exaggeration, hyperbole, understatement, parody, caricature, wit, and irony. Examples from Langston Hughes, Jonathan Swift, Philip Wylie, Dorothy Parker, Washington Irving, and Woody Allen. Good for satire unit in either fiction or nonfiction. Available for preview.

Women Writers: Voices of Dissent Series. Cassettes Unlimited.

Series of three filmstrips and cassettes using historic prints, dramatized quotations, and dramatized excerpts to provide a portrait of each writer and her work: *Edith Wharton: The Decadent New York Society, Ellen Glasgow: The Southern Myth,* and *Willa Cather: The Pioneer West.*

2

Teaching Drama

If any one genre receives universal acceptance by students, it is drama. Students may appear to dislike reading poetry or fiction or nonfiction aloud in class, but they usually jump right in when asked to read a play. Unfortunately, this success with drama may have kept drama study from advancing to student involvement with the dramatic process. Plays were never intended to be read cold by groups seated at desks arranged in rows. Dramatists write plays to be performed before audiences by living actors. Happily, students today have had more experience with plays than their parents and grandparents could have had. They have been exposed, although haphazardly, to numerous—some say to innumerable—plays on television and through films. This broad experiential background is a boon to teachers.

Drama study should go beyond the close analysis of plays read from books. James Moffett, in *Drama: What Is Happening*, declared that "Drama is the matrix of all language activities, subsuming speech and engendering the varieties of writing and reading."[1] In "Involving Students in the Drama Process, K–12," Sheila Schwartz explained that there is a difference between drama as subject and drama as process.[2] And Bea Morton, speaking before the Conference on English Education in 1974, argued that "Drama is neither theater, which requires an audience, nor the literary genre of scripted plays. The term is used to refer to specific activities such as pantomime, improvisation, role-playing, dramatic movement and speech, and the dramatization of poems and stories, published and original." Clearly, through its varied interpretations, drama is a means of understanding the world around us, of reacting to that world, and of understanding ourselves.

This chapter offers a variety of approaches to the study of drama, both as subject and as process. The five sections are:

1. creative dramatics

2. analyzing the elements of drama

---

1. James Moffett, *Drama: What Is Happening* (Champaign, Ill.: NCTE, 1967), p. vii.
2. Sheila Schwartz, "Involving Students in the Drama Process, K–12," *English Journal* 63 (May 1974), 32.

3. developing understanding of drama

4. ways to interpret drama

5. the evaluation of drama

The chapter does not suggest any particular sequence to the activities, since the authors see all the elements and approaches as basically interrelated. Only the teacher knows his or her class, and only the teacher can decide which activities are best for the class.

Assuming that students must be actively involved in the dramatic process to respond meaningfully to scripted drama, creative drama appears first, and the following activities depend upon students' willingness to participate in drama activities. An activity may not be successful if students feel threatened by it.

PERFORMANCE OBJECTIVES

As a result of the learning experiences in this chapter, students should be able to:
1. Create dramatic events through pantomime, improvisation, role playing, and writing.
2. Describe or design an appropriate setting for a play.
3. Identify the themes in a scripted play.
4. Summarize and evaluate the plot of a play.
5. Explain the characters' motivations and conflicts.
6. Understand techniques of producing plays.
7. Reinterpret aspects of plays for varying audiences.
8. Evaluate written and acted plays, as well as actors' interpretations of specific roles.

LEARNING EXPERIENCES

CREATIVE DRAMATICS

Creative dramatics is the epitome of drama as a process. Once students have been involved in creative dramatics to the extent that they feel comfortable performing in unique and inventive ways in front of their peers, then you can use the process as both a base and an adjunct to the study and development of all language arts skills and experiences with literature.

However, teachers must realize that not all students are automatically ready for creative dramatics. Secondary students in particular are wary of exposing their feelings before others and tend to be content to sit passively in classes, thus remaining safe from peer scrutiny and possible criticism. Thus, before beginning creative dramatics, you must know your class. What is the composition of the class? Are there more males than females? Do the ethnic groups represented have unique learning styles? Has the class had previous experience with drama? What are the linguistic abilities and emotional maturities of the students? If you know these characteristics, you can structure the creative drama experiences so that they become positive experiences for the students.

Warm-up Exercises

Warm-up exercises serve two important functions. First, they provide a nonthreatening way to begin creative dramatics with students who have never been exposed to the process before. Second, they are necessary before all creative drama exercises. Even professional actors do not perform before warming up. Remember, your students come to you from varying experiences: a math test the previous hour, a hard game in physical education, a fight with a girl friend or boy friend in the hall just before class, a big lunch, or even no lunch. Warm-up activities bridge the gap from such experiences to creative drama.

Although a number of different warm-up exercises are listed below, do not try all of them each time. Vary your choices. Invent new ones and let students suggest others. Spend only a short amount of time on them or they will become tedious and lose their stimulation potential.

1. A good way to begin warm-up exercises with a class for the first time is to seat all the students in one big circle or square and have them face out from the center of the room. In this way, they do not have to look at one another and they can perform the exercises within the relative security of the confines of their desks.

2. Moving their seats into a new arrangement can become a warm-up exercise. Ask the students to imagine that their seats weigh several hundred pounds, or to pretend that they are pushing a heavy load across thin ice or that the seat is a delicate bomb that may explode at any rough jar.

3. Have students close their eyes or cover their eyes so that they cannot see anything. Provide different sounds for them to listen to and then write about. Afterward, discuss what they write. For sound experiences, have the students:

   A. Crumple different types of material—tinfoil, tissue paper, cellophane, stale bread.

   B. Walk across the room in different ways—stamp as if in anger, tiptoe, hop, run out the door.

   C. Use noisemaking objects that range from the common to the exotic—bells of different sizes, wind chimes, willow whistles, rubber ducks, a recording of sandpaper rubbed across a microphone.

   D. Have students create "sound stories": a mystery with someone walking, a shot, a groan and a scream (a scream and a groan?), someone running, a police whistle, more shots, a thud.

   E. Play a brief musical selection and have students write about what it reminds them of.

   F. Make no noise—just listen to the normal, everyday sounds of school.

4. In the early phases of introducing students to creative dramatics, have them perform as a group. Later, move them to groups of two or three, and finally begin individual exercises.

5. To help relax the students, seat them in a circle facing away from the center of the room and direct them to:

A. Roll heads clockwise, then counterclockwise.

B. Raise the left arm up and stretch as high as possible; now do the same with the right arm.

C. Become as small as possible in the chair—scrunch up as much as possible.

D. Become as huge as possible in the chair—expand.

6. With palms together, the students are to place one palm flat on the desk in front of them and the other on top of it. Now reverse the procedure. How many first had the right hand on top? The left? How did it feel when the hands were reversed? Discuss why the feeling might be different.

7. Have all the students stand in a circle facing in one direction. Now have them start walking in a circle while you ask them to pretend the following:

A. You are walking in knee-high snow.

B. Now you are walking barefoot on hot sand.

C. You are carrying one very heavy suitcase.

D. Now you are carrying two very heavy suitcases.

E. Now you put the suitcases down, and you feel as though you weigh only ten pounds—you almost float away.

F. Wearing light clothes, you are caught in a sudden snowstorm and are hurrying to reach a warm building.

8. With students seated in a circle, but facing inward, have them throw an imaginary ball from one to another. Suggest various types of ball: a tennis ball, a football, a basketball, a huge but lightweight beach ball, a medicine ball.

9. In the numerically dominant Anglo-American culture, touch is ordinarily avoided. Secondary students are particularly self-conscious about touching one another. To break down the barriers to touching, have students perform the following exercises in pairs:

A. With arms outstretched, lean against each other, palm to palm. Push hard, but do not move the feet.

B. Standing back to back, link arms and walk around the room.

C. Arm-wrestle.

D. Seated on the floor with backs together, push against each other until you finally push yourselves to a standing position.

10. Create a very small "stage" area by forming the desks into a small circle. The area should be just large enough for the entire class to move around in.

A. Instruct the students to mill around without touching anyone else.

B. Switch to the game Atom Smasher. As the students are milling around, lightly push one of them in a particular direction. That student continues (not recklessly) moving until he or she ricochets off another student, who then continues to "bounce" in the direction propelled. Within a very short time, all the students should be bouncing off one another. (Caution: Do this only when you know your class is under control.)

Pantomimes

From warm-up exercises it is a very small step to pantomimes, which can also serve as warm-ups but which involve more individual performances. Move to this step as soon as you feel that the class has lost its inhibitions (if it ever had any).

1. Play charades. Students act out words, phrases, sayings, famous quotations, and the like, to their teams. The team has to guess the answer within a specified period of time to score a point.

2. In pairs, play mirror images. One student is the mirror; the other is the person before the mirror. The "mirror" has to follow the actions of the "person," but reversed laterally.

3. As individuals, pantomime the following situations before the class:

   A. A woman putting on makeup before a mirror.

   B. A football player getting into his equipment.

   C. A person standing in a shower trying to adjust the water temperature.

   D. A skier going off a jump for the first time.

   E. A space traveler trying to keep liquid in a glass.

4. Have students volunteer to pantomime an involved script that only they know. After each student finishes, the others write down what they believe has happened. The student who did the act judges which student's depiction is the most accurate.

5. Have students pair off and decide upon a set of antonyms, synonyms, or homonyms to pantomine before the class. See if the class can guess them correctly.

6. Have students write down a particular pantomime they would like to see someone perform. Put the slips of paper in a "hat" (box, bag, or whatever is handy) and draw out the pantomimes to be performed.

7. As a class, decide upon a situation to pantomime that would involve many people (the entire class). The situation might be a department store, a scene at the beach, a school-bus stop, or whatever appeals to them. Begin by having one person pantomime a role without telling the others. Each student then joins the mass pantomime with a new creation until the entire class is involved.

Improvisation

Once students have become familiar with pantomimes, improvisation becomes simply pantomime with sound. In improvisation, basic situations are mapped out, but no one know where they will lead. Again, depending upon the readiness of the class, you may want to begin with group improvisations and move to individual or small-group performances.

1. Play machine. In this exercise, you begin with one student performing a simple motion and making a simple sound. Then another student, or machine part, connects to the moving part, and also moves in a simple way and making a simple sound. Each member of the class adds a part to the machine until it becomes one huge machine with many parts and sounds. Instruct the students to close their eyes; when you touch one, he or she is to stop. The moment a student senses that a part has stopped moving, he is to stop. If the machine has been functioning as a unit, the group will have stopped within seconds. If not, some will still be moving when the others have stopped.

2. Play airport. The class outlines a runway with their desks. One student volunteers to be the airplane and is blindfolded at the end of the runway. Another student volunteers to be the air traffic controller who must talk the airplane down. Various obstacles that the blindfolded student cannot see are placed in the path of the airplane. The pair accomplishes their goal if the "plane" can be "talked down" without any part of the "plane" touching any of the obstacles. Do this with different pairs of students. It is a good exercise to use to emphasize the need for clarity when giving directions.

3. The theater of the absurd often puzzles students when they first encounter it. One way to convince them that there may be something to the form is to have them take note of absurdities they see around them or read about in the newspapers. Yet another way is to perform the following improvisations:

   A. Put three chairs in the middle of the room. Ask two students to sit in two of the chairs and carry on a conversation with a "person" in the third chair.

   B. Sit one student facing an empty chair. Have the student talk to the "person" in the empty chair about some problem. Then have the student switch chairs and respond to the problem, continuing until the conversation comes to an end naturally.

   C. Seat two students back to back in two chairs. Have them carry on a conversation without looking at one another. Then have them switch seats. Have one of them talk to the other without the other responding. Then have them switch seats again. Again ask one to talk to the other without the other responding. While that student is talking, motion to the silent student to slip out of the chair without letting the talking student know. After a minute or so, stop the talking student and ask the student how he or she feels about not getting a response; then instruct the student to turn around and again ask how he or she feels.

   D. Conduct a mass absurd-drama exercise by having students draw a particular role out of a "hat" at random and then have all students act out their roles together. Reproduction Page 1 contains a list of roles that can be distributed to students. You may designate a few students simply to be observers without telling them what is happening

ABSURD DRAMA EXERCISE

STAND UP, CLAP YOUR HANDS SLOWLY, AND, EVERY TIME YOU HEAR SOMEONE SAY, "OH, HOW I HATE STUDENTS," SHOUT, "I WAS A STUDENT ONCE!"

COUNT SLOWLY, USING THE NUMBERS *1* THROUGH *10*, BUT MIXING THEM UP, OVER AND OVER.

EVERY TIME YOU HEAR THE NUMBER 5, SHOUT, "OH, HOW I HATE STUDENTS!"

WHENEVER YOU HEAR SOMETHING NEGATIVE SAID, SAY, "OH, THAT'S AWFUL!" GO TO THE PERSON NEAREST YOU AND PAT THAT PERSON ON THE SHOULDER.

IF YOU SEE SOMEONE TOUCH SOMEONE ELSE, SHOUT FOR THE POLICE.

WALK AROUND THE ROOM RECITING ANY POEM THAT YOU CAN REMEMBER. IF YOU CANNOT REMEMBER ONE, MAKE ONE UP.

PRETEND THAT YOU ARE A LARGE CLOCK. WHENEVER YOU HEAR SOMEONE CALL THE POLICE, STRIKE WHATEVER HOUR YOU FEEL LIKE STRIKING.

THERE IS A PERSON SQUATTING IN THE MIDDLE OF THE ROOM. TRY TO SELL THAT PERSON A USED CAR.

YOU ARE A SHOE INSPECTOR. INSPECT THE SHOES OF EVERYONE IN THE ROOM.

YOU ARE TRAPPED IN A HAUNTED HOUSE. TRY TO FIND THE SECRET PASSAGEWAY OUT OF THIS ROOM.

STRIKE UP A CONVERSATION WITH AN EMPTY CHAIR. IF THE CHAIR BORES YOU, MOVE ON TO ANOTHER.

IF YOU SEE SOMEONE TALKING TO A CHAIR, GO SIT IN IT. IF HE STARTS TALKING TO ANOTHER CHAIR, PICK IT UP AND CARRY IT AWAY. IF HE TALKS TO ANOTHER CHAIR, CARRY IT TO THE PERSON WHO IS RECITING A POEM AND ASK THAT PERSON TO RECITE THE POEM TO THE CHAIR. CONTINUE THIS CYCLE AS NECESSARY.

SQUAT IN THE MIDDLE OF THE ROOM. IGNORE ANYTHING THAT IS SAID TO YOU.

YOU ARE A USED CAR. DRIVE AROUND THE ROOM AND FIND THE PERSON WHO IS TRYING TO SELL YOU. TRY TO CONVINCE THE POTENTIAL BUYER THAT YOU REALLY DO NOT WANT TO BE SOLD.

YOU ARE A POLICEMAN. IF SOMEONE CALLS YOU, GO TO THAT PERSON AND FIND OUT WHAT THE PROBLEM IS. TREAT THE PROBLEM IN THE WAY YOU THINK A POLICEMAN WOULD.

4. Have the class create basic situations that can be improvised. Each student writes down one setting, and these are put in a container, to be drawn out at random. Each student writes down one problem to be improvised and puts these into the container. Each student writes down three types of characters to be improvised. Then in groups of three, students draw out one setting, one problem, and three characters. They must try to improvise the result.

5. Divide the class into pairs. One member of one pair is sent out of the room while the other is given a specific task to accomplish: "Make him blush," "Make her laugh," "Make him sad," "Make her angry."

6. At a key point in the reading of a play (or story or poem), stop the class and ask students to volunteer to be the characters involved. Ask them to improvise what they think will occur next.

7. Ask a student to portray a character in a play (or story or poem) the class has been reading. Put that character in an entirely new situation and have the student

improvise how the character will act. For instance, how would Cyrano de Bergerac act on a date in this day and age? How would Huckleberry Finn behave if he were given this assignment? Imagine that the main characters in *Othello* were members of a school board that had to decide whether or not to bus students to achieve racial balance in the schools. How would they behave?

8. Use improvisation to help students who are having difficulties writing plays or short stories. Without telling the students whose creative-writing effort they were improvising, have volunteers improvise the scene from the writing that is giving the writer difficulty. Sometimes fine ideas and dialogue evolve. Tape-record this activity so that the student can review what has happened.

9. Some musical dramas help students improvise. Find a recording of a story that students can act out while the record is playing. They may want to listen to the entire recording before beginning. A couple of good examples are Stravinsky's *L'Histoire du Soldat* and Prokofiev's *Peter and the Wolf*.

10. Whenever students improvise, assign audience members to observe certain aspects of the improvisation and to discuss those afterward: for example, one character's gestures, one character's facial expressions, what characters did when they were not speaking.

11. If a real problem occurs in class, use the improvisational skills of students to work out a solution to the problem through creative drama. Students can portray themselves or, if the problem is too personal, pretend to be others. Be sure that the people who are involved in the problem agree to this procedure first. Consider with the class whether any literature they have read involves a similar problem.

12. Create an award for the most creative or "best" (let the class define this term) improvisation suggested by a student in the past month. Have the class vote at the end of each month.

13. Some plays, such as *Julius Caesar;* novels, such as *To Kill a Mockingbird;* short stories, such as "The Lottery"; or poems, such as "The Ancient Mariner," lend themselves to the creation of improvised courtroom dramas that serve as good reviews. Have the students determine the charges and take roles of the characters from the selection. You also need judges and attorneys; any students left over can be the jury. The actors must maintain the personalities of the characters and stick to the facts as they know them.

Role Playing

Role playing differs from improvisation in that role playing is intended to be serious and the exercise is more fully conceived by students before they proceed with it.

1. Charles R. Duke, in *Creative Dramatics and English Teaching*, establishes a number of cautions and procedures for employing role playing.[3] The serious teacher will read that work before attempting the form. Duke suggests five basic steps:

---

3.   Charles R. Duke, *Creative Dramatics and English Teaching* (Urbana, Ill.: NCTE, 1974), pp. 94–110.

A. Select a problem that is clear, specific, not too complex, and that has good dramatic possibilities.

B. Employ a warm-up period in which the entire class discusses what the facts are to be and what the characters are to be like.

C. When the players are selected, they should not be forced to take part, should not have an emotional involvement with the problem, and should take the assignment seriously.

D. The audience should be prepared by being specifically instructed to watch what occurs and to offer suggestions for alternative actions after the role playing ends.

E. There must be a debriefing session afterward in which the students discuss what happened, make suggestions for a new situation, and possibly repeat the role playing with new participants.

2. If the role-playing experience does not work, consider the possible reasons that Gene Stanford details in "Why Role Playing Fails."[4] 1. The students may not know each other well enough to be comfortable. 2. Secondary students may be self-conscious and afraid to move and touch one another. 3. The students may not have developed the necessary skills. 4. Regardless of prior preparation, students need a warm-up period before beginning role playing. 5. The teacher may not ever intervene to enable the role playing to proceed smoothly. 6. The students may not treat the role playing seriously. Be sure to consider all of these factors before moving to role playing.

Written Drama

1. Encourage students to submit written scripts whenever they want to. Establish an award for the best-written script. Have students be the judges.

2. Make arrangements with the drama teacher to have her or his students act out scripts created in your classes. They can perform before your classes, thus giving them training, or they can act selected scripts at assemblies. Ask the actors to talk about the script from actors' viewpoints.

3. Establish a creative-drama night in which the scripts written in your classes are acted. Have your students take charge of advertising, ticket sales, stage management, makeup, and acting.

4. Have students create their versions of chamber theater, originated by Robert S. Breen and well explained in James Moffett and Betty Jane Wagner's *Student-Centered Language Arts and Reading, K–13*.[5] Chamber theater does not employ a script but does have a narration and directions for the actors. Thornton Wilder's *Our Town* is a well-known example of the technique in popular theater. As an

---

4. Gene Stanford, "Why Role Playing Fails," *English Journal* 63 (December 1974), 50–54.

5. James Moffett and Betty Jane Wagner, *Student-Centered Language Arts and Reading, K–13*, 2d ed. (Boston: Houghton Mifflin, 1976), pp. 116–18.

assignment, have students write the narration from the points of view of different characters in a play or story they have read.

5. Story theater differs from chamber theater in that the actors pantomime what the narrator says as he reads a story. Have students create stories that can be pantomimed. Encourage them to practice beforehand and to select lighting and musical accompaniment.

6. Enable your students to write scripts that explain their ideas about something that English classes are concerned with. Stephen Dunning, in "Scripting: A Way of Talking," explains scripting both as a way of playing and as a means of student production.[6] He lists as examples some scripts written and performed by students: *Two Whys and One Wherefore of Punctuation; Kavalier Poets: Or the Karpe Diem Kids; What Real Student People Write About;* and *What You Always Wanted to Know About . . . Your Regional Dialect.*

7. Encourage students to submit their plays for publication. For possible sources, consult the current edition of *Writer's Market.* In addition, National Public Radio has conducted contests for plays on tape created by students aged six to eighteen. For details, write Young People's Radio Festival, 2025 M. Street NW, Washington, D.C. 20036. And don't ignore other sources of such "publishing": a local radio station, the community newspaper, and amateur theater groups. They may not pay money, but they do pay in encouragement and inspiration.

8. To develop students' awareness of and appreciation for production of television shows, let them write scripts that have directions for television cameras. See Reproduction Page 2 for terms commonly used in television scripts. Visit a television station to watch a program actually being shot. Provide books for writers as part of your class library, such as Irving Settel's *How to Write Television Comedy.*[7]

ANALYZING THE ELEMENTS OF DRAMA

1. Settings may vary greatly for the same play. In order to illustrate this point, distribute among the class clear transparency sheets and grease pencils or water-soluble felt-tipped pens. Ask the students to draw the set of the play that you are just beginning to read. Then, with an overhead projector, display the end results, having the class and/or the creator of the set explain what is there. Discuss with the class the appropriateness of each set design. Concentrate upon the positive aspects of each set—build the self-confidence of all students by valuing and welcoming their creations.

2. Collect slides of different stage sets. By writing to various acting companies, you may acquire publicity releases that contain photos of the stage sets they use. Use a copy stand and camera or a camera with close-up lens to photograph stage sets in magazines and theater books. Show the slides to your students to give them ideas for their own stage sets.

---

6. Stephen Dunning, "Scripting: A Way of Talking," *English Journal* 63 (September 1974), 32–40
7. Irving Settel, *How to Write Television Comedy* (Boston: The Writer, 1958).

TERMS EMPLOYED BY TELEVISION WRITERS

ANGLE—The angle or relationship of the camera to the subject. High Angle would be a bird's-eye view. Other angles include Wide Angle and Low Angle.

CLOSE-UP—A very close view of the subject, perhaps of the head only; sometimes this is a view of only the lips or the hands.

CRANE SHOT—A view taken from a moving platform.

CUT TO—Switching from one scene to another without any transition; as opposed to Dissolve or Fade.

DISSOLVE TO—The gradual fading out of one picture while another picture gradually appears.

DOLLY IN or BACK—Physically moving the camera closer to, or farther from, the subject.

ESTABLISHING SHOT—A large view with no particular focus. Used to set a scene usually.

FADE IN or OUT—To go from a completely blacked out picture to a full picture or vice versa.

FREEZE FRAME—Stop action; the picture is "frozen."

FULL SHOT—A complete view of the subject.

LONG SHOT—A distant view of the subject; sometimes Extremely or Medium Long Shot.

MONTAGE—A quick sequence of shots to indicate time passing rapidly or for emotional impact of some sort.

PAN TO—Remaining stationary, the camera moves horizontally from one side of the scene to another.

REAR PROJECTION—A film shown behind the subject. Television newsmen are sometimes superimposed over scenes of the news.

SLOW MOTION—All the action is artificially slowed down; extremely popular in playbacks of sporting events.

SPLIT SCREEN—The picture is separated into two or more scenes occurring at the same time.

STOCK SHOT—Film of something stored in the film library for use whenever a director may want, such as a view of stars for use in space programs.

SUPERIMPOSE OVER—The placing of one scene over another; often titles are superimposed over scenes.

ZOOM IN—To rapidly move in on a particular close shot; often used for sudden, dramatic effect.

Worth noting: Television writers do not give directions for every camera shot to be made. They usually include the directions that they believe are absolutely necessary to communicate their scenes best. Variations are usually left up to the director of the show.

3. In order to save money, certain repertory theater groups create one stage setting to serve for all the plays they present. With the class brainstorming ideas, create one stage set that will serve for all the plays the class has read or seen. Ask a model enthusiast to create a model that portrays the end result of your deliberations. Display the model in a prominent place. Individual members of the class might write explanations of how the model set would be employed for specific plays.

4. Encourage students to group the plays they have seen or read according to themes. Brainstorm to establish themes. List as many themes as possible. If students are keeping a notebook, ask that they list at least five television plays or films they have seen recently or plays they have read recently and state at least one theme for each play. At the end of a specified period of time, list all the plays seen or read and the themes for each. Have students group all the plays that have similar themes. Have them rank the plays with a similar theme according to how well those plays presented the theme. Then discuss with them how they decided upon that ranking. The important result will not be whether you agree with their criteria but whether they are able to develop their own criteria for judging plays in relation to their themes. (This exercise could also be conducted with characters and plots.)

5. After brainstorming with the class to determine many themes and listing the themes on the blackboard, write each theme on a piece of paper and have each student select one theme at random. Then have each student write a short skit based upon the theme he or she has selected. One page may be enough to accomplish this task. Then group the students and have each group pass its skits to another group. Ask each group to act out each skit within the group and after-

ward decide which skit best accomplished the task. If the class is ready for this exercise, have the group act out, perhaps in a Readers Theater technique, the skit they have selected as best.

6. Have the class pick one type of television show—detective mysteries, situation comedies, lawyer programs, or horror shows. Check the week's television listings and assign each student to write a plot summary of one show. When the students bring in their plot summaries, compare them to determine whether there are any similarities. Examine the plots for typical techniques, characters, conflicts, and resolutions. After having determined what similar elements appear over and over, isolate those shows that do not contain the similar aspects and decide whether they are good or bad and what makes them unique. Have the class determine standards they could use to determine if a television play were original or not. Later, apply those standards to plays they have read in class.

7. As students collect plot summaries, try to break the plots down into their most basic elements. Have the class determine whether in fact there are only a few basic plots in all plays. If they decide that there are, have them consider the same question with regard to short stories and novels they have read.

8. After the students have read a play, ask each to select one character and write a character sketch of that character. This process might be facilitated by assigning characters for each student to follow as they study the play. To guide students provide them questions for the character sketch. Joan Snyder, in *The Dynamics of Acting*,[8] suggests that actors be able to answer the following questions about specific characters (they are key questions for anyone studying characters):

What does the character want out of life?

What does the character do to get what he wants from life?

What does the character believe in? Does he have any convictions?

What was his childhood like?

What changes, if any, take place in the play relative to the actions of the character?

Snyder also provides other helpful questions you might elect to use:

What does the character do for a living? to pass his leisure time?

What does the character like and/or dislike?

What do the other characters in the play say about him?

How does the character feel about the other characters in the play?

9. After students have finished studying a play, have them portray characters from the play as though the characters were students in the class. Each student could pick whatever character he or she wanted to play, draw a character's name at random, or be assigned the character based upon your evaluation of the student's ability to portray the particular character. Give the students at least one night to prepare. After the students have pretended that they are the characters being students in class (the length of time would depend upon how long you thought they could successfully sustain the roles), ask each student to write down which

---

8. Joan Snyder, *The Dynamics of Acting* (Skokie, Ill.: National Textbook Co., 1972), p. 97.

character was being portrayed by which student. Discuss with the class the reasons for their conclusions. This will enable students to demonstrate their understanding of the characters.

10. To determine whether students can recognize stereotyping in drama, present the students with small groups of characters and ask each one to write plot summaries that would accommodate those characters. If the students develop similar plots, ask them why. Lead them to recognize that some characters and plots are not original in any way. Some students might create plots that are unique. Discuss with the class how even stereotyped characters can be present in nonstereotyped plots. Consider also whether a stereotyped plot can have nonstereotyped characters. Following are samples of groupings of characters you can present to the students:

A. a henpecked father
a nagging wife whose intentions are good
a boy-crazy daughter
a son whose main interest is sports

B. a sloppy, poor, honest detective
a suspicious police lieutenant
a beautiful girl

C. a young divorcée looking for a career
a laborer who lives in her apartment house
a smooth-talking lawyer

11. To prepare students to discuss the conflicts they find in plays they read, have them list in their notebooks the conflicts they observe in the following circumstances:

A. conflicts within themselves

B. conflicts between themselves and others

C. conflicts among their friends and relatives

D. conflicts reported on television news and in newspapers

E. conflicts on television shows and in movies

When the students have a wide variety of conflicts listed in their notebooks, divide the class into groups and ask the groups to categorize the conflicts listed by the group members. After each group has developed its categories, have the groups switch their lists to determine whether any conflicts listed by other class members deserve new and separate categories or whether they all fit the categories determined by the group. Continue doing this until all groups have seen all categories. Then ask each group to list its categories on the blackboard, compare them, and determine with the whole class whether one list of categories can be developed from the separate lists. Having categorized conflicts, the students are now free to apply the categories to the plays they have read.

12. The production of a play depends upon more than just the actors and the director. Assign students to learn more about the other people involved in producing a

play by finding such people and interviewing them if possible, following them at their tasks if possible, and observing what they do. If no theater group performs in your town, wait until the drama teacher produces a play in your school and, with his permission, make this assignment. Among the nonacting personnel that your students might choose to investigate are: the investors, the ticket sales personnel, the lighting personnel, the producer, the costume designer, the theater manager, and the public relations people.

13. If a local college or university has a drama department, plan a field trip to it before one of its major productions is given. Students will be surprised at the amount of effort and detail that goes into such a major production. Have them observe actors learning to put on makeup, visit the set designers at work, and wander through the wardrobe room. Arrange to have some of the drama majors talk to your students about the careers they are studying for.

14. In order to build a data bank of plays, have students keep a log of the television shows they view and the movies they go to. Such a log might consist of the following entries: "Title," "Type of Play" (situation comedy, police drama, classic play), "Theme," "Character Types," "Setting," "Conflicts," "Quality of Camera Work" (use of light, camera angles, editing). Ask students to suggest their own categories. As classes become more adept at evaluation, they will be able to suggest more subtle criteria. For less mature students, do not include too many categories of entries or you will discourage them. This log could be maintained throughout the year and referred to when class discussions or assignments warranted; or it could be maintained for a specific period, such as one full week, with the students assigned to specific hours of viewing on specific television channels. If students wished, they could turn some of the log entries into full formal reviews.

15. A simplified version of exercise 14 is the following: Have students write the title of a current film they have seen recently. In one sentence, they are to state the theme of that film. Have a group of students compile the themes and group them by categories. Do the same for films over five years old that they see on televisior Have the class decide whether there is any difference in the thematic concerns of the two groups. Speculate with them about the reasons for any differences. Might this indicate anything about the interests of audiences then and now? Have these differences influenced the quality of the productions in any way?

DEVELOPING UNDERSTANDING OF DRAMA

1. Prereading exercises may help students understand a play as much as the actual reading or postreading exercises. Following are listed three prereading activities that can help students get into a play. They are particularly important for less mature readers.

A. Ask students to speculate about how they would behave if they were in a situation that occurs in the play. For example, before they read *Macbeth*, ask them what they would do if they were an ambitious husband or wife who wanted to become king or queen. Or before they read *Raisin in the Sun*, ask students what they might think about before moving from an old but poor neighborhood to a better but strange neighborhood.

B. Have students improvise a scene in which they act out a situation that is similar to a key situation in the play they are about to read. For instance, before they read *Julius Caesar*, have students improvise a scene between a wife who wants her husband to stay home for a change and a husband whose primary concern in life is getting ahead in his work.

C. Discuss with students whether they have ever felt the way a character feels in the play they are about to read. Before reading Paddy Chayefsky's *Holiday Song*, discuss whether any of them ever lost faith in God after having believed in Him strongly. What did they do? Did they regain the faith? Why or why not? What advice would they give someone who felt the same way?

2. Whether or not a play is being produced in your community that your students have read, do more than encourage them to attend plays. Organize class trips to see live plays whenever you can. Write for special group rates—sometimes they are available. Make arrangements to talk to some of the actors, the director, and the stagehands or other production personnel before or after the play. If possible, have them come to class to discuss the play with the students. And if at all feasible have your students read the play prior to seeing it so that they will be more knowledgeable about what they are watching.

3. Allow some students to interpret a play through illustrations or cartoons. To do so successfully, they must be familiar with possible ways the characters look, dress, and move. They must know the setting, and above all they must know the play. This is a good way to encourage reluctant readers to read and a good way to reinforce the talents of artistic students in your classes.

4. As students read a play, ask each one to keep a notebook of significant lines. This collection of lines may be used to support the essays they write about the play Since immature readers have a hard time deciding which lines are significant direct them by either of the following methods: A. Select specific key lines to discuss with the class, either as they read the play orally, or after they have read sections silently. Direct the students to write these lines in their notebooks. B. Instruct the students to divide their notebooks into the following sections and write the lines which fit each section as they encounter the lines or realize their importance:

A. lines that foreshadow later events

B. lines that reveal a conflict

C. lines that reveal a character's personality

D. lines that explain why a character behaves that way

E. lines that refer to past events

F. lines that stick in my mind.

5. To demonstrate their understanding of characters, have students act out (improvise) how particular characters would behave in entirely new situations and settings. For instance, what might Macbeth do if he were vice-president of the

United States? How might Hamlet behave if he were a member of the school's student body? How would Miller's Willy Loman (from *Death of a Salesman*) behave if he were the coach of a losing football team? What would Saroyan's Joe (from *The Time of Your Life*) do if he were put in charge of the junior prom? Or, to reverse that process, put living people in place of characters in the plays the students read. Which class members would be most appropriate for the various characters in the classic play *Everyman*? What political figures could be substituted for the characters in Shakespeare's *Julius Caesar*?

6. When studying drama from a particular period, encourage students to examine other aspects of the same period. Assign research projects on such things as dress, music, events of the time, architectural styles, and military strategy Not all research has to be conducted in a library. Allow students to pursue their research in creative ways. For instance, a music student might enjoy studying specific musical styles of the period or examining musical instruments in museums. Other students might want to perform a dance of the period for their project. Yet another might want to make a model of a particular building, tool, or weapon. By becoming more familiar with the cultural entities of the period, students might gain more insights into the motivations and personalities of the characters.

7. Have students create a newspaper reflecting the period in which the action of a play takes place. For simplicity, the newspaper's style can be that of a modern newspaper, unless one student can investigate newspapers of the period and teach the class about them. News stories might report the events of the play as well as events that might have or could have occurred at that time. Other students might want to create ads reflecting the period. Have the class choose a complete newspaper staff and publish the newspaper for other students, teachers, and parents.

8. To reinforce students' understanding of the play or plays they are reading, John S. Simmons, Robert E. Shafer, and Gail B. West, in *Decisions about the Teaching of English*,[9] suggest that when students reach a climactic point in their reading they answer the following three questions orally or in writing:

   A. What has happened to this point?

   B. What effect has the action had on the people involved?

   C. What do you think will happen next?

9. For students to indicate how well they have understood the play, immediately before reaching the climactic scene, or denouement, stop the reading of the play and have each student write a brief summary of what will happen from that point to the end. Place the predictions in a sealed envelope (for dramatic effect, of course) and open them when the play is finished. Read them aloud and have the class decide which ones were most accurate. Reward the accurate prognosticators.

10. If some students do not want to act before an audience, encourage them to dress in appropriate costumes and pose for photos that illustrate particular scenes from particular plays. Perhaps you will find some student who is interested in, and

9. John S. Simmons, Robert E. Shafer, and Gail B. West, *Decisions about the Teaching of English* (Boston: Allyn & Bacon, 1976), p. 64.

capable of, taking and developing the photos. Encourage such participation. Collect the pictures and use them in future years as one more means of motivating students to read plays or to help them understand them better. Given the impetus, some students may elect to create slide and tape shows of specific plays. In such a case, the "actors" pose for the photographer but do not perform before an audience. Some students may be editors of the show, some narrators, some the "voices" of the characters, and some directors of background music.

11. Tests, oral or written, can determine students' understanding of plays they have read. Vary the types of question you employ. Examples of question types include the following:

   A. Identification: The student must identify a character from a quotation of that character.

   B. Short Explanation: The student must explain why something happened, why a character behaved as he did, or how one event led to another.

   C. Interpretation: The student must explain what a character means, how a scene might take place, why an author chose to include or omit a specific event.

   D. Imaginary—"what-if" questions: The student is asked to pretend he or she is an actor, a character, or a director of the play in order to answer the question.

12. To broaden students' comprehension of the wide range of play styles, give them lists of different types of plays; ask your librarian to develop a play collection if one does not already exist; and encourage students to read widely, ranging beyond the plays contained in their textbooks. Because some plays contain controversial subject matter, potentially offensive language, and values that may conflict with those of some communities, or because they are not well known, the plays may never appear in textbooks. For a beginning selection of full-length plays, musical plays, television plays, and one-act plays, read Anthony Roy Mangione's "Dramatic Touchstones Toward a New Cultural Pluralism."[10] Place this and similar annotated bibliographies where students may see them; pass them around to other teachers; and, of course, be sure your librarian sees them.

13. When reading long plays (three to five acts long), vary the type of exercise from class to class. Do not do the same thing day after day—especially, do not read the entire play cold from beginning to end. Among the possible activities are:

   A. Ask a student to memorize a key speech.

   B. Have a few students perform a readers' theater of a key scene.

   C. Have some students improvise something that may have happened "offstage."

   D. Have a student create a setting for the play or for a particular scene—a drawing or a model.

   E. Ask a student to prepare sound effects for scenes that lend themselves to such effects.

10. Anthony Roy Mangione, "Dramatic Touchstones Toward a New Cultural Pluralism," *English Journal* 65 (October 1976), 72-77.

F. Before beginning the study of the play, ask students to prepare oral reports on background information; for example, summaries of other works by the same author, historical or cultural background material, and biographical information.

G. Ask for a volunteer to write a skit of something that happens to one or more of the characters shortly after the play ends.

14. Emphasize oral reading to develop understanding. In particular (and this suggestion applies to understanding all genres), direct students' attention to *punctuation*. If a student reads without meaning (revealed by inappropriate intonation patterns), ask the student to state the punctuation mark while reading. Thus, Electra's concluding speech:

"No (comma) by the gods (comma) Orestes (exclamation point) No long speech from him (exclamation point) No (comma) not a single word (exclamation point)"

Electra, Sophocles

Don't overemphasize such reading. The point is to draw the students' attention to the punctuation and indicate that punctuation influences intonation and thus interpretation and understanding.

WAYS TO INTERPRET DRAMA

1. Students can rewrite plays into different genres. Rewriting plays as short stories is the easiest transition students can make. To do so, students must be aware of the limited amount of information a playwright provides to the reader or audience and must fill in details the playwright leaves to the director or reader. As a short story, the events in the play may have to be rearranged, specific scenery may have to be described, and new characters may have to be introduced. In addition to rewriting the play as a short story, some students may elect to rewrite the play as a long narrative poem, a ballad perhaps, or as a modern song set to the music of a current hit or set to music created by one of the students. Other students might want to rewrite the play as a series of newspaper articles reporting the events of the play. The students might then read their various interpretations to one another, gaining new insights into the features of the different genres.

2. After having studied a particular play, students may want to act out the play, present a Readers Theater version; or do a chamber theater version of it, for other English classes. In this way, several classes could study different plays, but all would share in experiencing the plays as live drama. Of course, one-act plays are more easily produced than three- or five-act dramas.

3. If several classes are studying the same play, each could elect to present the entire play to other classes, or all could share the presentation experience by selecting separate scenes and performing the entire play before an audience composed of the classes themselves. Afterward, in the individual classrooms, the students could discuss and evaluate the different interpretations and determine to what extent they provided insights into the play; into its characters, themes, conflicts; or even into play production itself.

4. Whenever your students perform a play (and whenever your school budget allows it), videotape the presentation. Videotape is easier to use than film, can be erased, and can reinforce students by allowing them to see their production immediately after completing it. Start a bank of videotape plays with other teachers. Show these videotapes when you want to motivate students to read a play (or other work that has been put into play form). You can show some or all of the play to students who have yet to read it. When different groups videotape the same play, the different versions can be compared and contrasted to enable students to develop evaluative criteria or to learn more about play production.

5. If you plan to videotape a particular class production of a play, encourage your students to do the videotaping themselves. The students might even want to assume special roles, such as those of director, set designer, lighting supervisor, and stage manager. In performing these roles, they will learn to view the play from different perspectives and thus will learn more about the living nature of drama. Afterward, encourage them to share their experiences, knowledge, and expertise with other students. They may even combine to write a "Guidebook to Videotaping Plays" for future classes.

6. In order to expand the potential boundaries of language interpretation, take important lines from a play the class is about to study, present them to the students without the context of the play, and ask the students to write a context around the individual lines, incorporating the lines into a wholly new context. When the students have turned in their new contexts, in the form of either brief skits, poems, prose, fiction or nonfiction, discuss how well the lines fit and what the lines mean in those contexts. Then proceed to read the play. When students read the lines in their original contexts, the lines will have greater impact. Reproduction Page 3, "The Well-Wrought Line," is a sample exercise.

REPRODUCTION PAGE 3

THE WELL-WROUGHT LINE

Directions: *The following famous lines are from well-known plays. You are to select one of these lines from a play you have not read or seen. Put the line into some dramatic situation. Then write the situation, including that line somewhere. You may write a play, a poem, a short story, or an essay. When you finish, find the line in the original play. Does it mean something different from your interpretation?*

A. She speaks, yet she says nothing. (Shakespeare, *Romeo and Juliet*)

B. Life . . . is a tale
Told by an idiot, full of sound and fury,
Signifying nothing. (Shakespeare, *Macbeth*)

C. Cowards die many times before their deaths;
The valiant never taste of death but once. (Shakespeare, *Julius Caesar*)

D. Though this be madness, yet there is method in it. (Shakespeare, *Hamlet*)

E. Excess of wealth is cause of covetousness. (Marlowe, *The Jew of Malta*)

F. He's a wonderful talker, who has the art of telling you nothing in a great harangue. (Molière, *Le Misanthrope*)

G. Though a man be wise,
It is no shame for him to live and learn. (Sophocles, *Antigone*)

H. I have to live for others and not for myself; that's middle class morality. (Shaw, *Pygmalion*)

I. . . . the strongest man in the world is the man who stands alone. (Ibsen, *An Enemy of the People*)

J. You see, we neither love nor hate in my world. We simply have hobbies. (Gore Vidal, *Visit to a Small Planet*)

---

7. Have students update an older play by changing the setting to one they may be more familiar with, by changing some or all of the characters into characters the students are likely to encounter in their daily lives, or by revising the plot or conflict to fit one that a modern character is likely to encounter. Students might want to rewrite the play and act out certain scenes to establish the validity of their script. While *Macbeth,* for example, concerns the overthrow and murder of a Scottish king, a modern version might deal with the rise of a dictator in a small country or even a more bloody version of *How to Succeed in Business without Really Trying.* After the final version is prepared and possibly acted, students can consider such things as how important setting and characterization are to establish the conflict or theme and how themes can be universal regardless of setting.

8. Have students volunteer to have their oral interpretation of a play—or one scene from the play—taped. Other students might volunteer to provide needed sound effects or musical background. If possible, find a professional recording of the same play. Compare the various versions. Be sure to praise the good points of the students' productions, realizing that, in certain aspects, their versions may be superior to the professional versions.

9. As a fun, creative exercise, encourage one or two students to tape their interpretation of a scene from a play in the following manner: From a professional recording, tape the recorded version of one character only. Have the students portray the other characters in the scene interacting with the professional actor. Mix up the student-professional actor combinations. Play back the versions for the class. After each listening session, ask the class if they gained any insights from the new version. Or, as a variation upon that exercise, tape only one recorded actor, leaving appropriate blank spots on the tape for student actors to reply, live, in class.

10. Provide an area where students may rehearse and possibly present dramatic interpretations of plays they have read or created. This may be a stairwell, an empty classroom, a storeroom, or an area in the classroom set aside for such activities (possibly separated from the rest of the classroom by a series of screens). If possible, keep materials there for simple props: colored cloths for "costumes," implements that may serve as weapons or tools, hats that establish character, and other items that encourage the students to use their imaginations. Some students have built raised platforms to serve as a stage. While this is not necessary, it does serve as a way of separating the actors from the audience.

11. Keep on hand materials for creating puppets. Many students who ordinarily will not go before an audience will gladly hide behind a screen or above a stage and manipulate puppets. These materials need not be elaborate; the simpler ones enable students to explore with their imaginations. Socks are traditional puppet "bases," with eyes, ears, noses and mouths easily sewn, glued, or taped on—keep buttons and pieces of colored cloth or paper on hand for that. Brooms, mops, boards, bags, and boxes also serve as good bases for puppets. Get students to suggest and contribute more ideas and materials.

12. Let students draw a cartoon series illustrating one of the plays they have read.

13. As a reaction to a play they have read, let students create a montage that relates

to the play. They can cut pictures from magazines. Save the montage or make a slide of it for future classes to see.

THE EVALUATION OF DRAMA

1. Establish a communication workshop such as the one described by Mary Colvario in "The Development of Classroom Workshops in Oral Communication." She describes twenty-five activities that range from establishing a warm atmosphere to expressing emotion to brief acting exercises. She advises that students be given credit at first just for participating and suggests that more specific evaluation criteria can be applied when "the class is functioning smoothly and the major traumas have subsided."[11]

2. Read a novel or a short story that has been turned into a film. After the class finishes studying the work, view the film. Before showing the film, ask the class to look specifically for the following aspects of the film: Was the story changed in any way? How? Why? Could the director have presented the story just as the author wrote it? If it was changed, was the end result better or worse than the original? Did the director emphasize specific events or characters more than the original author did? Why? Did the fact that a film shows scenes whereas an author describes them determine how the director would produce the film? After you have discussed these aspects with the class, consider whether the filmed play can be judged according to the same criteria as the written original or whether new criteria must be applied. If there are differences in criteria, list them on the board. Later the class might want to apply the two sets of criteria to a play which they read.

3. Have a number of dramas on hand, including taped radio and television plays. National Public Radio and Television often rebroadcast old plays. As long as you do not intend to make money on them, employ them for specific educational purposes, or use them year after year, you will avoid abusing the copyright laws. Examine catalogues of record distributors: They often have recordings of old radio programs. Discount houses offer special bargain prices when record houses unload slow-moving stock. Use these recordings for quick comparison-contrast exercises.

4. Encourage students to write reviews of plays they see on television or in the movies. Post the reviews in a prominent place, such as on the bulletin board or in the library, and suggest that students read each other's reviews. Make arrangements with the school newspaper to publish the best reviews. If your school does not have a newspaper, have your students publish their own newspaper or ask the editor of the local newspaper if the reviews can be published regularly there. For students who need guidelines for what should go into the review, run off copies of Reproduction Page 4, "Be Your Own Reviewer!"

---

11. Mary Colvario, "The Development of Classroom Workshops in Oral Communication," *English Journal* 63 (December 1974), 55–61.

REPRODUCTION PAGE 4

BE YOUR OWN REVIEWER!

Have you seen a television show or film lately that you would like to tell others about? Maybe it was an excellent production and you would like to recommend it to others. Or perhaps it was terrible and you want to warn them not to waste their time or money. The questions below are intended to be a guide to give you ideas to write about. You do not have to answer all the questions. Pick those that apply only to the work you are reviewing. Then write the review honestly from your own viewpoint. Remember, in order to convince people, you have to explain what you mean.

1. What is the name of this production?

2. If you know them, who are the main actors?

3. What was the main point of the production supposed to be?

4. Did it accomplish its purpose well or not?

5. Was the character portrayal good? Were the characters believable in that situation? Could other actors have done a better job? Who? Why?

6. Was the language believable? Did the characters speak as you would expect people to speak in a similar situation?

7. Was the action believable? Would people behave that way in real life?

8. Did you ever see a similar production that did a better job? A worse job?

9. Would you recommend this production to others? Who? Why?

---

5. A person interested in the quality of a particular play may consult three types of expert:

   A. The Literary Reviewer: This person makes value judgments for the consumer. Is a play worth spending money on? Consumers must determine whether the reviewer's value judgments coincide with their own.

   B. The Literary Interpreter: This person explains the play for the person who may have already seen it or read it. The interpreter enables the reader to discover more about the play by explicating it, unraveling and unfolding the intricacies of the play.

   C. The Literary Critic: This person makes value judgments about the play but is concerned with the sources of our values. The critic uses criteria that are broadly based, perhaps working from the perspective of what drama in general is and should be. The critic is concerned more with the text of the play itself than with the production of the play.

6. The relationship of the drama critic to the drama itself can be explored by students. Students can read and compare the writings of literary critics with the writings of popular-theater critics. This can be particularly useful when a classic play is produced for the modern theater, television, or movies. Different critics discuss the same play from entirely different perspectives. Would a modern critic of the Oedipus plays apply the same criteria that Aristotle used in his *Poetics*? What would a movie critic say about a Shakespearean play, and how would the critic's comments differ from those of, say, Coleridge? Advanced students might want to compare the views of such critics as Walter Kerr in *Tragedy and Comedy*; Edmund Wilson in *Axel's Castle*; and Martin Esslin in *The Theatre of the Absurd*.[12]

---

12. Walter Kerr, *Tragedy and Comedy* (New York: Simon & Schuster, 1968); Edmund Wilson, *Axel's Castle* (New York: Scribner's, 1931); and Martin Esslin, *The Theatre of the Absurd* (Garden City, N.Y.: Doubleday, 1961).

7. Have students compare movie or television reviews of the same production. What does each review emphasize? Do the reviewers agree? If they disagree, why? Does the reader know what the criteria of the reviewers are? If so, do the criteria match those of the reader? If several reviewers comment on the same production, which reviewer's comments most closely match the opinions of the students once they have seen the production? Have students write a review of the reviewers.

8. When studying a play by Shakespeare, or any other writer whose language may not be familiar to students, ask some students to translate into modern English lines from a scene, a key speech, or a brief interchange between characters. One group of students might elect to translate the selection into some formal variety of Standard English while another group translates the same selection into colloquial English, replete with slang and expressions that are currently "in" in your school. Then compare the three versions, noting whether key ideas are maintained or lost in the modern versions and whether the modern versions improve on the original version. Don't be afraid to let the students conclude that their versions are better as long as they can defend their criteria.

REPRODUCTION PAGE 5

A GLOSSARY OF DRAMA TERMS

ALLEGORY—A play (or story or poem) in which the characters and events have meanings other than the obvious surface meanings. For example, in the play *Everyman*, we encounter characters such as Good Deeds, Death, and Knowledge. They are portrayed as people, but they represent more. Yet they are also more than merely symbols, having both human character and qualities. For that reason, Ossie Davis's *Purlie Victorious* is an allegorical comedy.

ANTICLIMAX—The substitution of an unexpected, usually unimportant, event when one expects a play to build toward a climax. Used on purpose, it creates humor; used accidentally, it weakens the structure of the play.

ASIDE—A comment by a character onstage that is intended to be heard by the audience but not by the other characters.

CATHARSIS—Either (1) when the audience learns through the mistakes and behaviors of a character in a play how to avoid those wrong behaviors; or (2) when the audience is, according to Aristotle, purged or made psychologically whole by sharing the emotions of the main character but not the actual punishments.

CLIMAX—The point of greatest dramatic importance. Usually found near the end of a work, climax has been called the turning point of the action, when what has been going well suddenly turns against the main character (as in tragedy), or vice versa.

COMEDY—As opposed to tragedy, a type of drama that results in a pleasant ending. Comedy may be funny or not. Generally, in comedy the world is viewed as ultimately a good place. Humorous comedy results from incongruous speech and behaviors.

CONVENTION—The willing acceptance by both author and audience of certain procedures that are not realistic. Examples are: when an actor pretends to be dead, when days pass in seconds, when we accept artificial scenery and pretend it is real. It is also a convention, or an accepted practice, to applaud at the end of a production (assuming that we have enjoyed it).

DENOUEMENT—The final resolution or revealing of events in a play. In comedy, events fall together. In tragedy, events fall apart.

DRAMA—Either (1) any representation of life on a stage employing dialogue and conventions; or (2) a serious play but not necessarily a tragedy.

EXPOSITION—The point or points in a play in which the playwright provides needed information about characters or past events. Usually, but not always, it occurs at the beginning of the play.

FORESHADOWING—Hints to the audience of what will happen later. Characters typically provide foreshadowing without knowing they are doing so.

MELODRAMA—A funny tragedy in which the characters are stereotypes, having little motivation for their actions, and in which the plot is all-important, circumstances being more important than carefully structured actions.

MIME or PANTOMIME—In this form, the characters act through gestures, facial expressions, and other actions, but without talk.

MOTIVATION—The cause or reason for a character's behavior. By knowing the motivation of a character, we understand the character better.

SOLILOQUY—A relatively long speech in which the character talks to the audience or to no one in particular, expressing the character's innermost thoughts or providing background information for the audience. It is not common in modern plays.

TRAGEDY—A form of serious drama in which the main characters must commit themselves to specific courses of action in order to accomplish their goals, whether the goals are evil or good. Inevitably, the main character fails. In classic tragedy, this failure is the result of a *tragic flaw*, or important character weakness, which leads to the character's downfall.

9. Reproduction Page 5, "A Glossary of Drama Terms," provides students with the terminology they may need in evaluating plays. Pass it out as a guide but avoid testing the students on the definitions of the terms. If you want students to "know" the terms, find activities that compel them to use those terms.

10. Write to the Director, Utah Shakespeare Festival, Cedar City, Utah 84720 for study guides to the three plays that will be performed each summer in that southern Utah town. By increasing the background information available to your students, these guides will help them evaluate actual productions of the plays.

SUGGESTED RESOURCES

Print

Literature and Film. Audio-Brandon Films.
Presents films in the Audio-Brandon catalogue from works of literature. Includes a teaching manual for each film. Plays in the series include: *Our Town, Long Day's Journey Into Night, The Little Foxes, A Raisin in the Sun, A Doll's House, The Sea Gull, The Madwoman of Chaillot,* and *Murder in the Cathedral.*

Barnes, Douglas, ed. *Drama in the English Classroom.* Champaign, Ill.: NCTE, 1968.
Emphasizes both regular drama and creative dramatics activities. Excellent for teachers looking to integrate creative drama into regular drama programs.

Courtney, Richard, ed. *Play, Drama, and Thought.* New York: Drama Book, 1974.
Excellent work on the theoretical underpinnings for teaching drama. Courtney expands on the traditional approach to drama, with the addition of creative drama, creative movement, and the dramatic method. He relates dramatic education to philosophy, psychology, sociology, and cognition.

Duke, Charles. *Creative Drama and English Teaching.* Champaign, Ill.: NCTE, 1974.
An excellent first source on creative dramatics. Duke assumes you know little about the topic and proceeds. Includes an excellent handbook of resources for creative dramatics.

Evans, Bertrand. *Teaching Shakespeare in High School.* New York: Macmillan.
A traditional approach to teaching Shakespeare. Approaches, selection, presentation, and activities are included as well as individual plays. The best single source on the teaching of Shakespeare. Emphasizes the aesthetic approach.

Gray, Farnum, and Mager, George C. *Liberating Education.* Berkeley: McCutchan Publishing Co., 1974.
A handbook on improvisational drama. Firmly grounded in the authors' experience with this approach, especially at the junior high level.

Hawley, Robert C. and Isabel L. *Developing Human Potential.* Portland, Ore.: ERA Press, 1975.
Excellent source for creative dramatics. Includes motivation, self-awareness, interpersonal relationships, and creativity. Many, many exercises.

Hoetker, James. *Dramatics and the Teaching of Literature.* Champaign, Ill.: NCTE, 1969.
Examines the use of drama in the teaching of literature in British and American schools. Hoetker also makes tentative recommendations to teachers.

Moffett, James. *Drama: What Is Happening.* Champaign, Ill.: NCTE, 1967.
Moffett espouses considering drama as a focal point in the English curriculum. Good for both traditional and creative dramatics.

Spolin, Viola. *Improvisation for the Theatre.* Evanston, Ill.: Northwestern Univ. Press, 1963.
A classic in the field. Blends theory-of-theater games with numerous ideas for exercise.

Swenson, William G. *Guide to Great Themes in Drama.* New York: Bantam.
Meant to help teach a mini-course or elective in drama. Concentrates on Agamemnon, Ibsen, *The Crucible, Frogs,* and *Cyrano de Bergerac.* Provides goals and objectives, a course outline, a method for teaching dramatic form, and strategies. Very useful for the teacher with little background in drama.

Way, Brian. *Development Through Drama.* Atlantic Highlands, N.J.: Humanities Press, 1967.

Excellent source for creative dramatics at all grade levels. Especially valuable suggestions for beginning activities involving movement, the senses, and the emotions.

Nonprint: Films and Cassettes for Drama Study in the Classroom

The following selected films will provide you with a varied approach to the study of drama. The annotations indicate some possible applications for each film. See Appendix B for the addresses of university libraries with film collections.

Antony and Cleopatra. McGraw-Hill Textfilms; b/w, 33 min.
> If your students have time to read only one Shakespearean play, but you would like them to be familiar with some others, show them this brief reproduction of the play.

Creative Drama: The First Steps. University libraries; color, 28 min.
> A good introduction for the teacher interested in creative dramatics. The film introduces the concepts and helps free the students to become involved.

Hamlet. ACI Films; color, 14 min.
> After reading *Hamlet,* have students draw scenes and characters as they visualize them. Discuss their drawings and then show them this film, an animated selection of the play's highlights. This may be a good way to introduce the play to less mature readers.

Hamlet. Encyclopaedia Britannica Educational Corp.; color, 30 min. each.
> This series of three films is designed for students who have read the plays prior to viewing the films. *The Age of Elizabeth* treats the times, the theater, and the audiences. *The Poisoned Kingdom* deals with the meanings of the many poisonings and the weaknesses of the royal Danish family. *The Readiness of All* discusses the complexities of the main character: the ambiguity of man, reality versus seeming reality, the influence of environment and circumstance, and the imminence of death.

History of the Drama, The. Films for the Humanities.
> A ten-unit, year-long program on the history of the drama. Each unit focuses on a major play of the era. The basic program includes two filmstrips and cassettes for each unit. Films and text

of the plays are also available. Expensive but excellent. Available for preview.

How to Read Plays. Coronet Instructional Films; b/w, 14 min.
> Use this film as part of your introduction to the reading of plays. Since immature readers often have difficulty in visualizing a play in its printed form, this film stresses how to reconstruct a play: its physical construction, character movement, sounds, and content.

Macbeth, parts I, II, and III. Encyclopaedia Britannica Educational Corp.; color, 28, 28, and 33 min., respectively.
> The play must be read by your students before viewing these excellent analytic films. *The Politics of Power* concerns itself with the main characters, builds upon the idea that "Nothing is but what is not" and reveals the multiple meanings of lines and themes. *The Secret'st Man* develops the idea that good and evil reside in all, and Macbeth is a man with whom we can all sympathize.

Midsummer Night's Dream, A. University libraries; b/w, 14 min.
> Use this as an introduction to the play. The accessibility of *A Midsummer Night's Dream* makes it a good choice for late junior high.

Our Town and Our Universe and *Our Town and Ourselves.* Encyclopaedia Britannica Educational Corp.; color, 29 and 30 min., respectively.
> In the first, Clifton Fadiman discusses while the Stratford Shakespearean Festival Foundation of Canada acts out a summary of the play, the staging, the functions of the characters, and the theme. The second film, produced in a like manner, develops insights into the music, the variations of the themes, the condensations of theme, the use of time, and the play's import. Better readers will profit more from having read the play prior to viewing the film.

Romeo and Juliet. University libraries; b/w, 40 min.
> A condensed version of the play. It can be used either as another example of a Shakespearean play or, if the play has been read, as a culminating experience.

Stanislavsky: Maker of the Modern Theater. Films for the Humanities; b/w, 28 min.
> For an important aspect of the history of drama, this film shows us Stanislavsky in action, selections from several of his milestone play productions, and attitudes of others toward his work. Use the film in a discussion of how to present a play or ways to interpret characters.

Theater in Shakespeare's England Series. Encyclopaedia Britannica Corp.

For an introduction to Shakespeare aimed at students at any level, show these filmstrips: *Origins of English Drama, Theater in Elizabethan London, The Globe: Design and Construction,* and *The Globe: A Day at Shakespeare's Theater.*

Walter Kerr's Guide to Theater. Cassettes Unlimited. Six hours of tapes that trace live theater from its roots to the present. Topics are: *What Theater Is, Why Have Theater?,* and *How to Judge Theater.* Excellent for drama teachers.

Watts Tower Theater Workshop. University libraries; color, 27 min.

Through the use of improvisational techniques the group (black teenagers from a Los Angeles ghetto) uses everyday incidents to create a situation of active involvement of immediate importance for personal and social change. Three short acts are shown. Good for multiethnic literature, improvisational theater, or creative dramatics.

What Is Drama? Guidance Associates. Sound filmstrip program of two filmstrips and two cassettes or records. Traces drama from the beginning to present with a discussion by Paddy Chayefsky. Excellent for introduction to the drama. Available for preview.

3

Teaching the Short Story

Perhaps no other genre provides as much satisfaction in the classroom for both student and teacher as the short story. Students enjoy short stories for many reasons. Clearly, for many students the short story is a quick way of getting in to and out of literature: The short story can be read in a relatively brief span of time; it does not appear to be so mysterious as poetry; and the typical short story has a rather narrow focus—not the potential complexity of a novel, which might have many interweaving plot lines, numerous minor characters, and the potential for complicated theme structure. In addition, today's students have encountered the short story in many different forms, so it is not alien to them at all. They have seen short stories dramatized on television or converted into feature-length motion pictures. They have heard the short story in the form of jokes; in oral traditions handed down in their families; and even, when one considers it, as news reports on television or radio or in the newspapers. Realizing that students have had an extensive exposure to short stories, teachers ought to make use of them for comparison-and-contrast exercises and for gaining greater knowledge of the storyteller's art.

Numerous reasons justify the teaching of the short story as a genre. As mentioned previously, the first reason is that students tend to be more highly motivated to read short stories than any other genre. More importantly, however, the short story provides the teacher with a rather convenient vehicle for examining literary elements in a relatively limited context. In the short story, the elements of theme, plot, setting, characterization, tone, mood, and point of view interlock, but typically an author emphasizes one element more than another. Knowing that, a teacher can select one or several short stories that illustrate a given element. In addition, short-story writers may have different reasons for writing than, say, writers of novels, and there is some truth in the idea that a short story may create a particular effect. Focusing on both the reason and the effect may enable the teacher to consider the short story in an exciting lesson. Finally, the study of the short story is a good jumping-off point for introducing the other genres, since the literary elements contained in it are also present in the novel, drama, and poetry.

A word of caution applies to the teaching of short stories just as it would to teaching works in any other genre. Experienced teachers try not to teach everything about a short story simply because everything is there. True, the theme of a short story is developed by its plot, its characterization, and possibly by its setting. At the same time, irony may be worth noting, the climax might be evident; or the author may have developed the atmosphere through a particularly effective use of words, he may have employed foreshadowing, and he may have developed suspense through any of a number of different methods. But imagine the position of a student who has enjoyed reading an assigned story but who encounters a teacher who analyzes the story and points out all the elements the student has not noted. How impressed are college students the first time a university professor points out a fault in a footnote? A secondary student can be expected to realize only a limited amount upon first reading a short story. The more a teacher points out, the more inadequate many students begin to feel. So instead of treating the whole of the story and approaching it as an aesthetic experience, many students ask themselves, "What is it that the teacher wants us to know?" Many of them ask the teacher directly. Stories can be analyzed, but they should not be so thoroughly dissected and pinned to the literary analyst's board that nothing remains of them. For that matter, there are times when you, the teacher, will just want to let students read short stories for the sake of reading stories. The short story must not become something that only English teachers read and teach. These sentiments are echoed by teachers and students alike. For instance, Charles R. Duke's "Teaching the Short Story" offers a number of valuable short-story activities, and Duke warns us that

> ... the short story still presents some teaching problems, the most important of which is the difficulty of varying the classroom approach. Too many teachers handle the story as though they were teaching a shortened novel and do little more than engage in formal textual explication. Discussion of the short story text should occur, of course, and students should know something of what the short story genre is. But this does not mean that the activities leading to such understanding need to be routine or repetitive.[1]

Remember also that the teacher has other sources of short stories besides anthologies and magazines. Television shows, radio shows, and films provide convenient sources for approaching short stories visually and aurally, and they also enable the teacher to teach listening and viewing skills while studying the short story. Besides being studied as a separate genre, the short story can also be studied in chronological, thematic, or topical units. Thus, many approaches can work toward achieving the same end. Whatever approach you as a teacher take, remember this: Good teachers do not analyze a story to death; nor do they just throw a story out for students to read and hope that something may develop. Effective teachers—for that is what is meant by good—read possible selections carefully, asking themselves whether their students can profit by reading each story and what each story has to offer the students. Then they plan to use the short story for whatever purpose they may have determined. Then they determine the best possible way to introduce the story. That method may involve some prereading exercise, such as an improvisation or a class discussion; it may involve having the students read the story before doing anything with it; and it may even involve letting the students read the story without doing anything with it. As with all teaching, one teaches with a purpose, and one allows the purpose to determine the appropriate methods.

---

1. Charles R. Duke, "Teaching the Short Story," *English Journal* 63 (September 1974), p. 62.

PERFORMANCE OBJECTIVES

As a result of the learning experiences in this chapter, students should be able to:

1. Explain the term "short story," its history, and its types.
2. State what theme is and be able to identify themes and evaluate them in terms of the story itself and in terms of their own lives.
3. Identify the setting and discuss how it relates to other aspects of the short story.
4. Specify the purpose of characters in a short story and evaluate the author's characterization techniques.
5. Relate the plot, analyze its general structure, and consider it in relation to other aspects of the story.
6. Identify and evaluate the author's use of tone, mood, and point of view.
7. Evaluate short stories by being aware of the author's purpose and of the interrelationships among all aspects of the story.

LEARNING EXPERIENCES

Introductory mini-lectures: (Duplicate Reproduction Page 6 as a note-taking guide for your students.)

REPRODUCTION PAGE 6

THE SHORT STORY

I. Characteristics of the Short Story

II. History of the Short Story

III. Types of Short Stories

    A. The Plot Story

    B. The Action Story

    C. The Plotless Story

    D. The Episodic Story

E. The Character Story

F. The Thematic Story

G. The Psychological Story

I. WHAT IS A SHORT STORY?

A short story is a relatively brief fictional prose narrative, which may vary widely in length. In fact, it is often difficult to determine where a long short story ends and a short novel, or novella, begins. Edgar Allan Poe wrote that the short story should have unity, brevity, and singleness of effect. He even said that a short story could be read in one sitting, but that depends upon the reading ability of the reader and the length and complexity of the short story. W. Somerset Maugham described the short story as being a piece of fiction dealing with a single incident—material or spiritual—and having unity of effect.

As in a novel, the elements of plot, character, theme, and setting are interwoven. But unlike the novel, which may well ramble on for hundreds of pages, mixing plots, introducing and eliminating characters, developing several themes, and roaming from one setting to another, the short story does not have the space for doing so. Usually, the short story has one plot, one theme, possibly one setting, and one major character.

II. THE HISTORY OF THE SHORT STORY

Short stories have existed from prehistoric times until the present, but in forms vastly different from what we currently describe as the "short story." Prehistoric people probably told short stories to each other, for we have their magnificent paintings at such places as Lascaux and petroglyphs (carvings or inscriptions on rocks) and pictographs (paintings or drawings on rock walls) from around the world, art that clearly was intended to communicate. Egyptian papyruses dating from five to six thousand years ago tell stories of the Pharaohs and their people. The temples of the Mayans and other Mayan stone glyphs dating from five to one thousand years ago tell of rituals and rulers and the people. Unfortunately, many written records of the peoples of Central America were destroyed by the early European explorers, so we do not know all that they may have contained.

The Bible has many stories in it, some in the form of the parables of Christ. In fact, all cultures of the world told tales in their mythologies. In the Middle Ages in Europe, many fables and epics became popular. During the fourteenth century, two of the best-known writers were Boccaccio and Chaucer, who wrote a series of tales tied together with a loose structure. In Boccaccio's *Decameron*, a group of people escaping the plague in the city tell stories to pass the time. In Chaucer's *Canterbury Tales*, another group of people pass their time by telling stories as they travel together on a pilgrimage. In the fifteenth century, Malory collected and rewrote a number of tales about knights and King Arthur. It was never long before one author would use the ideas of another author to have a little fun. For instance, Cervantes wrote *Don Quixote de la Mancha* (1605-15) partly as a way of making fun of the knightly tales of his day.

And so the short story continued to develop, taking many forms. In the seventeenth century in England, Samuel Pepys wrote a diary that contains stories of his day. In the eighteenth century, satirists such as Addison and Steele helped the newspaper grow as a medium with their stories. In the United States, Washington Irving wrote a number of popular tales, such as the stories of "Ichabod Crane" and "The Headless Horseman."

Finally, in the middle of the nineteenth century, the short story developed into the form as we recognize it today. Edgar Allan Poe has been called by some the "father of the short story." His stories continue to fascinate us today. And in England, Charles Dickens wrote stories for Victorian newspapers, many of them serialized and later published in book form. Writers who were popular then remain popular even today.

What all of these stories have in common throughout history is that they are short. Unlike the earlier stories, the modern short story has what critics call a "tight" structure. The theme, setting, characters, and plot all fit together to form one single effect.

III. TYPES OF SHORT STORY

Short stories can be categorized in several different ways. It is possible that one short story may fit into several categories. Among those categories which have been identified are:

A. *The plot story:* This is what most people think of when they think of a short story. The plot story is a narration—a telling of a series of events—that has a traditional pattern of structure. A conflict is identified at the beginning, the action builds until it reaches a climax, and then the story either ends or gradually tapers off to the end. (Examples: Ambrose Bierce's "An Occurrence at Owl Creek Bridge," Ted Poston's "Rat Joiner Routs the Klan," Bruce Jay Friedman's "23 Pat O'Brien Movies.")

B. *The action story:* A type of plot story, the action story is dependent primarily upon what the characters do, not upon deep development of characters or theme. Most of the action is physical, and so typical examples are the television mystery or detective stories, cowboy or frontier stories, and some types of science fiction. (Examples: Arthur Gordon's "The Sea Devil," W. W. Jacob's "The Monkey's Paw," Richard Connell's "The Most Dangerous Game.")

C. *The plotless story:* In this type, there apparently is no action or very little action. The story appears to be mostly the description of a character or the creation of a mood. While this may seem like a useless type of story, in fact the author may have wanted to frustrate the reader or wanted not to come to a firm conclusion. The "plotless" story may well be more realistic than any other type, for life cannot always be said to be organized according to a tight structure. (Examples: John Galsworthy's "The Japanese Quince," Eudora Welty's "The Worn Path," J. F. Powers's "The Valiant Woman.")

D. *The episodic story:* This type of short story, also referred to as the "slice-of-life" type, consists of one main incident. What has happened before the incident may be told, hinted at, or not told at all. What happens after the incident is left up to the reader, although sometimes the author makes that clear. While the incident may not appear to be important, it may capture some aspect of life quite well, and, as an example, may reveal even more. (Examples: James Joyce's "Araby," Luigi Pirandello's "War," John Updike's "A & P," James K. Bowman's "El Patrón.")

E. *The character story:* The character story has as its main purpose the revealing of something about one main character. For that reason, there may be very little plot. The character may be involved in only one episode, and the character may be the only character in the tale. At the end of the story, the reader usually knows a good deal about that character. (Examples: Wilbur Daniel Steele's "Footfalls," William Saroyan's "The Poor and Burning Arab," Amado Muro's "Cecilia Rosas.")

F. *The thematic story:* In this type, the author's main purpose is to develop one particular theme. One type of theme may attempt to reveal a "great truth" about life, such as "Humanity is innately corrupt," or a simple statement about life, such as "Mothers are always worrying about their children." To develop the theme, there may be a heavy plot line or there may be little. In any event, the reader leaves the story feeling that the author had something meaningful to say. (Examples: Ernest Hemingway's "The Killers," Dorothy Canfield's "Sex Education," Shirley Jackson's "The Lottery," Stephen Vincent Benét's "By the Waters of Babylon."

G. *The psychological story:* Sometimes the character story fits this category well. Typically, any action in the story takes place within the character—changes in feeling, states of mind, beliefs, desires, drives, attitudes. One leaves such a story knowing a great deal about what the character is like internally. (Examples: James Thurber's "The Secret Life of Walter Mitty," William Faulkner's "A Rose for Emily," Jessamyn West's "Love, Death, and the Ladies' Drill Team," Katherine Anne Porter's "The Grave.")

INVOLVING STUDENTS WITH THEME

There is this about it: Teaching for theme can be much like Humpty Dumpty's use of words in *Alice in Wonderland*—one can make a story mean just about anything one chooses to have it mean if one tries hard enough. Not all short stories have themes worth noting, and many do not actually have themes.

But some do have themes. Why do we read literature that is not purely entertaining? Sometimes we stumble upon a work that, as some say, "speaks to us." We leave the selection asking what it has meant to us: Has it given us greater insight into the workings of the world, of humanity, or of ourselves? Has the author really had something worth communicating? If anyone expects all literature to do that, he may be upset or frustrated, for not all authors intend to teach anything or to reveal anything. To search for a moral in every short story is, simply put, wasteful of one's time; and for teachers, it is wasteful of the students' time. Theme searchers, like symbol hunters, or, in fact, like hunters everywhere, have as their ultimate goal the destruction of something that is living.

And teachers do owe students the opportunity to think about an author's words and creation when that creation does more than simply tell a story—when it somehow leaves the readers better people, or, if not better people, at least people who have thought, if only for a moment, about who they are, and about what everyone is doing in the world. When one finds a short story that does such things—a short story that presents the reader with an opportunity to discuss values or goals or methods to those goals; a story that is so emotionally powerful that it is moving; or a story that, while not emotionally powerful, at least jabs one in the ribs and says "Hey! What about this?!"—then one has a story that is worth presenting to students who are capable of reading it and of relating in their own ways to the experience of the story.

The teacher's activities should encourage students to become involved with the story, to interact with it personally. Students may want to compare the events of the story with events in their own lives. They may want to determine whether the theme of the story somehow means something to them personally. Or they may want to answer the question of whether the theme has value for anyone. Your task as a teacher is to give them the opportunity to do so.

Teachers need to keep in mind that theme does not exist as some entity that can be plucked out of the air and slapped on a story. Theme is dependent upon the tone of the author, and tone is dependent upon the point of view of the story—the way characters are described, the selection and arrangement of events, and other possible elements such as setting and the establishment of mood through words that appeal to our senses. Perhaps all of these will need to be discussed by the class before they can come to some conclusion about theme. Or perhaps the theme will be evident to all after a first reading. As long as teachers do not produce a class filled with "theme-seekers," they may be able to develop in the students an awareness that authors have at times something to tell people—a message for some, a moral for others, a special insight about how human beings behave or how the world functions for others.

Involvement with literature takes place on many levels and often from different perspectives. Human emotion at the time of reading cannot help but influence an individual's interpretation of a piece of literature. How will the young woman who just before school saw a dog killed by an automobile react if she reads (1) a story about machines; (2) a story about an animal; or (3) a story about man's cruelty to man? We cannot predict the results of those situations, but we can enable her to bring her special, and perhaps even momentary, insights into contact with those of the author. Then, if there is a theme worth considering, it will have meaning.

1. Theme is the basic idea of a short story abstracted from the fusion of setting, characters, and plot. One way of having students understand theme, and especially a way of distinguishing plot from theme, is to ask students whether they can draw out of the story some eternal truth or truths. This method may work best for younger, more immature readers, for while it is rather simplistic, it forces the students to realize that plot is tied in to a particular story but that a theme may exist in many stories, regardless of the form, and may exist in life without being tied to short stories.

2. Provide a list of questions about theme before students begin to read stories for their themes (see Reproduction Page 7).

3. Ask students to read as many stories as they can to determine which ones they

---

REPRODUCTION PAGE 7

THEME

Directions: *Read the following questions after you have read a story.*

A. Does the story say anything about life (the theme), or is the story simply a description of a character or tale of a series of events?

B. What does the story say about life?

C. How does the author reveal the theme? Does one of the characters state it? Does the author tell you? Do you have to realize it yourself?

D. Do you agree with the theme of the story, if there is one?

E. Is the theme an important theme for people to think about, or is it a very minor theme, appropriate to only a few people or for people in a limited period of time, or is the theme hardly worth considering?

F. Is the author trying to convince you of his point of view through his development of the theme, or is the theme something that many people can agree with?

G. Is the theme related very closely to the setting, to the plot, or to the characters? Explain your answers.

---

prefer. Then, when they have selected their favorite stories, have them state what the themes of those stories are. Next, have them group the stories that have common themes. Then ask the students, "Why are these your favorite stories? Do you enjoy them for the plot, for the way the author uses his words, for the theme—or for something else?" Some students may respond very well when asked to put together a collection of stories based upon theme for younger students to read.

4. Have students bring to class their favorite records. The students can provide the lyrics for the songs. Then ask them whether there are any themes present in those songs. After the students have determined what the themes are, have them read stories with the same themes. Discuss: In what ways are the songs different from the short stories in presenting the themes? Do the songs present the themes better than the short stories? Why or why not?

5. Compare the short stories of modern writers with the stories written by writers in the nineteenth century for their treatments of theme. Given the same basic problem, do the authors develop the same theme, or are our attitudes toward life different today from those of people in the last century?

6. After reading a number of short stories written by writers of the United States, and after listing the themes found in those short stories, students can read the stories of writers from other countries and list the themes revealed by those stories. Are the themes different from those of U.S. writers, or are they the same? Do writers from different countries emphasize different themes, or does the occurrence of particular themes appear to be equally distributed in stories regardless of the national origin of the writer?

7. Have students read short stories written by representatives of different ethnic groups in the United States. Ask them to list the themes that seem to be common to the writers of the specific ethnic groups. Do the groupings of themes differ from ethnic group to ethnic group, or are they common to all ethnic groups? Do these findings reveal anything about the differences or similarities of different ethnic groups?

8. Assign students to find a proverb or maxim that best illustrates the theme of a particular short story. This activity forces students to concentrate upon theme and not upon story line. If some stories do not suggest proverbs or maxims, discuss with the students why. Perhaps the stories are not intended to reveal a particular theme.

9. Give your students the following themes. Ask them to brainstorm possible plots that would support these themes. Do this as a class or have groups compete against each other to see which group can develop the greatest number of, or the most original, plots.

"Power corrupts."

"Greed ultimately makes one unhappy."

"Love conquers all."

"We seldom appreciate our friends until it is too late."

"The rich get richer, and the poor get poorer."

"People are seldom what they appear to be."

"All the world loves a clown."

"Money isn't everything."

"Money does buy happiness."

Or, have students suggest their own themes for this activity.

INVOLVING THE STUDENTS WITH SETTING

Many students will skip right over the descriptive passages in a short story, trying to get directly to the action. To these students description is just padding added by an author to make the story longer and harder to get through. More materialistic students may even suggest that the author was probably paid by the word and so wrote all those extra words for money, not for a purpose. Add to those students the ones who have a hard time reading, who plod along word by word and thus grasp little meaning from any sentence, and you have two groups for whom setting may have to be emphasized.

Not all authors create extensive settings. Perhaps the author manages to encompass all that needs to be said by simply writing one sentence, or two, as in the opening of Ted Poston's "Rat Joiner Routs the Klan": "There had never been a Ku Klux Klan in Hopkinsville, Kentucky. So it was sort of surprising how our leading colored citizens got all worked up when they heard that *The Birth of a Nation* was coming to the Rex Theater down on Ninth Street." Or the setting may be summarized by a single word or a simple phrase, as in Bruce Jay Friedman's "23 Pat O'Brien Movies": "... on the sixteenth-story hotel-room ledge...." In such cases, the student can grasp the essence of the setting simply, quickly, and with little exploration. But when an author does include an extended setting or scatters pieces of the setting throughout the story, then students may need some guidance.

"Who cares about the setting?" Faced with a question such as that, the teacher can be dogmatic: "I do—and you'd better." Or the teacher can be coy: "Why don't we find out whether we do, class?" Or the teacher can be silenced by the sudden realization that some people may actually not care, not be fascinated, not be swept up in the magnificence of the author's words—or, as the students may view it, verbosity. When the teacher knows beforehand how students *may* feel about reading a short story in which the setting is meaningful, then the teacher can plan some activities that will involve the students with the setting—*and the way the setting relates to other aspects of the story.*

Let students realize that many different elements fit into the setting. Setting refers not only to place but also to time. As an artist with words, the skillful author uses setting to help the reader gain insights into the characters who populate the story, into the moods that run through the story, into the possible sudden twists in plot, into the attitude the author hopes to share, and even—and many times—into the meaning that underlies the tale. Teachers will not help students appreciate literature by telling them how setting may relate to all those elements. They must find ways to allow the students to discover those things so that an encounter with a short story becomes a voyage of discovery, or a puzzle in which the pieces begin to fall into place, revealing something they may not have thought about.

1. Before students read the stories selected to emphasize setting as an element of the short story, pass out a questionnaire for students to use such as the one on Reproduction Page 8.

REPRODUCTION PAGE 8

SETTING

Directions: *Setting may tell us something about a story that we may not have noticed. After you finish reading a story, answer the following questions:*

A. When and where did the story happen?

B. Could the story have happened somewhere else? At another time?

C. How long a period of time is encompassed by the events of the story?

D. Would it have changed the story any if the author had shortened or lengthened the time period?

E. Does the author follow one time line from beginning to end or jump back and forth in time (flashbacks)?

F. If the author does jump around in time, would the story have been different if the story were rewritten with time moving chronologically from beginning to end?

G. Is the setting important to the story? Why or why not?

H. Does the setting influence the plot or the characters in any way?

I. Is the setting believable?

J. Does the setting help create a particular mood? Is that mood essential to the story?

K. How much time does the author spend describing the setting? At what points in the story? Is this done on purpose?

---

2. Find a story in which setting is strongly depicted and read it to the students. Ask them to draw the setting or to find pictures in magazines that best portray the setting. Ask each student to explain to the class why that illustration seems most appropriate to the story.

3. After reading a series of short stories, ask students to copy or cut out an illustration from a magazine that portrays the setting of a particular short story. Display these illustrations around the room without revealing which story they represent. Ask the students in the class to match the illustration with the appropriate short story.

4. Pose the following problem to your students: You have been asked to design a stage set for a one-act play based upon the short story. You cannot change the scene because that would take too much time and cost too much. Create a model of the stage set you would design or draw a picture of it. Then explain how the action of the story would take place in that set.

5. Select two short stories in which setting is important to the theme or characterization or plot. Ask students to respond to the following question: If the plot and characters of story A were to be placed in the setting of story B, would anything necessarily change? Why?

6. After the students have read a number of short stories, have them go back through the stories and write down the exact words the author employs to establish the setting. (It would be more convenient if the students could underline those words, but since most schools must use their textbooks over and over, underlining obviously has its drawbacks.) Then have them classify the author's descriptions on a scale from the most abstract to the most specific. Does the author talk of the setting as being "gloomy" without describing what causes that gloom? Does the author describe the leaves of the trees as "glistening with dew!" and let us come to our own conclusions about the mood? Have the students consider whether the abstract descriptions are as appropriate to their stories as the concrete and specific descriptions, and why or why not.

7. Before students actually read a short story in which the setting is important to character development or mood or theme, read aloud to the students the paragraph or paragraphs that actually describe the setting. Then ask them questions which will force them to think about what the setting will lead to. In some stories, you may be able to ask, "What type of event will probably happen in this story?" In others, your question may have to be oriented toward mood: "What sort of feeling do you get from this description? What kinds of things could happen in this type of setting?" Consider, for example, the first paragraph of D. H. Lawrence's "Tickets, Please"[2] (see Reproduction Page 9).

   There are many places for a teacher to begin with such an introduction. Beyond the initial questions—What will happen here? What is the mood? and so on—the teacher may have to ask some specific things of the students in order to cause them to focus upon keys to understanding the passage; for instance:

   A. Notice (perhaps list on paper) the adjectives which the author employs (*black, ugly, stark, grimy, cold, gloomy, fat,* etc.). What sort of mood is the author creating? (somber, melancholy). And in this case, do the adjectives change in feeling anywhere? (Suddenly we are faced with *perky, jaunty, daredevil, green,* etc.) Why does the author include both categories of adjective? (Develops contrast.) Which indicates what the story might be like? (Possibly both.) How do you know? (Let students argue both ways if they so choose.)

   B. List all the adverbs. What do they indicate to us? (Answers will depend upon the specific instances.)

   C. List all the things (objects, people, animals, machines, etc.) that the author

2. From "Tickets Please," *The Complete Short Stories of D. H. Lawrence,* Vol. II. Copyright 1961. By permission of Viking Press, Inc.

SETTING

Directions: *Read the selection below from D. H. Lawrence's "Tickets, Please." Then answer the questions that follow and be prepared to discuss your answers.*

There is in the Midlands a single-line tramway system which boldly leaves the county town and plunges off into the black, industrial country-side, up hill and down dale, through the long ugly villages of workmen's houses, over canals and railways, past churches perched high and nobly over the smoke and shadows, through stark, grimy cold little market-places, tilting away in a rush past cinemas and shops down to the hollow where the collieries are, then up again, past a little rural church, under the ash trees, on in a rush to the terminus, the last little ugly place of industry, the cold little town that shivers on the edge of the wild, gloomy country beyond. There the green and creamy coloured tramcar seems to pause and purr with curious satisfaction. But in a few minutes—the clock on the turret of the Co-operative Wholesale Society's shops gives the time—away it starts once more on the adventure. Again there are the reckless swoops downhill, bouncing the loops: again the chilly wait in the hill-top market-place: again the breathless slithering round the precipitous drop under the church: again the patient halts at the loops, waiting for the outcoming car: so on and on, for two long hours, till at last the city looms beyond the fat gasworks, the narrow factories draw near, we are in the sordid streets of the great town, once more we sidle to a standstill at our terminus, abashed by the great crimson and cream-coloured city cars, but still perky, jaunty, somewhat dare-devil, green as a jaunty sprig of parsley out of a black colliery garden.

A. Notice (perhaps list on paper) the adjectives the author employs. What sort of mood is he creating? And in this case, do the adjectives change in feeling anywhere? Why does the author include both categories of adjectives? Which indicates what the story might be like? How do you know?

B. List all the adverbs. What do they indicate to us?

C. List all the things (objects, people, animals, machines, etc.) that the author includes. Do they have anything in common? If not, are they placed there for contrast? Why does the author choose to talk about those things and only those things?

From "Tickets Please," *The Complete Short Stories of D. H. Lawrence*, Vol. II, Copyright 1961. By permission of Viking Press, Inc.

includes. Do they have anything in common? (Mostly man-related.) If not, are they placed there for contrast? (Even what is pleasant is part of the ugliness.) Why does the author choose to talk about those things and only those things? (Perhaps to establish mood, perhaps to tell much in a short space.)

This exercise is available on Reproduction Page 9.

8. Find a long descriptive passage in a short story (such as in number 7) and ask students to summarize the paragraph in one sentence. The important reason for this exercise is to enable them to indicate whether they have grasped the purpose for such a setting. Follow-up activities include:

A. Read all sentences aloud. The class then decides, after some discussion, which sentence best captures what the author was trying to accomplish.

B. Contrast the single-sentence examples with the author's original, extended version. Which does more for the story? Is it possible that the author has written too much? Or are the single sentences too concise to be able to develop the mood or create a meaningful setting for the events to follow?

C. Ask the students to draw the scene, or part of it, based upon the single-sentence examples. Then ask them to do the same based upon the author's version. Discuss which was easier to do and why. Do not assume that the author's version will be the easier to draw from. Allow the students to come to their own conclusions. Indeed, the very complexity of the author's version may confuse the student artist, and that just may suit the author's purpose. If so, it is worth considering.

9. Sometimes characters become part of the setting. Ask students to relate the characters to the setting: Do the characters belong there? Are they part of the setting? Or is there something strange about those characters being in that particular setting? Note, as an example, this paragraph from E. M. Forster's "The Machine Stops":

> Imagine, if you can, a small room, hexagonal in shape, like the cell of a bee. It is lighted neither by window nor by lamp, yet it is filled with a soft radiance. There are no apertures for ventilation, yet the air is fresh. There are no musical instruments, and yet, at the moment that my meditation opens, this room is throbbing with melodious sounds. An arm chair is in the center, by its side a reading-desk—that is all the furniture. And in the arm chair there sits a swaddled lump of flesh—a woman, about five feet high, with a face as white as a fungus. It is to her that the little room belongs.[3]

INVOLVING STUDENTS WITH CHARACTERIZATION

Since the characters in a short story are typically involved closely with the plot, students seldom experience difficulty in being aware of character types. But how do students judge characters? Do they judge the characters in the same way, according to the identical standards that they would judge their friends and people they meet? They may, and that may be just the sort of reaction and judgment that a teacher needs to begin study of a story. But some authors may place their characters in very special situations, situations that demand of the reader new ways of viewing the characters. The students need ways of considering characters both as typical—to them—human beings and as special people whom they may never have met and may never ever meet.

For the study of characterization in short stories, the obvious question is, "What is the purpose of the character in the story?" That may be the teacher's primary question; it may be the question that captures the essence of the tale. But it may not be the question to begin with. Think about it. The answer to that question involves a number of other considerations, answers and conclusions to more basic questions. And some of those questions may have little to do with the story itself. For instance, to what types of character will students react positively and negatively? What determines such judgments on their parts? Their experience? A good deal of their judgment will be related to their past experience, and that is to the teacher's advantage, for it means that the students are applying standards of evaluation. Other underlying questions are: Will the students identify, sympathize, or empathize with the characters? Are the characters believable, stereotyped, or both? What do we know about the characters, and how do we know it? Is one character speaking for the author? (Conversely, is the author speaking through the character?) The answers to these questions may not come easily to students, but the answers must be sought.

Consider the possibility of treating characters out of the context of the story, especially before the students encounter them in the context of the story. Prereading exercises, such as improvisation or role playing, may give students greater insights into characters and

---

3. From "The Machine Stops," *The Eternal Moment and Other Stories* by E. M. Forster. Copyright 1970. By permission of Harcourt Brace Jovanovich.

thus enable them to understand the characters better within the confines of the author's setting and plot. This is especially true when characters' motivations and drives are vastly different from those of the students. If your students have never encountered a Mexican American woman from the mountains of northern New Mexico, such as Mana Seda in Fray Angelico Chavez's "Hunchback Madonna," a woman who has dedicated her life to God, they may judge her harshly as one who has no meaning to them. On the other hand, they may believe strongly in religion or in some cause, or they may have had relatives or friends who did, even in the factory towns of the Northeast, and that may provide insights into Mana Seda.

On the other hand, prereading exercises dealing with characters may work against an appreciation of characterization. In some stories, the characterization is the essence of the tale, and how the author develops the character depends upon the choice of images, events, and specific words. With characters such as Maggie, Dee, and Mama in Alice Walker's "Everyday Use" or Mrs. Wilson in Shirley Jackson's "After You, My Dear Alphonse," the students may gain more by reading the stories first and coming to their own conclusions about the characters.

Helping students judge characterization in the context of the specific short story is an important goal. Immature readers might not recognize stereotypes when they encounter them and thus might miss an important aspect of the short story. More mature readers might recognize the stereotypes and dismiss the story out of hand without considering the author's purpose for stereotyping. And, at the final extreme, stereotypes may ruin the impact of a story. If stereotyping is the teacher's concern, perhaps some exercises which will develop students' awareness of stereotyping will help. For example, the teacher could have students respond to the following:

A teacher is _____ .

Adults are _____ .

Football players are _____ .

Women should _____ .

American Indians live _____ .

The communists _____ .

After students have individually filled in the blanks, they can compare responses. Are those responses alike or not? If alike, are the similarities true? Always? If all short stories were about the categories of people portrayed them in such ways, would the stories still be interesting? Would they tell us anything new? Why should we read stories in which a type of character is always portrayed in the same way?

Such exercises are helpful in isolating specific considerations relating to characterization. If the students do not need to go through a particular type of exercise, do not put them through it. But be aware that some exercises may help the students interpret and eventually evaluate short stories according to criteria they arrive at themselves. The value of particular exercises may thus be inestimable. Ask the teacher who, year after year, has encountered the knee-jerk reaction from students—"That character is dumb!"—how to overcome such a reaction. If the teacher says nothing can be done about it, then he or she has not planned for the reaction ahead of time or has not planned to make use of it the moment it arises—and it will.

The following exercises are designed to cope with the knee-jerk reaction:

UNDERSTANDING THE CHARACTER

1. Take any character out of a short story and ask students to predict how that character will behave in the new situation. Situations can be developed that relate closely to the situation of the short story or that are unique. By employing a unique situation, the teacher can force students to consider the total personality of the character. Examples of possible situations are contained on Reproduction Page 10.

REPRODUCTION PAGE 10

CHARACTER

Directions: *Pick one of the characters from a short story you have just read. Where the questions below say CHARACTER, substitute the name of the character you have picked. Then answer the questions.*

A. CHARACTER has just been given a ticket for speeding. How will CHARACTER respond?

B. In a contest sponsored by a commercial company, CHARACTER has won $100,000. Describe what CHARACTER will do with the money.

C. CHARACTER is thinking about getting married (after a divorce, after the death of the spouse, etc.). What characteristics will CHARACTER look for in a marriage partner? How do you know?

D. CHARACTER wants to buy a new house. What type of home will CHARACTER look for? Where will it be located? How much will it cost? What kind of landscaping will it have?

E. You offer to give CHARACTER a ticket to any type of sporting event CHARACTER would enjoy seeing. What type of sporting event will CHARACTER choose? Why?

F. You are the director of a movie based upon the short story which you have just read. Whom will you cast in the role of CHARACTER? Why?

G. CHARACTER has just entered a restaurant that serves every type of food in the world. The waiter asks CHARACTER, "What would you like?" CHARACTER replies: _____ . Explain the choice.

---

2. Ask students to write tombstone epitaphs for the characters in the short story. For guidelines, the students might want to visit a local cemetery, or read such semiserious collections of epitaphs as *Comic Epitaphs from the Very Best Old Graveyards* and *Over Their Dead Bodies: Yankee Epitaphs & History* by Thomas C. Mann and Janet Greene.[4] For those students who prefer writing poetry, you can suggest that they read Masters's *Spoon River Anthology* as a guide. Have the students draw their tombstones complete with epitaph and post them around the room or in the school hallway.

3. As a variation upon exercise 2, direct students to the obituaries in the local newspaper. Discuss with the students elements that are common among all obit-

---

4. Thomas C. Mann and Janet Greene, *Over Their Dead Bodies: Yankee Epitaphs & History* (Brattleboro, Vt.: Stephen Greene Press, 1962). *Comic Epitaphs from the Very Best Old Graveyards* (Mt. Vernon, N.Y.: Peter Pauper Press, 1957).

uaries. (Have the students determine what they are.) Then ask the students to write obituaries for selected characters.

4. Pass out the list on Reproduction Page 11 and require the students to justify their answers. These forced questions compel students to think about the qualities of characters. You may want to add literary characters such as:

A. Macbeth, Moll Flanders, Willy Loman, or Mrs. Mike.

B. Tom Sawyer or Huckleberry Finn.

REPRODUCTION PAGE 11

CHARACTERIZATION QUALITIES

Directions: *Pick a character from a short story you have just read and answer the following questions. Be prepared to discuss your answers.*

Is CHARACTER more like:

A. May or December?

B. A Subaru or a Mercedes Benz?

C. Brown or blue?

D. A snowstorm or a rainy day?

E. The letter *A*, the letter *M*, or the letter *Z*?

F. Vanilla ice cream or charlotte russe?

G. New York, San Francisco, Salt Lake City, or New Orleans?

H. A hammer or a nail?

I. A short story or a poem?

J. White, rye, or pumpernickel bread?

K. A TV quiz show or a news report?

L. Soap or dirt?

M. Fire, water, earth, or air?

N. A cathedral, a pup tent, or a log cabin?

O. Africa, Asia, Australia, Europe, or South America?

P. A horse show, a hockey match, or a track-and-field event?

Q. A filing cabinet or a garbage pail?

R. A lock or a key?

S. A forest fire or a mountain stream?

T. The comics, the sports section, the business report, or the editorial page?

U. A wood lathe or a kitchen stove?

---

5. After having students read a short story, present them with the following problem: "You are the garbage collector who visits CHARACTER'S house on your regular route. You have found throughout the years, as you have come to know the people along your route better, that their garbage is a good indication of their personalities, likes, and dislikes. Describe the types of garbage you are likely to find at CHARACTER'S house and what that garbage reveals about CHARACTER."

6. Provide your students with checklists of adjectives that describe the short-story characters they have read about. One such checklist is on Reproduction Page 12.

Ask your students to check off the descriptive words that best characterize any given character in a short story. Have them bring their checklists to class and share their perceptions with their classmates. Several ways of doing this include:

A. Break into small groups. Have the students in each group compile totals of each characteristic checked. Then rank the totals in order of most to least

REPRODUCTION PAGE 12

QUALITIES OF A CHARACTER

Directions: *Either check the words below that describe a character in a story you have just read or use the most appropriate ones in your written character description:*

Mental Qualities

intelligent	unintelligent
educated	unschooled
smart	dumb
wise	ignorant
gifted	simple
clever	puerile
ingenious	obtuse
brilliant	vacuous
learned	narrow-minded
scholarly	shallow
astute	dull
competent	incompetent
sensible	unreasonable
talented	incapable
intellectual	bigoted
precocious	ignorant
rational	irrational

Moral Qualities

moral	immoral
kind	cruel
considerate	inconsiderate
idealistic	unprincipled
innocent	corrupt
righteous	vile
upstanding	deceitful
truthful	lying
honest	unscrupulous
honorable	dishonorable
loyal	untrustworthy
helpful	self-centered
virtuous	dissolute
pure	vulgar
puritanical	degenerate
austere	sensual
polite	insulting
respectable	base

Physical Qualities

strong	weak
healthy	sickly
handsome	hideous
beautiful	ugly
pretty	graceless
cute	emaciated
robust	clumsy
hardy	awkward
dainty	grotesque
delicate	odious
charming	coarse
ravishing	repulsive
adroit	ungainly
skillful	unkempt
lively	decrepit

Social Qualities

cooperative	contentious
hospitable	inhospitable
congenial	impolite
cheerful	sullen
supportive	antagonistic
urbane	boorish
worldly	provincial
debonair	brusque
suave	obsequious
elegant	unpolished
courteous	petulant
tactful	crude
cordial	crabby
convivial	critical
encouraging	caustic
merry	grumpy

often checked. Finally, compare their ranking with the rankings of the other groups. If the groups have been working on the same character, some disagreements may result. If so, good. Have each group defend its list. If time permits, ask the groups to combine their rankings and come to some consensus. Individual students need not agree with the class result and should be encouraged to defend their opinions.

B. Ask each student to write a brief paragraph in which the character is described by employing the most appropriate adjectives from the list. As a variation, request that the name of the character be omitted from the description. Read the descriptions to the class. Can they determine which character is being described? If not, why not? Are some of the adjectives too vague? Could the same adjectives fit other characters in the story? How can the characterizations be improved?

C. Obviously, such adjective lists are limited in scope. Ask the students to add adjectives to the lists that better describe the characters in the short story they have read. Or, prior to reading the short stories, pass out the adjective lists and ask students to improve them by adding new adjectives or making those on the list more descriptive.

7. Some students are unable to detect stereotyped characters in their reading. In order to make them more aware of possible stereotypes, discuss television shows in which stock characters are employed. Examples include the soap operas, cowboy shows, family situation comedies, and detective mysteries. Then present the students with the following snatches of dialogue and ask them to describe the plot in which such dialogue is likely to occur:

A. Doctor, I wouldn't tell you this if I didn't respect you so, but there's something you ought to know about your wife.

B. John, no man has ever tried to reach that sunken ship and survived to tell about it. Surely you can't be thinking of trying that.

C. Well, Lieutenant, it looks like no one is going to be able to get through to that trapped patrol. Lieutenant? Lieutenant! Where are you?

D. I don't know, Martin. I've had this funny feeling about this house since we first saw it. I guess it's just my nerves.

E. I know the ranchers have always hated us sheepherders, but that land is free and out there waiting for us.

F. Her? She's just a woman! What can she possibly know about driving a race car? Believe me, automobile racing is for men—strong men.

After they have described the plot, ask them to list the characters who will be in the story. In order to strengthen the idea of stereotyping, direct the students to do the above tasks in small groups, and then compare the results. The more likely a character is to be stereotyped, the more likely that character will show up in more than one group.

8. To concentrate on the short-story characters, students can use Reproduction Page 13, which could apply to any short story.

REPRODUCTION PAGE 13

UNDERSTANDING CHARACTERS

Directions: *Use the following questions whenever you have to analyze and understand characters:*

A. Who are the characters in the story?

B. What are these characters like?

C. Is there a common problem that all of the characters must face?

D. Do the characters fall into particular groups? Are these groups against one another?

E. Is one of the characters the main character, or are there several main characters?

F. Do the characters change or grow as individuals, or are they alike throughout the story?

G. If the characters change, is there a good reason for their change? If so, what is it?

H. If there are any minor characters, what is their purpose in the story? To help move the plot along? To provide a change of pace in the story? To balance one character against another, or to provide a contrast to a main character? To help explain the motivations of the main character or characters?

I. Are the characters realistic? Stereotyped? Unbelievable? Romantic?

J. Are all the characters necessary to the story, or could the author have left some of them out?

K. Does the author let you know a great deal about the characters, or does the author tell you about one main characteristic only?

L. How important is our knowing more about the characters, or do we appreciate the story without knowing much about the characters? Does this factor indicate something about the author's purpose in writing the story?

9. Direct each student to pick a character who has a major problem and to write a letter offering advice on how to handle that problem. If a student feels uncomfortable giving such advice, have that student pretend to be another character in the story who is writing the letter.

10. Have some students volunteer to improvise a scene from the short story, each student selecting a particular character to portray. They might do a better job if given the assignment a day ahead of time. Ask the remaining members of the class to consider the following:

    A. Did the scene turn out the way it did in the short story? If not, which version was better—the short story version or the improvised version? Why?

    B. Did the actors portray the characters in the way that you visualized them? If not, how were the portrayals different? After discussing the last question, did the improvised version help you understand the characters better? If so, how?

11. A variation is to have the students improvise a scene between characters in the short story, but in a setting or about a problem that does not exist in the short story. For a more interesting approach, bring two characters from different stories together and improvise what would happen. Then ask the students whether they have gained further insights into the characters.

12. Ask students to go through magazines to find pictures of people who look like given characters in a short story. Compare the pictures they bring in. Do they have any common features? If so, what does this indicate about the characters? Are they drastically different in any way? If so, does this tell us anything about the way the author has developed the character?

13. Have students think of some well-known historical figures or celebrities of today

who resemble one or more characters in a short story. Discuss why they are alike. Do they differ in any significant way? If the historical figure or current celebrity were in the place of the character, would the story change in any way?

14. Ask students to visualize one character in a new setting. For instance, if the character were a student in this class, what would the character be like? Would other students like the character? How would the character dress, think, behave? Would you want that character for a friend? Why or why not?

15. Check the values-clarification suggestions in Sidney Simon, Logan P. Howe, and Howard Kirschenbaum's *Values Clarification.*[5] We are indebted to Linda Shadiow of Bozeman, Montana, for bringing the following applications of values-clarification techniques to our attention. Students can be asked to apply these techniques to characters they encounter in short stories—or poems, novels, biographies, and plays, for that matter—just as they can be applied to the students themselves.

Developed by Joe Luft and Harry Ingham, "The Johari Window" (see Reproduction Page 14) is a technique used to illustrate the difference between the way

---

REPRODUCTION PAGE 14

JOHARI WINDOW

	Self Blind	Self Aware
Other blind	Character or others in story not aware of these aspects of the character; an omniscient author would be.	Character is aware, but does not let other characters know about these aspects of character.
Other aware	Other characters realize this about the character, but the character does not.	Both the character and others in the story are aware of these characteristics.

	Self blind	Self aware
Other blind		
Other aware		

---

5. Sidney Simon, Logan P. Howe, and Howard Kirschenbaum, *Values Clarification* (New York: Hart, 1972).

a person views himself and how others view that person. It also indicates those traits to which the person or others may be blind. The "Coat of Arms" (see Reproduction Page 15) is a device for considering any number of ways in which a character may be considered. Students can either write what is asked for in each segment or draw pictures that represent the items. The motto of the character may be included or left out, but if included it can summarize the essence of the character under consideration.

REPRODUCTION PAGE 15

COAT OF ARMS

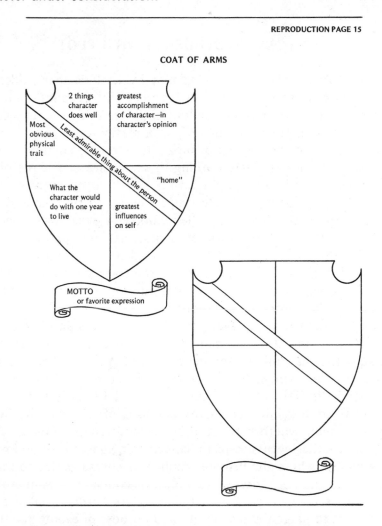

Possible items for inclusion in each section might be:

A. One thing the character does very well.

B. The greatest accomplishment of the character (from his or her point of view).

C. Three words the person would use to characterize himself or herself.

D. The most influential person in the character's life.

E. The most memorable physical trait of the character.

F. The place the character considers home.

G. The item that most other characters associate with this particular character.

H. What the character would do with only one year to live.

Another variation or an addition to the shield, might be a "bar sinister," a diagonal space running across the shield. On this might be placed the most ignominious or degrading or immoral thing the character has ever done. Again, this is optional, for it will not apply to all characters.

INVOLVING STUDENTS WITH PLOT

A word of warning: The danger of studying plot by itself is that students may gain too trivial a notion of what is involved in a short story. A plot depends upon the characters to carry it to a worthwhile conclusion. It enables the writer to tie events together in an effort to communicate the theme. It may occur only in a particular setting. Or, it may be only a series of events strung together with no apparent purpose, employing characters of no particular worth and having absolutely nothing to say to the reader. A story may be tightly structured and highly dependent upon plot to hold itself together, or it may be "plotless," aimed particularly at developing characterization or mood or theme. Younger students, particularly those in the junior high or middle school, enjoy reading stories with strong plot lines. Selecting stories that will give these students what they prefer is important, for the teacher must find ways to encourage students to read before any discussion and evaluation can take place. For senior high school students, more complex stories can be employed; for hopefully, after having explored manipulations of plot in their earlier school years, they will be more capable of handling intricate variations.

Possibly every student who has ever gone through a secondary school English program has been asked to diagram plot according to the Aristotelian model. Such a model is included in the activities that follow. And yet the act of applying this model to a short story is valuable only if it helps explain the structure of the story and if it makes the story more accessible to the students. To force it or any other model blindly upon a short story is to sidetrack students from the important considerations of whether the plot is potentially believable or improbable, whether the author has ordered the events with extreme and purposeful care, or whether events seem to happen coincidentally—you know the type—the deus ex machina ending where the heroine, Pauline of course, is tied to the rails in front of an onrushing train and the hero, dressed in white, of course, rushes in at the last second to save her. Those stories may be great fun, but they are hardly great literature. Exercises should enable students to judge the probability and purpose of events in a short story.

Again, less mature readers are going to need more guidance. Once in a creative-fiction-writing class, a sophomore student turned in the first story of the semester with the following plot: Jane has decided to run away from home. She travels by bus to a new and unfamiliar town. While getting off the bus, she sees a baby about to be run over by a car in the middle of the street. She rushes out and saves the child. A young man hurries over to thank her, saying that the baby is his sister. He invites her home. After supper, she retires to bed, and the young man's father says to the young man, "Why don't you ask her to marry you—I saw how you looked at her." The next day, her parents come to get her after seeing newspaper pictures of her taken when she saved the child. They are contrite for having mistreated her. She and the young man know they love each other. The end. Now, some of the students in the class immediately recognized the extreme coincidence and shallowness of the plot and said so. But others disagreed. Only after more maturing and more reading did the author begin to write stories with less improbable plots—good ones, too. The moral: The teacher must meet students at their level of maturity and experience and move them from there.

We are accustomed to thinking of stories as having a clear beginning, middle, and end. The beginning ought to make the setting clear, introduce the characters, and establish the conflict that will develop in the remainder of the story. Clearly, students need to consider that beginning carefully. The middle should develop from the beginning, and the end ought to result from what has gone on before. That seems to be about as basic a series of realizations as we need. But it is not enough.

What happens when the student encounters an unclear plot in a short story? Perhaps the author tells the aftermath first, then shifts to the earliest relevant series of events, interjects some foreshadowing, refers again to the aftermath, comes back to the main chronological line of events, gives us some more foreshadowing, sustains the suspense for a few pages, and finally reveals the ending that led to the aftermath. In such a case, less mature readers will have to pay close attention to the chronological order of events and may have to outline those in order to grasp what has happened. Even more confusion may arise when apparently nothing happens in the story. John Galsworthy's "The Japanese Quince" is an excellent example of such a story. Students may read this three-pager and come back to class saying, "I turned the page over and there wasn't any more! What happened?" In this story, the main character goes out, looks at a Japanese quince, feels uncomfortable, and goes back to his apartment. That is all. Or, as some students might say, "That is *all*!!!" But there is more to the story, and only through considering the separate elements the author presents can the students begin to comprehend what it is all about. Plot, as we normally consider it, is inconsequential.

Thus, the teacher should take students to and through stories in an effort to find the reason for the elements of plot, if those elements are there. It does not matter that the story has a climax and that the climax occurs at the very end. What does matter is whether the climax has a purpose related to the rest of the story. Nor does it matter if the main character is stereotyped or not as long as the portrayal in the plot is clearly purposeful.

The following exercises are designed to make students aware that plot is more than a mere list of events and that all the elements of a plot ought to be related to the purpose of the author. Then the students ought to be able to evaluate the plot according to criteria that relate to the story in question.

1. With the entire class, list all the events of the story on the board. Discuss whether this is the plot or not. Does there have to be something besides events in order to make a plot? If the students still cannot make the distinction between plot and events, try the following: Mention a movie or TV show which most of the students have seen. First, ask what it was about. Then ask the students to list the events which occurred in the movie or TV show. Compare the responses to these two questions. What is the basic difference between them? Return to the original list of events in the short story. Ask the following questions: Could any of the events be left out? Why or why not? Why are the events that cannot be left out essential to the story? This time ask the students to tell what the story is about. Then ask them to explain plot in their own words.

2. A more direct approach is simply to ask students to tell what the story is about in one sentence. If they have captured the essence of the plot, tell them that they have just described the plot and then ask them to define plot in their own words.

3. Ask students to create their own story by listing the events of the story on the board. Allow students to ask such questions as "What is the story about?" or "What characters are going to be in it?" Come to some conclusions with the class about what must go into a short story besides events alone.

4. Have students create a montage based upon their reading of a short story by having them cut out pictures from magazines and newspapers that portray the events in a short story. Ask each student to inform the class how each element of the montage relates to the plot.

5. A plot-completion exercise enables students to consider a variety of elements of plot in an attempt to evaluate different types of plot. Basically, the teacher reads a brief story outline to the students with several endings suggested. The students choose the ending they feel is best and justify their answers. The following is an example of such an exercise:

Mouse, whose father was Mexican and whose mother was Paiute, tried working in the mining towns of southern Nevada when he was young. No matter how hard he tried to please his Anglo American employers, they still refused to promote him because he was a "half-breed." One day, when he was insulted by two miners along the Colorado River, Mouse flew into a rage and killed them.

A. Feeling a sudden elation after killing the miners, Mouse realized that Anglo Americans were his enemies and vowed to kill them all until his people were free of them. He hid outside White Hills, Arizona, and began to kill miners as they returned to their homes at night. The miners banded together, trapped Mouse, and hanged him.

B. Hearing of what Mouse had done, and realizing that he had not been punished, the Paiutes in the area rose up against the white man. The whites, realizing that they had been unjust to the Paiutes, swore to change their ways and began creating laws that gave the Paiutes equal rights. The whites did not prosecute Mouse, and eventually he became chief of his tribe.

C. Mouse ran off into the desert. The whites were enraged. They spread the word that Mouse was a renegade and that he had to be stopped. A reward was posted for his capture, dead or alive. One day, after stealing a cabbage for food, Mouse was recognized by another Paiute and was killed by him.

Walter Loban, Margaret Ryan, and James R. Squire, in *Teaching Language and Literature*, report such an exercise developed by Sara Roody of Nyack, New York.[6] Several exercises are also supplied by Dwight Burton in *Literature Study in the High School*.[7]

6. Read a story to students that is clearly a story where plot is important. But stop before you finish the story. Ask students to finish the story. Read the student versions to the class and discuss with the class which ones are the most likely endings and why. Then read the original version to the students. Discuss whether they prefer any of their endings over the original author's ending and why.

---

6. Walter Loban, Margaret Ryan, and James R. Squire, *Teaching Language and Literature*, 2d ed. (New York: Harcourt, Brace & World, 1969), p. 562.

7. Dwight Burton, *Literature Study in the High School*, 3d ed. (New York: Holt, Rinehart & Winston, 1970), pp. 91–98.

7. Have students decide how a story might be changed if a current TV character were to be one of the main characters instead of the main character which the author has created. For instance, how would Mr. Spock of "Star Trek" handle any of the situations which Ray Bradbury creates in *Martian Chronicles*? Or how would a current television detective handle a Sherlock Holmes mystery in place of Sherlock Holmes? Does the substitution of a different main character substantially alter the plot? Discuss also how important a particular character may be to a particular plot.

8. Ask students to create simple outlines of the plot of a short story. Compare the outlines, checking to see which ones may include events other students leave out. Discuss the differences with the class. How essential are all the events to the plot? Which are the key events—which events cause the story line to move in very specific directions? In order to illustrate a difference between the novel and the short story, do the same exercises with a novel the students have read. Discuss the importance of events in a short story as contrasted with the importance of events in a novel.

9. In order to illustrate the importance of the beginning of a short story, read several first paragraphs from short stories your students are not likely to have read. Ask them to describe what the author has done in each of the first paragraphs. A variety of answers are likely to be developed: The author has established the scene, introduced a main character, presented the main problem present in the story, and so on. Then read the first two paragraphs of each story, then the first three, and so on until all the important elements necessary for getting into the story have been established. Have the students list the important elements of a good short-story beginning.

10. Once students are aware of the essential elements of a short-story beginning, read them the beginning of one short story and ask them to predict the possible courses the story may take from there. Some key questions for you to ask are:

    A. What is the story about?

    B. What is it not about?

    C. Who is the main character?

    D. Is the main character involved in a problem? If so, what is it?

    E. Do we have any indication of how the problem may be resolved?

11. When reading a story that is not strong in plot, or that seems almost plotless, students often wonder what it is about. Because immature readers may react negatively to relatively plotless stories, have your students write character descriptions first and then discuss with them what sorts of events could reveal those same character traits to a reader without telling the reader what the characteristics are. For younger students, concentrating upon only one characteristic may be more effective than asking them to handle a variety of characteristics.

12. In stories with a strong plot line, the turning point, or climax, typically occurs when the author stops presenting the problem and begins presenting the solution. Collect a number of stories from magazines such as *Redbook, Ladies' Home*

Journal, or *True*—stories with a strong emphasis upon plot. Run off copies of one or two of the stories and ask one half of the class to read the stories to determine when the author stops presenting the problem. Ask the other half of the class to determine when the author begins presenting the solution. Then have the two halves of the class compare their results. In most cases, they will have determined the climax themselves. Tell them so afterward, not before you begin the exercise.

13. Comic strips provide a valuable source for illustrating the variety of ways in which plot may be developed. Save a series of comic strips that are concerned with one particular plot. Continuing serious strips such as *Steve Canyon, Dick Tracy, Mary Worth,* and *Apartment 3-G* provide some good contrasts. Display an entire comic-strip series on a bulletin board or make copies for each member of the class. Examine how the cartoonists develop their stories in different ways. Which ones have many events and many characters? Which are predictable? Which get right into the story, and which take a long time developing it? Ask students to pick one cartoon story and turn it into a written short story. Compare their results with the original version, the cartoon. Reverse this exercise. Ask students to turn a short story into a cartoon. Stories with a strong plot line will lend themselves readily to this exercise. If students pick their own stories and find that they cannot easily draw cartoons based upon some, this would be a good opportunity to discuss the different emphases of different short stories: the explicit versus the implicit plot line, the plot versus the character versus the thematic short story.

14. Have students pretend that they are newspaper reporters reporting the events in a short story. Compare their articles with the short story. How do they differ? Can the differences be justified? This is a good opportunity to discuss the purpose or intent of the writer.

15. Divide the class into groups and have each group present a different version of the same short story: One group is to do a slide and tape show; another, a dramatized version of the short story; another, a newspaper account; another, an 8 mm film re-creation; another, an improvisation of two men gossiping about the events while standing by their office coffee pot on a break; and another, rewrite the story from the point of view of another character besides the main one. When evaluating all of these presentations, discuss how some of the groups may have emphasized different elements of the plot. Consider why this may have happened. Does the medium influence the selection of events?

16. In order to understand conflict as a struggle between two opposing forces, students can be asked to list as many types of conflict as possible, in groups or individually, and then classify the types of conflict they have listed as a class. Or, if the class needs more guidance, the teacher can list the types of conflict, giving examples of each. Such a list would look like the following:

A. Man against man: Two men are fighting to win the love of the same woman.

B. Man against nature: A woman has to fight her way through a storm to rescue her hiking companion who has fallen down a cliff and is unconscious.

C. Man against himself: A student who wants an A on a geometry test finds a copy of the test beforehand: Does he read it and assure himself of the A, or does he turn it in to the teacher?

D. Man against society: A politician discovers that her colleagues in the state senate are under the influence of a major oil exploration firm. She tries to convince the voters that the influence of this firm is immoral.

17. After discussing conflict with students, bring up the terms "protagonist" and "antagonist." Explain to the students that the protagonist is the main character of the story, whether the character is morally good or bad; whether the character is human, animal, or vegetable; or even, in a symbolic or metaphoric tale, for instance, whether the character is a concept, such as truth. Whoever or whatever is opposed to the main character is the antagonist. Brainstorm with the students possible protagonists and antagonists. For example:

   a. a football team against a football team

   b. a manta ray against a fishing net

   c. a husband against a wife

   d. a tarantula against a rattlesnake

   e. a student against the beliefs of all her classmates

   f. a man with only one match fighting to survive in a snowstorm

18. Consider diagramming the plot structure of a short story. A traditional way of viewing the plot structure of a short story is the Aristotelian plot structure.

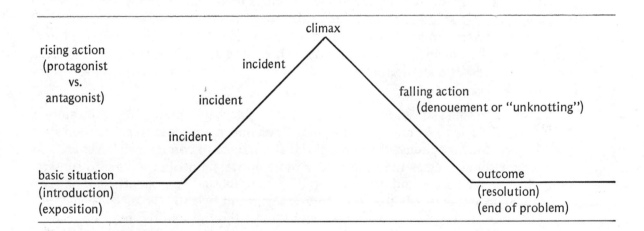

Draw the diagram on the board and relate it to a story which is well known by all the students. Traditional fairy tales often provide good examples, such as "The Three Pigs" or "Little Red Riding Hood." Follow up the examples by asking students to diagram the stories they have read according to this model. Some stories may not lend themselves to this type of analysis. For instance, some stories may have a series of climaxes.

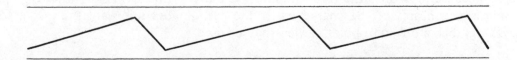

Some stories may build up to one climax and end there, such as Shirley Jackson's "The Lottery" or Saki's "The Interlopers." Since many modern stories are often "plotless," consisting of what might be a series of apparently meaningless incidents or simply a character description, the accompanying diagram often helps students understand such stories more clearly and can be applied to almost any short story.

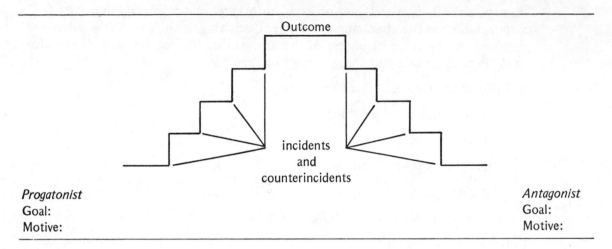

Outcome

incidents
and
counterincidents

Progatonist
Goal:
Motive:

Antagonist
Goal:
Motive:

Notice that this diagram for a short story is not dependent upon a clear plot. Essentially it explains the conflict or conflicts of the story or the ways in which the opposing forces meet each other. Whether there is a climax or not, there will be an outcome to the story, even if the outcome brings the two opposing forces back to the starting point. By employing both diagrams in attempting to explain a story, students may begin to realize that while plot may not be essential to a story conflict is.

19.   Evaluating some stories may be very difficult. One way of determining if a story is worthwhile is to examine the conflict. Have students discuss Reproduction Page 16. As students discuss these questions, allow them to come to whatever answers they wish, as long as they can justify those answers. Encourage them to consider whether the nature and presentation of the conflict alone is a sufficient basis on which to evaluate whether the story is significant, worth reading, or believable. Have the students ask those three questions of the short stories they are reading.

INVOLVING STUDENTS WITH TONE, MOOD, AND POINT OF VIEW

"Point of view" is considered because it provides insights into how well the author has created his or her own special world and enables the reader to appreciate the particular selection of events the author has made. An author who selects an omniscient point of view does so because he wishes the reader to know as much as possible about what is going on in the minds and hearts of the characters. If the author does not want the reader to know everything, then a different point of view may be used.

CONFLICT

Directions: *Answer the following questions and discuss your answers in class:*

Is the conflict significant or trivial?

Consider the following examples for discussion:

A. Your alarm clock goes off in the morning. Should you get up or not?

B. You see a classmate cheating on an exam. Should you report him or not?

C. You want money from your parents to buy a new record or tape. You know they consider that an unnecessary purchase. You could tell them that the money is for school supplies. Should you? Suppose you know that your parents cheat on their income tax report every year?

D. You believe in saving the environment. Every demand for new electricity justifies more strip-mining and power-plant pollution. Yet, you would really like to have a stereo component outfit or a radial arm saw.

E. If you move away from your family, you can get a better job and move up in the world. Yet, by moving you are leaving your parents and other members of your family.

F. You know that stealing is wrong, but if you do not steal a little food from the food stand, you may starve to death.

Is the conflict worth writing about?

Consider the following examples for discussion:

A. Football team A is leading football team B by a score of 62–0 in the last quarter.

B. Football team A is leading football team B by a score of 14–13 in the last quarter.

C. A heavy snowstorm has just covered the tulips, which are blooming. One of the tulips struggles to keep its stalk from breaking.

D. The army of Napoleon has just met the army of Wellington.

E. George Washington does not consider Gen. Charles Lee to be a good officer. Gen. Charles Lee is very popular with the Continental Congress.

Is the conflict believable?

Consider the following examples for discussion:

A. The beautiful belle of the ball has to leave her prince charming at the dance or else her fine carriage will turn into a pumpkin, her prancing horses into mice, and she into a scullery maid.

B. Having lost all his money in a bad investment, the businessman is considering committing suicide.

C. The teenage girl has just met a new boy in school. Should she tell him that she has fallen in love with him?

D. An ant has found the largest bread crumb he has ever seen. Should he struggle to bring it in by himself, or should he get help and lose some of the glory for the find?

E. The spaceman must disentangle himself from the clutches of the mile-high space monster.

F. The president of the United States has just asked you to accompany him to Russia on a diplomatic visit as his key adviser. Should you accept?

The discussion of "tone" provides the teacher with a way of knowing whether students have grasped the author's purpose. The term "tone" provides students with a word that refers to the way the author feels or thinks about the subject of the story. "Mood" is a useful term for enabling students to discuss the particular feeling they may derive from the short story. Thus, "mood" and "tone" are technical critical terms we teach students, hopefully as timesaving devices in literature discussions. The distinction between the two terms can help students grasp the difference between the underlying attitude of the author (tone) and a method by which the author communicates this attitude (the creation of a particular mood).

Tone and mood are easily confused by students, so the teacher should prepare for that confusion by developing exercises that will treat those terms clearly and separately. The student must be able to comprehend that while an author may feel one way about a situation, his or her attitude may not be immediately apparent to the reader because the feeling created by the literary work may be contradictory to the attitude of the author. In his short story "Socrates Wounded," Bertolt Brecht admires the philosophical consistency of Socrates, but Brecht wrote the story in a light, amusing way. Conceivably, an immature reader might believe that Brecht was mocking Socrates. An author may be very angry at the stupidity of army life but may write a very funny story emphasizing its idiocies, inequities, and illogicalities in order to drive home the main point better than an angry diatribe would. While awareness of tone and mood may be valuable, do not dwell upon these terms in class if the end result will be more confused students.

When teaching a short story in terms of tone, mood, and point of view, the teacher may feel the need to introduce more critical terms. The term "satire" may have to be explained, which may lead to consideration of the term "irony" and the various types of irony. "Realism" may have to be contrasted with "romanticism" or even "naturalism." "Sentiment" may have to be distinguished from "sentimentality." But to bring up any of these terms without a clear purpose and out of context is to risk confusing students unnecessarily and perhaps convincing them that only English teachers and other such "experts" can possibly understand literature. The teacher's purpose should be, not to produce more English-literature majors, but to enable students to enjoy literature, to evaluate it, and to continue reading throughout their lives. If teachers must be missionaries, then let them produce a multitude of readers, not a coterie of critics.

Use the following activities selectively and meaningfully. Allow tone, mood, and point of view to develop from the context of specific short stories.

1. In order to teach students about tone (the author's attitude toward the story or the subject of the story), provide students with the following list of tones, or attitudes, and ask them to provide some oral examples. For the sarcastic tone, students might suggest such verbal satire as "Boy, are you smart!" to indicate that the person referred to is really the opposite of smart. After the first step of this activity, break the class into small groups and ask them to create a short paragraph that exemplifies one kind of tone. When they have done that, pass the paragraphs from group to group and direct each group to indicate what they believe the tone to be for each paragraph. After each paragraph has been read and categorized by each group, ask the originating group to verify the correctness of the other groups' classifications of their paragraph's tone. Here is a list of "tones" your students can work with:

whimsical	angry
joking	bitter
solemn	upset
portentous	joyous
sad	awed

2. One clue to the tone of an author is whether or not the author is sympathetic with any of the characters. If a class is unable to determine the degree of sympathy an author has for any of the characters, give the class the questions on Reproduction Page 17 to answer in relation to any of the characters.

3. The narrator's language gives us very good clues to the author's tone. Have students go through the story and note the following items:

TONE AND CHARACTER

Directions: *Answer the following questions about a story you have just read:*

A. Would the author be sorry to see this character die?

B. Would the author invite any of the characters in the story to a party at the author's house?

C. If the character is the opposite sex from the author, is the character the type of person the author would be likely to marry, assuming author and character to be capable of doing so?

D. Would the author trust the character with the author's life?

E. Would the author want the character to handle the author's money?

F. If the author knew the character, would the author want to help the character?

G. Do you believe the author would ever consider the character a friend?

H. If this short story were made into a movie or TV show and if the author could choose the person to play this character, whom would the author choose?

I. How does the author feel about the situation this character is in?

J. Does the situation relate in some way to the central problem (or problems) of the story?

K. How does the author feel about the character's behavior in the story?

L. What is the author's attitude toward this character?

A. What adjectives does the author use to describe each character?

B. Note all the metaphors the author uses. To what things or to what person does the author apply the metaphors?

C. Does the author use any allusions? If so, what is the context in which the allusions occur?

D. After you have answered these questions, consider whether your answers reveal anything about the author's attitudes toward what he writes about.

4. Provide your students with the following explanations. One of the first decisions a short-story writer must make when beginning to write is what point of view to use. The point of view of an author determines how much and how an author can write about the subject. Generally, points of view may be grouped into four main categories:

A. *Third-person omniscient:* It is omniscient because the author knows everything that goes on, including what the characters think and feel. The story is third person because the "narrator" does not appear in the story. Therefore, the narrator does not use "I" to talk about himself or herself.

B. *Third-person limited:* The narrator does not appear in the story. The author does not know what is going on in the minds and hearts of the characters. The author can only describe what the characters do. This point of view is often referred to as "objective."

C. *First-person participant:* The narrator tells the story as though he or she were actually taking part in the events. Therefore, we know what the narrator thinks, but we do not know what the other characters think.

D. *First-person observer:* The narrator is a bystander, one who has seen or heard of the events, but has not taken part in them.

5. When the first-person points of view are used, the reader must be able to determine whether the author and the narrator are one and the same, or whether the author is simply pretending to be the narrator. Students' ability to determine what the tone of a story is may hinge upon this knowledge. If students confuse narrator and author—and if the distinction between the two is important to their understanding the story—have students answer the following questions:

A. Could the author have been the narrator? How do you know?

B. Would the author want to be the narrator? Why or why not?

C. Did the events in the story actually take place? If you cannot determine that, could they have taken place?

D. Find a biography of the author. Was the author alive when the events of the story took place? Was the author ever involved in the events of the story?

E. Would it make a difference to your interpretation of the story if the author were the narrator? If the author were not?

6. Students sometimes confuse tone, the author's attitude, with mood, the feeling they, the readers, get from the story, and, as a result, with their own attitude toward the story. The following activity will help students distinguish tone from mood. Hand out a checklist with these directions:

A. Circle the way you feel about what happened in the story:

> happy   other:
> sad
> satisfied
> upset
> angry
> amused

B. Circle your feelings toward the protagonist:

> like   other:
> dislike
> hate
> love
> neutral
> sympathetic

C. In items A and B, put a check next to the adjectives that describe how the author feels. When the students have done this, compile the results and discuss them with the students. Was there any disagreement among the students? If so, why? When the class has been able to come to some conclusion, inform them that the author's feelings are the tone and the reader's feelings reveal the mood.

7. Use sounds to portray moods:

   A. Ask several students to walk across the classroom in different ways. Ask the class to close their eyes as they listen to the different types of walking. Then have them write down the feeling they had while listening to the walking or to write down the way they thought the walker felt. Afterward, compare and contrast the results.

   B. Do the same as in item A, but tape-record the sounds beforehand.

   C. Instead of walking, as in items A and B, have some students knock on the classroom door to represent different moods. If they need ideas, give each a slip of paper with one of the following moods written on it:

      1. Angry (perhaps you are the police trying to get a suspect to open the door).

      2. Optimistic (you are a door-to-door salesman trying to catch the person inside in a good mood).

      3. Furtive (you have to apologize to your next-door neighbor for accidentally backing your car over his prize chrysanthemums).

      4. Mysterious (you want to scare the inhabitant).

   D. Play records of music that set different moods. For instance, you might want to use a military march, a love ballad, a symphony, and the background music to a Japanese No drama. Have students write what event or events the music is trying to portray.

8. Reverse the activities in number 7 and ask students what sound effects they would use if the story were turned into a radio play. What background or introductory music would they use? Why? Without mentioning mood, allow students to discuss mood. Have them actually create the radio play based upon the story, complete with sound effects and music.

9. In order to indicate how point of view is important to a story, ask students to rewrite the story (even a brief plot summary will suffice here) in several different ways:

   A. If the point of view is omniscient: Pretend that the person telling the story does not know what is going on in the minds and hearts of the characters.

   B. If the point of view is first-person participant: Assume that you know everything going on in the minds of the participants.

   C. If the point of view is first-person observer: Pretend that you have been dragged into the action of the story at some point. Or pretend that you suddenly can read the minds of all the characters.

   D. If the point of view is third-person: Pretend that you are one of the characters in the story telling the story. Ask students to write the story from the perspectives of different characters in the story.

   After the students have accomplished these tasks, ask them whether they had to change the story in any way to complete the assignment. If so, how? Is the story completely different now? Which do they prefer, the new version or the old one? (Allow them to prefer the new one if they do. Then discuss why.) Has anything else changed as a result of changing the point of view? Do you now get a different feeling from the story (mood)? Have you developed a different attitude toward the events or characters of the story (tone)? Now summarize why an author might choose a particular point of view in writing a story.

10. Two stories that have the same tone and are about the same subject may not be alike in quality and may not create the same mood in the reader. Find two stories from widely divergent sources, such as an anthology of short-story "classics" and a magazine of the confession or modern romance variety; and two stories about the same subject, such as the love of a man for a woman, and ask students to read them together. Ask the students which author is more serious or more sincere. They may not be able to decide. Then ask the students whether the stories are essentially the same. Here, differences in opinion will emerge, and that is to your advantage. Then list the differences between the two stories on the board. Consider, finally, the question, "If two stories have the same tone and are about the same subject, why do we prefer one over the other?" At this point, if students do not agree with you about which is the "quality" story, do not worry. The important point is that they will be developing their evaluative skills and will be considering tone in the context of very specific stories.

11. If a story has a large amount of dialogue, the following exercise may help the students distinguish between the attitudes of the characters and the attitudes of the author.

Have a group of students read the story aloud. One student reads everything except the dialogue. The other students take the parts of the characters and read what they say as though they were reading a play (in effect, they are). Discuss with the class the attitude of the student reading the nondialogue sections. Did he or she read the words the way the author would have? If not, why do the students think the author would have read the words differently? At this point, the class will have to be considering the tone of the story.

As a variation of this exercise, ask students to read the dialogue without the intervening words. Then discuss with the class whether anything has been lost from the story, and, if so, what.

12. Use improvisation to establish tone based upon point of view. For instance, have two students improvise the following scenes:

A. A student is trying to get a teacher to change a grade.

B. A son tries to convince his father that the son should be allowed to buy his own car.

C. A daughter explains to her mother that she doesn't have a date for the most important school dance of the year.

D. A car salesman tries selling a car to a buyer.

E. A husband and wife talk over their recent discovery that one of them is dying from cancer.

F. A girl breaks a date with a boy.

After each improvisation, reverse the roles of the characters. Does the change in characters' points of view influence anything else about the presentations? Allow students to discuss as many aspects of the improvisations as they want. They will be integrating those aspects into a more complete, more valid evaluation than if they had discussed the aspects singly. Thus, as they read their short stories, they will be more aware of the interrelationships of all the aspects of the stories.

13. Another improvisational device that enables students to perceive more about tone and point of view is the use of the "alter ego." Two students still improvise scenes based upon conflicts such as those in activity number 12. But two other students act as alter egos for the two doing the improvising. This activity may be carried out in two ways:

A. In the first way, the alter ego tells the improvisor what to say. The improvisor cannot speak until the alter ego has given directions.

B. In the second way, the improvisors say what they want, but after each has spoken the alter egos explain what they "really meant."

After the improvisations, discuss with the class how the use of the alter egos influenced the events. Did the audience gain greater insights? Did the people doing the improvising realize a change in their roles? How do the alter egos and the improvisors relate to the four ways of categorizing point of view? What does this indicate about point of view in short stories?

14. After students have read a particular short story, show them a film based upon the short story. "An Occurrence at Owl Creek Bridge" is a good possibility. Ask the students which they preferred, the story or the film. Then ask them why. Was something changed in the film? What? Who made the decision to change the story—one of the characters, or the director of the film? Is the director's attitude the same as the author's? If the same, which communicates the attitude best, the film or the short story? Why? Has the tone been changed? How and why? Reverse the procedure the next time you do this exercise with the class—show the film first. Then ask the same questions. Students may conclude that the director is actually another author telling the same story. If so, the tone, mood, and point of view may all be changed. For a deeper examination of this possibility, read a short story or play or novel and see several films produced at different times by different actors and directors. *Hamlet*, for example, is an often-produced play. Do not be concerned that you are using a different genre or medium to get at one aspect of the short story. Anything which develops the students' literary appreciation skills is well justified.

15. Laurence Perrine, in *Story and Structure*, presents a segment of the fable of the grasshopper and the ant as told from three different points of view.[8] Read the examples to your students, discuss them, and ask your students to write a fable or children's fairy tale from more than one point of view.

16. To develop student awareness of the difference between tone and mood, have students list a series of attitudes they may have toward such things as:

---

8. Laurence Perrine, *Story and Structure* (New York: Harcourt Brace Jovanovich, 1974).

a. school (disgusted with it, excited by it, bored, etc.)

b. politicians (angry, frustrated, admiring, etc.)

c. litterers (hate, feel sorry for, apathetic toward, etc.)

The list of subjects can be quite extensive and vary from abstractions such as *war* and *love* to specifics such as *your mother* or *your textbook*. The second step is to list next to each of the attitudes the different ways in which those attitudes may be revealed by a writer, such as:

School: disgusted with it—
    make fun of ignorant behavior of teachers
    show teacher bowing to principal's demands
    tell funny tale about registering for classes
    tell sad story about a dropout

17. Give the students these imaginative situations as a brief writing assignment to exemplify point of view:

A. You have just been in a fight. Explain to your parents what happened.

B. You have just witnessed a fight but did not take part in it at all. Tell a friend what you saw.

C. You were told about the fight several days later. Write about the fight for the school newspaper. Give a straightforward account. Do not editorialize.

D. Imagine that you were God and witnessed the fight. Write an account of what happened indicating everything that the participants in the fight thought and felt.

INVOLVING STUDENTS IN THE EVALUATION PROCESS

Ultimately, the teacher hopes that his students will be able to judge what they read after they have left his classes and will continue to enjoy reading. But the individual has to develop a set of criteria about quality that will suit him or her, not some idea that an English teacher may promote. In fact, each individual will develop criteria for judging literature despite everything the English teacher does. Hopefully, those criteria will be well considered and justified.

The best the teacher can do in the realm of evaluation is give the students as many different ways of evaluating short stories as he can: discussion, surveys, voting, public affirmation through speaking and writing, and indirect methods that grow out of the study of the short story. By being required to judge short stories from many different perspectives, the students' criteria will be established upon a firm foundation. For this to happen, the teacher dares not impose his or her judgment upon the students. In a free classroom environment, the teacher may and should feel free to state an individual opinion. In fact, if the teacher does not, students may wonder at the reason why the teacher wants them to make judgments. When students mature, they gain new life experiences. As they do, their judgments will change. To expect a seventh grader to view marriage, for instance, in the same way that a twelfth grader does is to be very naive. A teacher must allow students to make judgments based upon their own understandings of life and literature. At the same time, he or she can interject additional information and ways of viewing literature the students may not have thought of but can surely understand.

Evaluation of short stories in the classroom should also be undertaken in many different forms. Sometimes the students should be required to justify their evaluations; doing this enables their thinking skills to grow. At other times, however, simply a gut-level reaction may be all that we can expect. Hasn't everyone felt some way about a particular event or person or selection of literature without being able to explain that feeling? In short, a varied choice of evaluative exercises, chosen with careful regard to the stories the class has read and aimed at developing the already present skills of the students, will go a long way toward improving the students' abilities to evaluate literature.

1. If students have developed evaluative criteria for literary quality, they should be able to compare and contrast two short stories, arrive at some decision as to which is the better, and justify their conclusions. Since practice in such an activity is an essential step to success, provide your students with a list of questions that will compel them to consider the relative merits of short stories. One such list, designed to help students evaluate one short story in relation to another, is on Reproduction Page 18.

REPRODUCTION PAGE 18

EVALUATING LITERATURE

Directions: *Use the following questions to help you evaluate literature you have read:*

A. Theme

1. What is the theme of each short story?

2. Which theme means more to you as a human being? Why?

3. Which theme has more meaning for mankind in general? Explain.

4. If you were asked to argue against one of the themes, which would you choose to argue against and why? What would you say?

5. State whether you believe the following elements of each story were chosen by the author in order to illustrate the theme well: (a) the characters; (b) the setting; (c) the plot.

6. In general, which author develops the theme better?

B. Plot

1. Summarize the plot of each short story.

. .which plot is more true to life? Why?

3. Which plot is more interesting? Why?

Is there anything unbelievable about either plot?

5. Do you believe that the characters involved in each plot would have behaved the same way if the events had happened in real life?

6. Is the plot of each story likely to happen in the setting the author chooses? Why or why not?

7. Is the plot predictable? If so, when did you first realize how it would turn out? Did you enjoy the story less because of that? If the plot was not predictable, was the ending a complete surprise? If so, was the surprise justified, or did the author end the story just to get it over with?

8. In general, which plot is developed better?

C. Setting

1. Describe the setting used in each story.

2. Is the setting essential in each story, or could any setting be used?

3. If the setting is essential, why? Does the setting enable the plot to develop? Does the setting influence the behavior or personalities of the characters? Is the setting related to the theme?

4. Is the setting believable? Is it realistic? After answering the first two questions, consider whether your answers reveal anything about the author's purpose in writing the story.

5. In general, which story makes the better use of setting?

D. Characterization

   1. Describe the main characters in each short story.

   2. Did you find each of those characters to be believable? Explain.

   3. If any of those characters were not realistic, was there a reason for that lack of realism?

   4. Explain why each of the characters was essential to the plot. If any were not essential, explain why not.

   5. Was each character fully developed or shallow, round or flat, or stereotyped or realistic? Did the author develop them that way on purpose, or was his portrayal of the characters weak?

   6. Did any of the characters relate in some way to the theme? If so, how?

   7. Did the setting have any influence upon any of the characters? If so, how?

   8. In general, which author makes the better use of the characters?

E. Summary Evaluation

   1. If you had to decide which of the two stories was the better, what would your decision be, and why? In order to help yourself answer this question, reread your answers to the last questions in sections A, B, C, and D.

2. Pass out pairs of stories to small groups of students in your class. Ask each group to evaluate the stories in their groups and come to some conclusion about which one is better and why. Have each group report orally to the class. Record the results on the blackboard. After all the groups have reported, note which of the two stories received the larger number of votes. If the groups disagree, ask each group to reconsider its choice of story as the better of the two.

3. Sometimes students can be involved in the evaluation process without being told specifically that they are evaluating short stories. One method of doing this is to employ some imaginative questions for discussion or writing, such as:

A. If you could have one of the authors of the stories we have just read as a friend of yours, which one would you pick? Why?

B. In which of the stories we have just read would you like to be involved? Why?

C. Which of the characters in the stories do you think you would be most likely to meet in this school? In this town? In your own home? Explain.

D. Pretend that you were a minister getting ready to deliver a Sunday sermon. You cannot decide what to talk about. You have just read these stories, and now you think that one of them will give you an idea for your sermon. Which one will that be? What is the idea? Why did you pick that story?

E. Imagine that you are the editor of a literature anthology for this class. You have been told that you must drop one of the stories in the book but that you can add another story in its place. If the stories we have just read were already in the book, which one would you drop? Why? If they were the stories that were not in the book, which would you choose to include in the anthology? Why?

F. You are a movie producer, and you want to make a great deal of money on your next picture. Which of these stories would you pick to turn into a motion picture? Why?

G. You are a movie director who does not care about the amount of money your pictures make. For your next picture, you want to direct a picture that will have the greatest influence upon humanity. You have been given the short stories we have just read to choose from. Which one will you choose? Why?

H. Who is the most popular motion-picture actor today? The most popular actress? If you were selecting the cast for movies based upon the short stories we have just read, into which stories would you place the actress and actor? Explain why.

I. One of your best friends is sick in a hospital and has asked you to bring and read him a short story. Which one will you bring? Why?

J. A person you know, or a famous personality you know of, bothers you very much because of the way he behaves. You believe that reading one of the short stories might help him see himself better, and so change. Pick a short story to send to that person. What is that person like, and why have you chosen that particular short story?

K. If you could only read one short story in this class this year, what short story would that be? Why?

4. In order to begin a discussion evaluating a series of short stories the class has just read, poll the class on which story they liked best or which they thought was the best short story. The poll could be public, requiring students to raise their hands, or it could be private, requiring students to pick one of the stories on a mimeographed list or to rank the short stories from best to worst. If the latter method is employed, a couple of students could tally the results before the class discussion.

5. An indirect way of determining the impact of the short stories upon the students is to give them one of the following assignments:

A. Create a motion-picture billboard advertising one of the stories that has just been turned into a movie.

B. Write a review of one of the short stories for the school newspaper.

C. Create an advertisement for next year's class to convince them that they ought to read one of the short stories we have just read. (Save them and use them next year before beginning to read the short stories. Put them on the bulletin board or mimeograph them and pass them out to the students.)

D. Write a letter to the author of the short story you enjoyed the most or the least and tell that author why.

E. Write a letter to the editors of your anthology and tell them which stories they ought to keep and which they should throw out. Explain why in all cases. (Or send these letters to the anthology's publisher. Publishers want to know how students react to selections in their anthologies.)

6. One of the most effective ways of having students evaluate their own knowledge of the short story is to have them create plot outlines, together with character sketches, descriptions of appropriate settings, and conclusions as to possible appropriate themes. Let students work in groups, creating their own short-story outlines, and then have them share their outlines with other groups in the class. Some groups or individuals may actually elect to write the short story, but this should not be required.

7. Stephen Moro and Donald Fleming, in "Video Short Story," describe a procedure

for having students create their own videotape versions of their own short stories.[9] The authors explain that such a creation not only fosters creative writing but also develops students' appreciation for the story and the medium.

8. Read Geoffrey Summerfield's "What Is a Good Story?"[10] After doing what Summerfield asks you to do—evaluate a brief story—ask your students to do the same. Compare your responses with those of your students.

9. Develop opinion surveys to which students may respond simply by checking responses. Some formats include the following:

A. Story A was a well-written story.

    1. Agree strongly

    2. Agree

    3. No opinion

    4. Disagree

    5. Disagree strongly

B. Check the point along the continuum that indicates how you feel:

The main character of story B was:

Static ＿＿＿ ＿＿＿ ＿＿＿ ＿＿＿ ＿＿＿ ＿＿＿ ＿＿＿ Dynamic

C. Do "real" people behave the way character A does:

Yes＿＿ No＿＿ Sometimes＿＿

D. The tone of author A in story C was:

    1. Angry

    2. Satiric

    3. Glad

    4. Sad

E. What effect does author B accomplish in story D with his first sentence?

    1. He creates a feeling of suspense.

    2. He makes the reader laugh.

    3. He puzzles the reader.

    4. He puts us on the side of the main character.

F. Number in order of preference (1 being highest) the stories you enjoyed the most:

Story A ＿＿＿＿

Story B ＿＿＿＿

9. Stephen Moro and Donald Fleming, "Video Short Story," *English Journal* 65 (March 1976), 60–63.

10. Geoffrey Summerfield, "What Is a Good Story?," *English Journal* 63 (May 1974), 12–13.

Story C _____

Story D _____

While these surveys may not probe the students' abilities to support their judgments, they do enable the teacher to begin discussions that will develop students' evaluative powers; and they will also help the teacher consider what selections to teach in the next short-story unit.

SUGGESTED RESOURCES FOR THE TEACHER

The following materials are helpful for the teacher thinking through the issues involved in the teaching of short stories and planning the specific lessons.

PRINT

Beachcroft, T. O. *The English Short Story*. London: Longmans, Green, 1964.
> The history of the short story and criticism of the forms it has taken make this book worthwhile for background information.

Brooks, Cleanth, Jr., and Warren, Robert Penn. *Understanding Fiction*. New York: Appleton-Century-Crofts, 1943.
> This is a classic in the close analysis and interpretation of intent, theme, plot, and characterization. Advanced students and teachers will find it profitable reading.

Chicorel, Marietta, ed. *Chicorel Index to Short Stories in Anthologies and Collections*. New York: Chicorel, 1974.
> For the teacher searching for specific stories in planning the study of short stories, this index will be particularly valuable.

Current-Garcia, Eugene, and Patrick, Walton R., eds. *What Is the Short Story?* Glenview, Ill.: Scott, Foresman, 1974.
> A collection of critical essays and short stories, this anthology provides good, selective insights into authors' crafts.

Dunning, Stephen. *Teaching Literature to Adolescents: Short Stories*. Glenview, Ill.: Scott, Foresman, 1968.
> A good how-to book written from the perspective of one who has taught. Dunning lists principles of teaching and explains the principles through a few detailed examples.

Fenson, Harry and Kritzer, Hildreth. *Reading, Understanding, and Writing about Short Stories*. New York: Macmillan, 1966.
> The authors lead the reader through analysis to composition about the short story.

Ingram, Forrest I. *Representative Short Story Cycles of the Twentieth Century*. The Hague: Mouton, 1971.
> "A story cycle is a set of stories so linked to one another that the reader's experience of each one is modified by his experience of the others." A critical discussion of a genre somewhere between the novel and the short story, the text can add dimension to the teacher's repertoire.

Kempton, Kenneth P. *Short Stories for Study*. Cambridge: Harvard Univ. Press, 1953.
> The stories were selected as guides for aspiring writers, for readability, and for appeal to readers. The critical comments are helpful to the teacher.

O'Donovan, Michael (Frank O'Connor). *The Lonely Voice, a Study of the Short Story*. Cleveland: World, 963.
> A series of lectures given at Stanford, these approach the short story as the unique form it is. Teachers will broaden their perspectives by reading O'Connor's critical responses.

Perrine, Laurence. *Story and Structure*, 4th ed. New York: Harcourt Brace Jovanovich, 1974.
> An anthology of better-known short stories, each section containing a good introduction to techniques. Subjects include: escape and interpretation, plot, character, point of view, symbol and irony, emotion and humor, fantasy, and analysis and evaluation.

Young, James H. *101 Plots Used and Abused*. Boston: The Writer, 1946.
> Don't let the date throw you off this. These

plot outlines can be used for enjoyable activities with students. Discuss stereotypes, originality, believability. Use them in creative writing exercises.

Collections of Short Stories for Students

The short-story collections below are not intended to be inclusive but only to sample a field which is enormous. The teacher should seek out many of the fine collections that are available on the market, many of which are selected according to theme, subject, and/or quality, thus simplifying the decision process for the teacher.

Alwin, Virginia, ed. *Short Stories I* and Scheld, Elizabeth, ed. *Short Stories II.* New York: Macmillan, 1961.
> Brief advice on reading the short story, biographies of authors, and interesting short stories.

Ashley, L. R. N., ed. *Classic British Short Stories.* Woodbury, N.Y.: Barron's, 1975.
> The better-known writers are contained in this collection.

Boynton, Robert W., and Mack, Maynard, eds. *Introduction to the Short Story,* 2nd ed. Rochelle Park, N.J.: Hayden, 1972.
> A traditional collection of short stories that can be readily structured into the curriculum.

Freeman, Mildred, ed. *Street Sounds.* New York: Globe Book Co., 1970.
> Short stories designed for the inner-city student. Easy reading, with questions relating to the selections and vocabulary exercises at the end.

Haupt, Hannah Beate, ed. *Man in the Fictional Mode.* Evanston, Ill.: McDougal, Littell, 1970.
> Books 1 through 6, designed for grades 7 through 12, include short stories designed to appeal to current interests of students with appropriate photographs illustrating selections. No exercises or explanatory material.

Hopper, Vincent F., ed. *Classic American Short Stories.* Woodbury, N.Y.: Barron's, 1964.
> The style, content, and literary backgrounds of these stories by well-known authors are discussed.

Kaplan, C., ed. *Critical Approaches to the Short Story.* New York: Holt, Rinehart & Winston, 1969.

> This collection, intended for grades 10 through 12, is clear and easily employed in the classroom.

Liebman, Arthur, ed. *Masterworks of Mystery* series. New York: Richards Rosen Press.
> Historical and literary commentary plus the stories: *Thirteen Classic Detective Stories* (1974), *Classic Crime Stories* (1975), and *Tales of Horror and the Supernatural* (1975).

MacNeill, James A., and Sorestad, Glen A., eds. *Sunlight & Shadows.* Ontario, Canada: Thomas Nelson & Sons, 1975.
> Short stories arranged thematically: life or death, folly, anguish, of the heart, *and* and beyond.

Madden, David, ed. *Creative Choices.* Glenview, Ill.: Scott, Foresman, 1975.
> The stories are taken from contemporary magazines and literary quarterlies. The emphasis is upon what the author is trying to accomplish and how.

Miller, James E., Jr.; Hayden, Robert; and O'Neal, Robert, eds. *American Models.* Glenview, Ill.: Scott, Foresman, 1973.
> This is a good anthology of modern American short stories, including discussion questions, biographies, and a pronunciation key.

_____. *British Motifs.* Glenview, Ill.: Scott, Foresman, 1973.
> The student will find this an interesting collection of modern British short stories, including biographies and discussion questions.

Mirer, Martin, ed. *Modern Black Stories.* Woodbury, N.Y.: Barron's, 1971.
> A good collection with an introduction and general commentary.

Nadel, Max, ed. *American Jewish Writing.* Woodbury, N.Y.: Barron's, 1975.
> Notes and discussion questions, as well as a discussion of the key events in Jewish history and the impact of those events on the Jewish people.

Paredes, Americo, and Paredes, Raymund, eds. *Mexican-American Authors.* Boston: Houghton Mifflin, 1972.
> Although this collection also contains drama and poetry, it is a good introduction to Mexican American short stories.

Rees, Robert, and Menikoff, Barry, eds. *The Short Story,* 2nd ed. Boston: Little, Brown, 1975.
> Through selections from around the world, students are encouraged to consider plot, set-

ting, character, point of view, and tone.

Stone, Wilfred; Packer, Nancy Huddleston; and Hoopes, Robert, eds. *The Short Story: An Introduction*. New York: McGraw-Hill, 1976.

The stories are organized in three sections: the early period (forebears of the modern short story), the first true short stories, and contemporary short stories. The book also contains information on techniques of fiction, biographies of authors, and critical assessments of the form.

Ungerer, Tomi, ed. *A Storybook: A Collection of Stories Old and New*. New York: Franklin Watts, 1974.

Ungerer's unique illustrations accompany stories that range from the classic folk tale to the very modern tale.

NONPRINT: Films for Short-Story Study in the Classroom

The following selected films will provide you with a varied approach to the study of the short story. The annotations indicate some possible applications for each film.

All Gold Canyon. Weston Woods Studios, color, 21 min.

This is a rather free adaptation of the Jack London short story, but that should enable students to compare and contrast one with the other.

Chickamauga. McGraw-Hill Textfilms, b/w, 33 min.

The images selected to portray Ambrose Bierce's short story would be interesting to compare with the images that students have in their own minds after reading the short story.

Christmas Carol, A. Coronet Instructional Films, b/w, 25 min.

The film attempts to re-create Charles Dickens's style as closely as possible. Students working in language studies might enjoy comparing the language of the film with Dickens's own words. For fun, if you can obtain a copy of the out-of-print version by Teaching Film Custodians (b/w, 43 min.), the comparison of film styles would be worthwhile.

Discussion of Dr. Heidegger's Experiment. Encyclopaedia Britannica Educational Corp., color, 11 min.

Clifton Fadiman talks about the Hawthorne short story. Use this film with the companion film of the story, or present it after students have read the story, or both.

Discussion of The Lady, or the Tiger? Encyclopaedia Britannica Educational Corp., color, 11 min.

Clifton Fadiman discusses the short story in this companion film to *The Lady, or the Tiger?*

Discussion of The Lottery. Encyclopaedia Britannica Educational Corp., color, 10 min.

Professor James Durbin discusses the short story in this companion film to *The Lottery*.

Discussion of My Old Man. Encyclopaedia Britannica Educational Corp., color, 11 min.

Professor Blake Nevius discusses the short story in this companion film to *My Old Man*.

Dr. Heidegger's Experiment. Encyclopaedia Britannica Educational Corp., color, 22 min.

This version of Hawthorne's short story will fit beautifully into a unit on science fiction, ecology, or morality. Students can compare it with the written original and discuss which was better, whether the director captured the story accurately, or whether a modern audience can appreciate an "old" story.

Father, The. New Line Cinema, b/w, 28 min.

Based on the Chekhov story "Grief," this film is an excellent vehicle for discussing such aspects as realistic plot and characterization.

Garden Party, The. ACI Films, color, 24 min.

This adaptation of the Katherine Mansfield short story would work well in a unit on death, or in lessons about point of view and mood.

Gift of the Magi. Teaching Film Custodians, b/w, 20 min.

This classic story by O. Henry, typically taught for its portrayal of irony, is presented in this film by a segment of Twentieth Century Fox's *O. Henry's Full House*.

Happy Prince, The. Pyramid Films, color, 26 min.

This animated film, based upon the Oscar Wilde short story, provides a good opportunity to discuss theme, in this case embodied by the conflict between greed and selflessness.

Lady, or the Tiger? The. Encyclopaedia Britannica Educational Corp., color, 16 min.

Ask your students how they would rewrite Frank Stockton's short story if it were set today. Then ask them how they would write it if the setting were in the future. Finally, show them this space-age version.

Last Leaf. Teaching Film Custodians, b/w, 20 min.

> This segment from the Twentieth Century Fox *O. Henry's Full House* is introduced by John Steinbeck. Students can compare it with the original written version.

Lottery, The. Encyclopaedia Britannica Educational Corp., color, 18 min.

> Shirley Jackson's story is one of the all-time favorites of English teachers. Have students read the story first and then ask them whether this film version is a faithful re-creation. For variation, show the film to one class before they read the short story and compare their reactions with those of the students using the first approach.

Mr. Pickwick's Dilemma. Coronet Instructional Films, b/w, 24 min.

> Students may find this version easier to follow than the original by Charles Dickens. Have students read the tale, describe the characters, and then determine whether they have imagined the characters as the director of the film did.

My Old Man. Encyclopaedia Britannica Educational Corp., color, 27 min.

> Hemingway's story is an excellent vehicle for considering the conflict of right versus wrong. Joe's youthful idealism wars with the evident corruption of the father he loves.

Occurrence at Owl Creek Bridge, An. McGraw-Hill Textfilms, b/w, 29 min.

> Ambrose Bierce's short story depends upon a shock at the end for its effect. Consider with the class whether this film accomplishes that or whether the style of the photography gives away the ending or hints at it more strongly than the story does.

Reading Stories: Characters and Setting. Coronet Instructional Films, b/w, 11 min.

> What do characters look like, sound like, and do? How do they influence one another? How does an author communicate all this? Basically a teaching film, this film employs examples from "Fawn in the Forest," "Captains Courageous," "Myeko's Gift," and "Onion John." Appropriate for junior high and middle school.

Reading Stories: Plots and Themes. Coronet Instructional Films, b/w, 13 min.

> This film examines the interrelationship of plot and theme by employing examples from "A Summer Adventure," "My Brother Stevie," "The Borrowers," and "A Dog on Barkham Street." Appropriate for junior high and middle school.

Selfish Giant, The. Weston Woods Studios, b/w, 14 min.

> A giant builds a wall around his garden to get away from the children, but in doing so he finds loneliness. This film may fit well into the study of parables. Different ages and abilities of students may bring something different to the viewing.

Short Story, The. Grover, color, 20 min.

> A historical tracing of the short story from colonial times to the present, this film also will fit well in a chronological study of American literature.

Stories. Coronet Instructional Films, b/w, 10 min.

> A writer helps a young boy plan a puppet show. In doing so, he helps the boy visualize characters, settings, and plots as he reads well-known stories. Basically a teaching film, it is appropriate for junior high and middle school.

Tell-Tale Heart. Columbia Picture Corp., color, 8 min.

> James Mason narrates this surrealistically animated film of Poe's short story. Show this film and the Films, Inc., version (1946, b/w, 20 min.) for a good contrast of interpretations.

Up Is Down. University of Southern California, color, 6 min.

> This animated film is an excellent example of the film as a short story. The little parable tells of a boy who is happy seeing the world upside down but who, upon being righted, realizes that the world can be ugly. Society evaluates him and turns him to see the world its way, but in the end he reverts to his original position.

What's in a Story? BFA Educational Media, color, 14 min.

> By employing Thurber's "The Unicorn in the Garden," this teaching film points out that every story has something to say and that by thinking about the plot, readers can discover a number of possible things a story says.

Writers on Writing. General Learning Corp., color, 17 min.

> Four writers talk about their objectives and how they work toward them. Ask your students to write a short story or a short-story plot, discuss with them how they proceeded, and then show them this film.

4

Teaching the Novel

Teaching the novel is one way to influence our students' future reading habits. For most adults, which our students will soon be, literature means the novel. If our students are to read anything beyond the newspaper and popular magazines after they leave school, it will be the novel. Poetry and drama are seldom read by adults, although much is written.

The benefits of reading novels go beyond appreciation and enjoyment, the two most popular justifications. Exploration, the opportunity to look into the past or future as well as to explore alternative life-styles in the present, is important. Bibliotherapy—assimilating psychological or sociological objectives with the reader's personality—can help students understand their own behavior and that of others, assist in the formation of ethical values, offer opportunities for identification, and provide an understanding of the many motives for human behavior.

The novel has a central place in the literature program. It can stand alone or be part of a thematic unit or topical unit that may incorporate poetry, drama, short stories, and nonfiction. Regardless of where it is in the program, it must be selected carefully because of the time investment required to read and teach the novel. A short story or poem that is unsuccessful costs only a day or two, but an unsuccessful novel can cost weeks.

This chapter deals with several major issues or topics related to teaching the novel. Primary is the problem of selection; a successful literary experience ultimately depends on what is read. When choices have been made, the teacher must decide how to teach. Broadly, novels may be taught extensively, intensively, or by a free reading approach. Finally, the teacher must decide what kind or kinds of novels will be read. The types of novel discussed are adolescent, multiethnic, science fiction, and adult—both classic and popular.

The problem of selection is magnified by the quantity of novels to choose from. Probably because the number of possible choices is so great, few novels are actually read in English classes. We cannot read them all, so we teach the same ones year after year. This chapter emphasizes selection based on interest, need, and ability.

All novels cannot be taught extensively, intensively, or through free reading. Just as it is foolish to spend three weeks on a novel that can be read in an evening, such as H. G. Wells's *The Invisible Man*, it is also difficult to deal with Ralph Ellison's *The Invisible Man* in a few days. Similarly, novels that deal with a specialized theme or appeal to specialized interests may work very well in free reading situations but not so well with a whole class.

Choices also extend to the type of novel to be read. Adolescent literature may be neither the panacea that many experts claim it is nor the bane of literature that others call it. However, it does have a place in the literature program, especially at the junior high-middle school or early senior high level. Multiethnic literature, whether viewed narrowly, as black, Mexican American, and native American literature, or widely, as literature that deals with all ethnic groups in the United States, may also be appropriate for the literature program. Science fiction is a type of literature growing both in popularity and in academic respectability. Finally, adult fiction—the traditional type of fiction taught in secondary schools—is an important group from which choices can be made.

PERFORMANCE OBJECTIVES

1. Students will read novels with enjoyment.
2. Students will voluntarily read novels.
3. Students will select appropriate novels for personal reading.
4. Students will be able to classify novels as realistic or romantic.
5. When reading the classics, students will be able to discuss with understanding what makes a good novel good.
6. Students will be able to relate their values to those of specific characters in novels.
7. Students will be able to respond to dilemmas presented in novels.
8. Students will be able to ascertain the theme underlying a given novel.
9. Students will be able to discuss whether or not characters are consistent.
10. Students will be able to state their personal objectives for reading a novel or novels.

LEARNING EXPERIENCES

SELECTION

The objective of selecting appropriate novels is simple to state—the right book for the right student at the right time—but complex to achieve. Students' needs, interests, and abilities as well as the teacher's objectives, interests, and the constraints of time are all factors in determining what novel or novels will be read. Most choices, because of these variables, will be a compromise.

For students in the junior high-middle school grades, as well as for senior high students inexperienced with the novel, the choice should be a relatively simple novel. Simple, in this context, does not refer to children's literature but to simplicity of plot, character, and theme. The plot will usually concern a physical or physical-psychological conflict rather than a purely psychological one. Characters will often be stereotyped rather than individuals whose personal motives determine action. The theme will usually deal with values of immediate concern to the reader rather than with universal values. As students mature and become more experienced with literature, novels with complex plots, characters, and themes should be read.

Interest is of prime consideration if only because the teacher's first objective is to get the students to read the novel. An old adage, "You can lead a horse to water but you can't make him drink," may have been first spoken by an English teacher about student interest. Unfortunately, what interests adults and teachers of English is not necessarily what interests students. A brief comparison of two studies reinforces this assertion. The first, directed by Ted Hipple,[1] lists the most frequently taught novels in 308 high schools.

The Adventures of Huckleberry Finn	*The Great Gatsby*
A Separate Peace	*The Pearl*
To Kill a Mockingbird	*Animal Farm*
The Scarlet Letter	*The Old Man and the Sea*
Lord of the Flies	*Catcher in the Rye*

The second[2] lists those novels chosen by students in a metropolitan area as their favorites. Only one novel from the teacher-selected list above appears among the students' choices.

Junior High Boys	**Junior High Girls**
Star Trek	*The Outsiders*
The Outsiders	*Go Ask Alice*
The Call of the Wild	*Love Story*
Papillon	*Mr. and Mrs. Bojo Jones*
The Godfather	*My Darling My Hamburger*
	Joy in the Morning

High School Boys	**High School Girls**
Lord of the Rings	*The Outsiders*
The Exorcist	*Catcher in the Rye*
The Godfather	*The Pigman*
Patton	*My Darling My Hamburger*
	Go Ask Alice
	Love Story
	Mr. and Mrs. Bojo Jones
	Gone with the Wind

Teachers wishing to determine which novels or types of novel may be successful with students might want to use the "Reading Interest Inventory" (Reproduction Pages 27 and 28). Given at the beginning of a year or term, such inventories can help the teacher make choices based on student interest. Using a good annotated bibliography (see suggested resources), teachers can match students with several appropriate books.

When trying to choose the right book for the right student at the right time, one should consider a student's ability. To select a particular novel or group of novels, the

---

1. Theodore W. Hipple, Faith Z. Schullstrom, and Robert G. Wright, "The Novels Adolescents Are Reading," *Research Bulletin of the Florida Research and Development Council* 10, 1 (Fall 1975) 12.

2. Dennis Badaczewski, "2396 Kids Can't Be Wrong Twice: Reading Interest of Adolescents," *Ohio English Bulletin* (June 1976).

READING INTEREST INVENTORY

1. Name one novel that you did not enjoy reading.

2. What was your favorite novel? Why?

3. What is your favorite nonfiction book? Why?

4. What magazines do you read regularly?

5. What is your favorite television program? Why?

6. What was your favorite movie? Why?

7. Do you have any hobbies? If so, what?

8. Do you work at a regular job? What?

9. If you could choose the career that you would have for the rest of your life, what would it be?

10. What do you enjoy most about English class?

11. What activity do you enjoy least in English class?

12. Name three living people that you admire most in the world.

    A.

    B.

    C.

13. If you could be like one historical person, who would that be?

14. What subject do you enjoy most in school?

15. What subject do you enjoy least in school?

16. If you had three wishes, what would they be?

17. If you ever wrote a book, what would its title be?

18. What would you like to change most about conditions in the world today?

19. Do you read any newspapers or magazines regularly? If so, what are they?

20. If there is anything special that you feel like writing about now, go ahead.

_____

_____

REPRODUCTION PAGE 28

READING INTEREST INVENTORY

Please put an X in the column that best describes how you feel about reading these books.

	1 Like	2 Like a little	3 Dislike	4 Dislike very much
1. Reading books	( )	( )	( )	( )
2. Reading books about real people	( )	( )	( )	( )
3. Reading books that are funny	( )	( )	( )	( )
4. Reading adventure books	( )	( )	( )	( )
5. Reading books about hobbies	( )	( )	( )	( )
6. Reading books about the same problems you have	( )	( )	( )	( )
7. Reading mystery books	( )	( )	( )	( )
8. Reading books about family life	( )	( )	( )	( )
9. Reading books about romance	( )	( )	( )	( )
10. Reading science-fiction books	( )	( )	( )	( )
11. Reading sports books	( )	( )	( )	( )
12. Reading books about teenage problems	( )	( )	( )	( )
13. Reading books about animals	( )	( )	( )	( )
14. Reading books about the past	( )	( )	( )	( )
15. Reading books about the present	( )	( )	( )	( )
16. Reading books about love	( )	( )	( )	( )
17. Reading books about religion	( )	( )	( )	( )
18. Reading books with a lot of violence	( )	( )	( )	( )
19. Reading books about social problems	( )	( )	( )	( )
20. Reading books about people like you	( )	( )	( )	( )
21. Reading books about different people	( )	( )	( )	( )
22. Reading books about people younger than you	( )	( )	( )	( )
23. Reading books about people older than you	( )	( )	( )	( )
24. Reading books about people near your age	( )	( )	( )	( )
25. Reading books about people in cities	( )	( )	( )	( )
26. Reading books about people in the country	( )	( )	( )	( )
27. Reading books about people in the suburbs	( )	( )	( )	( )
28. Reading books that seem real	( )	( )	( )	( )

29. What is your favorite magazine? _____

30. What is the best book you have ever read? _____

readability level should be taken into account. The range of reading abilities in a class may be quite wide. In an average ninth-grade class, for instance, the spread in reading ability may be ten years. Teachers should attempt to use a book or books most of the students can read. The Fry Readability Graph[3] (see page 96) is an easy and quick tool for estimating the grade level equivalent of a particular book. Many readability measures are available, but they should not be used as strict guides for matching students with novels or other forms of prose. Less able students may read difficult materials if these materials interest them. Able students may read at a frustration level even though they consider the material dull.[4]

_____

3. Edward B. Fry, "A Readability Formula That Saves Time," *Journal of Reading* 11 (April 1968).

4. For a valuable series of articles on reading, consult *Language Arts* 54 (February 1977).

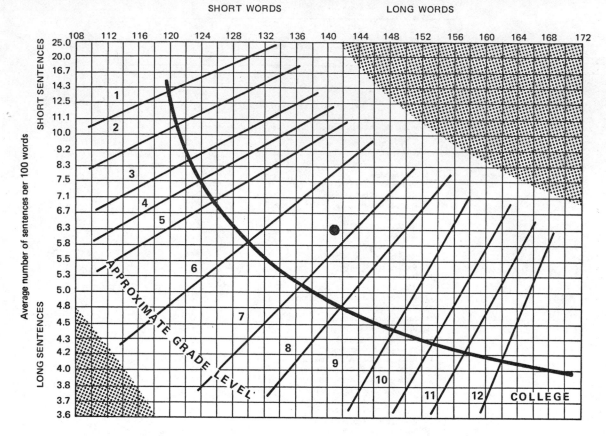

Average number of syllables per 100 words

SHORT WORDS   LONG WORDS

DIRECTIONS: Randomly select 3 one hundred word passages from a book or an article. Plot average number of syllables and average number of sentences per 100 words on graph to determine the grade level of the material. Choose more passages per book if great variability is observed and conclude that the book has uneven readability. Few books will fall in gray area but when they do grade level scores are invalid.

Example:	Syllables	Sentences
1st Hundred Words	124	6.6
2nd Hundred Words	141	5.5
3rd Hundred Words	158	6.8
AVERAGE	141	6.3

READABILITY 7th GRADE (see dot plotted on graph)

DIRECTIONS FOR USING THE READABILITY GRAPH

1. Select three hundred-word passages from near the beginning, middle, and end of the book. Skip all proper nouns.

2. Count the total number of sentences in each hundred-word passage (estimating to

nearest tenth of a sentence). Average these three numbers (add together and divide by 3).

3. Count the total number of syllables in each hundred-word sample. There is a syllable for each vowel sound; for example: *cat* (1), *blackbird* (2), *continental* (4). Do not be fooled by word size, for example: *polio* (3), *through* (1). Endings such as *-y*, *-ed*, *-el*, or *-le* usually make a syllable, for example: *ready* (2), *adapted* (3), *bottle* (2). I find it convenient to count every syllable over one in each word and add 100. Average the total number of syllables for the three samples.

4. Plot on the graph the average number of sentences per 100 words and the average number of syllables per 100 words. Most plot points fall near the heavy curved line. Perpendicular lines mark off approximate grade-level areas.

Example	Sentences per 100 words	Syllables per 100 words
100-word sample page 5	9.1	122
100-word sample page 89	8.5	140
100-word sample page 150	7.0	129
Divide total by 3	3)24.6	3)391
Average	8.2	130

Plotting these averages on the graph we find they fall in the fifth-grade area. Hence the book is about fifth-grade difficulty level. If great variability is encountered either in sentence length or in the syllable count for the three selections, then randomly select several more passages and average them in before plotting.

Other constraints on selection are time and purpose. Short novels have obvious appeal; they look less imposing and can be read quickly. Nothing is more stifling than teaching a novel chapter by chapter, day after day. While this approach may get at the important elements, it will probably prompt many students never to read another novel after they leave school. After all, how many people would go to baseball games if the teams played an inning a day for nine days? If teachers wish to acquaint their students with many types of novel, three novels of 175 pages each may be better than one 500-page novel.

Purpose influences selection when the English class is organized around broad course titles: "American Literature," "English Literature," "World Literature," or mini-courses and electives, such as "Man and Imagination," "Existentialism," "Sports Literature," "The Religious Quest," and so on. Whatever other elements are considered, the novels selected must fit the organization of the class.

APPROACHES

Novels may be taught extensively, intensively, or through free reading. The first approach emphasizes quantity; the second, quality; and the third, need or interest. While each approach has advantages and disadvantages, most teachers will base selection on suitability and variability. The good literature program probably uses all three.

Teaching novels extensively emphasizes both wide reading and reading for pleasure. A common approach is to introduce the novel on Thursday and provide some background on the author, pass out study questions, attend to new or difficult vocabulary, and so on. Friday is spent reading the novel in class so that the students are well into it by the weekend. On Monday all students are expected to have finished the book. Completion may be checked by a factual test. Monday, Tuesday, and Wednesday are spent on activities dealing with the novel.

Using the extensive approach limits the teacher to relatively short, simple books. Two hundred pages may be the maximum length for a book taught extensively. Language, concepts, theme, plot, and character should be simple enough for most of the class to read with understanding. Attempting a too-difficult novel defeats the purpose of reading for pleasure.

The analytical system of literary analysis often taught in college English courses may present barriers for immature or unsophisticated readers. Good readers, with a high interest in literature, can probably benefit from a close study of a difficult work. However, the study of any novel is successful only if the reader can react to it intelligently. If the work is too far removed from the student's experience and background, the study will be an empty exercise in labeling and parroting pat answers. Intensive study of the novel, if used at all, should be reserved for high school juniors and seniors. Care should be taken that the novel selected for intensive study is able to withstand close scrutiny. Students involved in this kind of study should also be familiar with novels and enjoy reading them.

Choice will often dictate what approach to use. If the curriculum requires, or the teacher chooses, *Moby Dick*, then the intensive approach is in order. If *My Darling My Hamburger*, is to be read, then the extensive approach is appropriate. To spend three weeks on *The Red Pony* is a waste of time and intellectually dishonest. To spend a day or two discussing *The Scarlet Letter* does not do it justice.

Free reading, as used in this chapter, may be a misnomer. It is actually three approaches, only one of which is "free." The first is a grouping concept in which three, four, or five novels are being read by various groups in the class. The second has each student in the class reading a different work but within a common rubric. The third approach bases selection on individual student need, ability, and interest with a minimal attempt by the teacher to conduct group reading. The common element in all free reading is choice.

Paul Zindel's *I Never Loved Your Mind*, Maureen Daly's *Seventeenth Summer*, Ann Head's *Mr. and Mrs. Bojo Jones*, and June Jordan's *His Own Where* all deal with boy-girl relationships, a common concern of adolescents. The novels differ in point of view, problem resolution, characterization, and difficulty. By using a Reading Interest Inventory, teachers can assign students one of the four novels. Because the general topic is the same, many activities can be used to compare, contrast, discuss, and evaluate the novels. Hopefully, each student will have an enjoyable reading experience and a meaningful contact with the novel.

Many themes or topics are general enough that hundreds of novels are available. Besides man versus man, man versus society, man versus nature, and man versus himself, what else is there? Choosing one of these or a more specific topic—multiethnic literature, war literature, Canadian literature, classics, or the like—would allow each student to read a different novel based on his ability and interest while allowing activities to center on a particular topic or theme.

The final kind of free reading is usually taught as an elective of three, six, or nine weeks, or as part of the regular English program, as in "free reading Friday." The emphasis is on enjoyment, as we attempt to give all students several successful experiences. Specific selections can be based on student interest, on the teacher's attempt to move students to progressively more complex works, or on bibliotherapy. This approach is successful with remedial groups, enrichment classes, or as part of the regular program.

ADOLESCENT LITERATURE

Until recently, preconceptions and misconceptions about adolescent literature have relegated it to a status of subliterature. Now, however, acceptance by colleges, universities, and professional organizations has brought the adolescent novel to a prominent place in the secondary school English program. The adolescent novel is now viewed by many as an effective bridge between children's literature and adult fiction.

Early novels for adolescents were usually of the Hardy Boys, Jack Armstrong, Nancy Drew variety. They focused on the good, the true, and the beautiful. The villain was always punished; the white, middle-class, upwardly mobile hero always won. Hard work always paid off; success was always hard won; and the only single-parent homes were caused by death, not by divorce. It is no wonder that the Commission on English found that "for classes in remedial reading a resort to such books may be necessary, but to make them a considerable part of the curriculum for most students is to subvert the purposes for which literature is included in the first place."[5]

Recent adolescent novels are usually written by serious writers addressing serious themes to the teenage reader. The same issues current in adult fiction—premarital sex, broken families, race relations, death, mental problems, and homosexuality—are common in adolescent literature. Unlike many adult novels, they are treated sensitively and in good taste. Traditional adolescent themes of initiation, family life, sports, and peer relations are also treated.

The growing interest in this type of novel makes it difficult for the teacher to select and/or recommend appropriate titles to students. As with adult novels, no teacher can read them all. Many colleges and universities now offer courses in adolescent literature, usually at the graduate level. Two leading professional organizations, the National Council of Teachers of English and the International Reading Association, have subgroups with newsletters to keep teachers up-to-date on current issues and new titles. ALAN (NCTE) and SIGNAL (IRA) can assist the teacher interested in the adolescent novel. Two annotated bibliographies prepared by English teachers, *Books for You* and *Your Reading*, are also available from NCTE.[6]

The popularity of the "new" adolescent novel is based on a need fulfilled. The characters are real—they have real problems, real families, go to real schools, and do not always live happily ever after. They provide vicarious experiences—living in another place, being of a different socioeconomic group, getting into trouble, living in the future, living in the past, having a large family, having no family, and so on. They also give students alternative

---

5. Commission on English, *Freedom and Discipline in English* (New York: College Entrance Examination Board, 1965), p. 49.

6. Kenneth Donelson, ed., *Books for You* (Champaign, Ill.: NCTE, 1976) and Jerry L. Walker, ed., *Your Reading* (Champaign, Ill.: NCTE, 1975).

solutions to problems they may have: a broken home, a drinking parent, peer pressure, disabilities, boy-girl relationships. The adolescent novel, because it speaks to teenagers, can be an excellent vehicle for starting the student on a lifelong reading habit.

MULTIETHNIC NOVELS

Multiethnic novels are now a legitimate part of literature study. The recent interest in ethnic or cultural heritage has led to the publication of many fine books that deal with aspects of our polyglot heritage. Given this body of literature, teachers must decide how to teach it. Three approaches are possible: as literature, as awareness, and as ethnic pride or understanding.

Teaching ethnic novels as literature is academically respectable, but seriously limited in terms of choice. Wright's *Native Son* or Ellison's *Invisible Man* can be taught as good literature that happens to be written by black authors about the black experience. Cather's *My Antonia* deals with the experience of a Bohemian girl in Nebraska, and Undset's *Kristin Lavransdatter* with life in fourteenth-century Norway, besides being multiethnic novels that are considered significant literature. If only serious novels can be considered for ethnic studies, the choice is limited, not because multiethnic novels are poorly written, but because most serious fiction deals with universal rather than with specific themes. While multiethnic novels often deal with universal themes, teaching them as multiethnic fiction places their ethnicity before their universality.

Teaching multiethnic novels as awareness broadens the choices considerably. In this approach, the teacher attempts to make students aware of ethnic groups in U.S. culture that may not be represented in a specific school population. The novel is a vehicle for cultural awareness. Common broad topics are "Black Literature," "Native American Literature," and "Mexican American Literature." A large number of annotated reading lists available for black, native American, and Mexican American literature are cited in the Suggested Resources.

A final approach to multiethnic literature is that of ethnic pride or heritage. In this approach, students explore their own heritage through novels. Many turned-off readers will often enjoy a novel that speaks of their heritage. In the past, multiethnic literature has usually meant black, native American, or Mexican American literature. While the majority of the population of the United States has European roots, little has been done with the ethnic literature of these peoples. Included in the Suggested Resources is an annotated list of European ethnic literature that can serve as a starter.

The teacher should also be aware of two distinct types of multiethnic novel: those written by, and those written about, the ethnic group. Usually, a novel written by a member of an ethnic group will more truthfully portray that group. Novels about ethnic groups range from truthful portrayals to thinly drawn books that may be about a black experience but could easily be portraying a Swedish, Portuguese, or Polish experience. The latter type of ethnic portrayal is often found in adolescent novels.

The approaches to multiethnic literature roughly parallel the approaches to teaching all novels. Multiethnic novels considered as literature should usually be taught intensively; as awareness, extensively. Reading for cultural pride or heritage can succeed through a free reading approach.

SCIENCE FICTION

Like adolescent literature, science fiction has recently emerged as a legitimate branch of literature. The pulp magazines of the 1920s and the space comic operas of Edgar Rice Burroughs and others put a mark on science fiction that is only now being erased. Early science fiction was fairly easy to categorize as gadget stories or adventures on other planets. Current science fiction can be loosely classified in three categories: social science fiction, scientific science fiction, and alien science fiction. The increased sophistication of science-fiction writers and readers has led to a movement to change the name of science fiction to "speculative fiction" or "imaginative fiction" to get away from the old connotations.

Social science-fiction novels, though they may be set in the future or on other worlds, deal with problems of the present: overpopulation, racism, pollution, war, famine, religion, and so on, often in a satirical manner. The authors are looking back at the present and are either offering solutions or are predicting what they think are logical conclusions to man's problems. The novels are often grim and may or may not offer hope for the future.

Scientific science fiction is closest, at least in theme, to the old science fiction. It deals with gadgets, inventions, and technological and medical breakthroughs. Much fine science fiction that has crossed over to modern fiction best-seller lists is scientific science fiction. *The Terminal Man, Andromeda Strain,* and *Flowers for Algernon* all sold well beyond the science-fiction market.

Alien science fiction involves an alien or otherworldly presence in human society. Aliens in a human host, interplanetary or intergalactic contact, peaceful aliens, hostile aliens, monster aliens, and further-advanced aliens are all common topics. These novels usually conclude with the aliens serving to bring men together in a common cause.

This rough categorizing is not discrete. Many novels spread over two or all three categories: Heinlein's *Stranger in a Strange Land* concerns a Martian-raised half human (alien) who starts a new religion (social) with the aid of some technological advances (scientific). If you are a science-fiction buff, selecting appropriate novels is no problem. If you are uninitiated, an "All-Time All-Star Science Fiction Book List," divided into categories, is included.

The major reason for including science fiction in the English class is interest. For the adolescent, science fiction is probably the most popular type of fiction. The popularity comes from two sources: escapism and a concern with the future. While still considered by some a spurious candidate for inclusion in the literature program, science fiction is a useful vehicle for increasing reading appetites as well as for exploring current social problems and the future.

ALL-TIME ALL-STAR SCIENCE FICTION BOOK LIST

(All books on the list are available in inexpensive paperback editions.)

Social Science Fiction

Ray Bradbury, *Fahrenheit 451,* Ballantine, 1953

John Brunner, *Stand on Zanzibar,* Ballantine, 1968

John Christopher, *No Blade of Grass*, Avon, 1975

Harry Harrison, *Make Room, Make Room*, Berkeley, 1973 (film version, "Soylent Green")

Frank Herbert, *Dune*, Ace Books, 1974

Ursala K. Le Guin, *The Left Hand of Darkness*, Ace Books, 1969

Walter Miller, *A Canticle for Leibowitz*, Bantam, 1961

Alien Science Fiction

James Blish, *A Case of Conscience*, Ballantine, 1975

Pierre Boulle, *Planet of the Apes*, NAL, 1968

Arthur Clarke, *Childhood's End*, Ballantine, 1974

Samuel Delaney, *The Einstein Intersection*, Ace Books, 1971

James Gunn, *The Listeners*, NAL, 1974

Robert Heinlein, *Stranger in a Strange Land*, Berkeley, 1968

Larry Niven, *Ringworld*, Ballantine, 1970

H. G. Wells, *War of the Worlds*, Berkeley, 1975

Scientific Science Fiction

Michael Crichton, *Andromeda Strain*, Dell, 1971

____, *The Terminal Man*, Bantam, 1974

Gordon R. Dickson, *Sleepwalker's World*, Daw Books, 1972

Robert Heinlein, *I Will Fear No Evil*, Berkeley, 1971

Aldous Huxley, *Brave New World*, Harper & Row, 1969

Daniel Keyes, *Flowers for Algernon*, Bantam, 1970

Robert Merle, *Day of the Dolphin*, Fawcett World, 1973

Andre Norton, *Judgment on Janus*, Ace Books, 1973

John Sladek, *The Muller-Fokker Effect*, Pocket Books, 1973

H. G. Wells, *The Invisible Man*, Airmont, 1964

____, *The Time Machine*, Bantam, 1968

CLASSICS

A classic novel is one that has stood the test of time. It continues to be read while most of its contemporaries have long been forgotten. A classic may also fit Mark Twain's definition, "something that everybody wants to have read and hardly nobody reads." The teacher choosing classics for use in the English classroom usually offers the following justifications. First, the teacher can be sure they are first-rate because generations of critics and scholars have said so. Second, classics are part of our cultural heritage and, as such, need to be read. Finally, any modern novel, no matter how critically well acclaimed, may be a temporary abberation. Therefore, the teacher cannot be sure his time is being spent judiciously unless he teaches the old masters.

A handful of novels, relatively speaking, have endured for generations. Their enduring qualities—universality of theme, ageless symbolism, word choice, ordering of detail—lead to a pleasing aesthetic experience. Classics, when examined closely, stand up to scrutiny in a way lesser works cannot. Because they represent humankind's finest use of language, they should be studied intensively. Knapton and Evans's *Teaching a Literature Centered English Program* offers the following list of classics suitable for use in the secondary classroom.[7] They all are works that critics and scholars have deemed first-rate.

9th Grade

Charlotte Brontë, *Jane Eyre*
Charles Dickens, *David Copperfield*
____, *Great Expectations*

Stephen Crane, *The Red Badge of Courage*
Edith Wharton, *Ethan Frome*

10th Grade

Charles Dickens, *A Tale of Two Cities*
Thomas Hardy,
    The Mayor of Casterbridge
Victor Hugo, *Les Miserables*

Joseph Conrad, *The Secret Sharer*
Gustave Flaubert, *A Simple Heart*
Leo Tolstoy, *The Death of Ivan Ilyich*

11th Grade

Jane Austen, *Emma*
____, *Pride and Prejudice*
Honore de Balzac, *Pere Goriot*
Emily Brontë, *Wuthering Heights*
Gustave Flaubert, *Madame Bovary*
Thomas Hardy, *The Return of the Native*
____, *Tess of the D'Urbervilles*

Joseph Conrad, *The Heart of Darkness*
Henry James, *The Turn of the Screw*
Franz Kafka, *The Trial*
Herman Melville, *Billy Budd*
Katherine Anne Porter, *Noon Wine*
____, *Pale Horse, Pale Rider*
Leo Tolstoy, *Anna Karenina*

12th Grade

Charles Dickens, *Bleak House*
Fyodor Dostoevsky,
    Crime and Punishment
Henry James, *Portrait of a Lady*
____, *Washington Square*
Herman Melville, *Moby Dick*
Stendhal, *The Red and the Black*
William Thackeray, *Vanity Fair*

Henry James, *The Aspern Papers*
____, *The Beast in the Jungle*
____, *Daisy Miller*
____, *The Spoils of Poynton*
James Joyce, *The Dead*
Thomas Mann, *Death in Venice*
____, *Tonio Kröger*

Literary classics are a part of our cultural heritage and as such should be read to pass on the literary experiences of our predecessors. By reading classics we share a common

---

7. James Knapton and Bertrand Evans, *Teaching a Literature Centered Program* (New York: Random House, 1968).

experience with those who have gone before. The best novels of the past are a very suitable vehicle for exploring our literary heritage.

To teach only modern popular fiction may be to waste the students' time. While the classics have stood up to generations of critics and scholars, modern fiction has yet to withstand the test of time. *Uncle Tom's Cabin* (1852) was a best-seller in the 1850s, while *Moby Dick* (1851) was hardly noticed; of the books published in the United States between 1880 and 1935, Charles M. Sheldon's *In His Steps* (1896) outsold them all, while the novels of Henry James had a small audience. Melville and James are now considered great American novelists, while Stowe and Sheldon are forgotten. Will the same happen to the authors of *Jaws, The Godfather*, and *The Exorcist*? Will Steinbeck, O'Hara, Hemingway, and Dos Passos be read fifty, a hundred, or two hundred years from now? The teacher can be sure of teaching first-rate literature if the classics are used.

A commitment to the classics seems to involve more than just a liking for particular kinds of novel. It aims for an enjoyable literary experience at the highest level—the aesthetic. Classics are not read simply as sociology, bibliotherapy, exploration, escape, or political science, but more importantly, for their value as art. The comitment also implies a faith in eternal as opposed to relative values. Finally, student interest, immediate need, and ability may be only incidental. Classics are read, not because they are easy or fun or because they relate to the present, but because they should be read.

GENERAL ACTIVITIES

The following are general questions and activities that can be used with almost any novel:

1. Katherine Lever defines the novel as "a form of written prose narrative of considerable length involving the reader in an imagined real world which is new because it has been created by the author."[8] Does the novel you have read fit this definition? Is it prose? Is it written in narrative form? Is it of considerable length? Does it involve the reader in a real imagined world? Is the imagined real world new? Is it created by the author? Can a book still be a novel if it does not meet all the criteria?

   This basic discussion can be either oral or written. The process can be used for individual reading (student-teacher conferences), as a group assignment if several novels have been read, or as a whole-class discussion about a novel.

2. The narrator is fundamental to most novels. For this reason it is important to speculate why a particular narrator was chosen. Is the narrator a central character? A minor character? Outside the action? An eyewitness? All-observant? Is the type of narrator important to the novel?

3. Try to define novels you have read recently as either romantic or realistic. Do you find you favor one kind or the other?

4. Good novels follow the dictates of relevance and economy. Every episode or description should have reasons for being. Choose several episodes from a particular

---

8. Katherine Lever, *The Novel and the Reader* (New York: Appleton-Century-Crofts, 1961), p. 16.

novel and discuss why they are necessary. Ask students to find any unnecessary episodes or descriptions.

5. Does the world of the novel seem real to you? Are the places, settings, and scenes in keeping with the novel?

6. Does the novelist accept the moral standards of any of his characters? Do you? Are there any characters that specifically seem to reflect the novelist's moral views? Are characters opposed to the novelist's or your own moral standards?

7. What do you, as a reader, know that the people in the imagined world do not know? Why does the novelist let you know? Does it enhance or hurt the effect of the novel?

Characters

1. Does each character seem to be a distinct individual who has lived before he or she appears in the novel? Do some characters appear "unreal"?

2. Do you feel as if you were an inhabitant of the world of the novel, participating vicariously in the action through identification with one character? If so, is it because the character is like you, like you wish you were, or a sympathetic character?

3. Do you understand why the characters act as they do? Are there reasons, as portrayed by the novelist, for the actions? Do any actions seem unbelievable?

4. Do you have a clear and vivid image of the inhabitants of the imagined world? If not, is it a flaw in the novel, or does it serve a purpose?

5. As we read novels, we usually form mental pictures of what certain characters look like. Using the novel you are now reading, cast it as though you were making a movie. Actors may be taken from television or the movies. Try to cast it again with classmates and acquaintances.

ADOLESCENT LITERATURE

Adolescent novels are extremely flexible in that they can be read by individuals, small groups, or the whole class. For individuals they can be part of a free reading program or an attempt by the teacher at bibliotherapy. For groups, the teacher can assign several novels on a given theme and let students group themselves according to interest. For novels that are particularly important, the teacher can assign them to the whole class. The following topics or themes can be used in any of the three situations:

1. A popular theme in literature is the individual versus society. An interesting unit can be developed by taking advantage of adolescent literature and classic literature to meet various needs and abilities. The following novels vary in difficulty and maturity, but all deal with the individual in conflict with society:

Robert Cormier, *The Chocolate War*, Dell, 1975

Ken Kesey, *One Flew Over the Cuckoo's Nest*, NAL, 1975

Harper Lee, *To Kill a Mockingbird*, Popular Library, 1974

Sinclair Lewis, *Main Street*, NAL, 1961

Jack London, *Martin Eden*, Airmont, 1970

Robert McKay, *The Troublemaker*, Dell, 1972

2. Women's liberation and the spirit of feminism appear in many adolescent novels. The following are good choices for the teacher who wishes to expose students to this important social issue:

Carole Bolton, *Never Jam Today*, Atheneum, 1972.
Maddy Franklin is a suffragist in 1917. Good novel on the struggle for women's voting rights.

Hope Campbell, *No More Trains to Totenville*, Dell, 1972.
Jane's mother begins to discover the inequalities in society after dropping out to India.

Hila Colman, *Dangerous Summer*, Bantam, 1966.
Gaby gets a newspaper job and must decide whether to be a career woman or play girl.

Elizebeth H. Friermood, *Focus the Brightland*, Doubleday, 1967.
Set in the nineteenth century, this is an interesting novel about a young woman trying to make a career as a photographer.

R. R. Knudson, *Zanballer*, Dell, 1974.
Preceding Title IX, a story of a girl's struggle to have girls' sports accepted in her high school.

Ira Levin, *The Stepford Wives*, Random House, 1972.
The ultimate male chauvinist scheme. Why are the wives so docile? Popular movie.

Lila Perl, *That Crazy April*, Seabury, 1974.
Eleven-year-old Cress faces issues of marriage versus college, and girls in masculine roles.

Sylvia Plath, *The Bell Jar*, Harper & Row, 1971.
The feminist equivalent of *Catcher in the Rye*—excellent.

Alix Kate Shulman, *Memoirs of an Ex-Prom Queen*, Bantam, 1973.
Sasha searches for self amidst society's sexist values. Mature fiction.

Richard Peck, *Representing Super Doll*, Viking Press, 1974.
Sexism as seen in a teenage beauty contest.

3. The increase in divorce in our society has had an effect on adolescents. Students are either living in a one-parent home or know fellow students who are. Many recent adolescent novels have dealt with divorce in a realistic way. The following novels can assist students in dealing with this social phenomenon:

Judy Blume, *It's Not the End of the World*, Bradbury, 1972.
The reactions of the three Newman children, aged six to fifteen, to their parents' divorce.

Lynn Hall, *Sticks and Stones*, Dell, 1972.
Tom and his mother move to Iowa after her divorce. He is suspected of being a homosexual because he is a pianist and sensitive.

Norma Klein, *Mom, the Wolfman and Me*, Avon, 1974.
Brett doesn't mind having an unmarried mother who wears jeans and keeps irregular hours until the wolfman comes into their lives.

Peggy Mann, *My Dad Lives in a Downtown Hotel*, Doubleday, 1973.
Joey thinks his parents' divorce must be his fault.

Harry Mazer, *The Dollar Man*, Delacorte, 1974.
Marcus is raised by his unmarried mother. At fourteen he decides to find his father.

——, *Guy Lenny*, Dell, 1972.
Twelve-year-old Guy has lived with his father for seven years, but the father wants to remarry and his mother wants him to live with her.

Norma Mazer, *I, Trissy*, Dell, 1972.
Trissy's reaction to her parents' divorce is erratic behavior. She asks, "Who will I be?"

Mary Stolz, *Leap Before You Look*, Dell, 1973.
Fourteen-year-old Jimmie is too wrapped up in herself to realize the growing antagonism between her parents. Their divorce comes as a shock, especially when she learns she will be living with her grandmother.

4. Premarital pregnancy is an increasing problem in U.S. society. A teacher may wish to deal with it on an individual basis, with certain groups, or with a class from a social-problems perspective. The following novels deal with the problem in an unpatronizing manner and offer various solutions—marriage, abortion, or adoption:

Patricia Dizenzo, *Phoebe*, Bantam, 1970.
Sixteen-year-old Phoebe comes to terms with her pregnancy and searches for a way out.

Blossom Elfman, *The Girls of Huntington House*, Bantam, 1973.
A young teacher takes a job at the home for unwed mothers.

Jeannette Eyerly, *Bonnie Jo, Go Home*, Bantam, 1973.
A story that realistically reflects the experiences of many girls in the past before laws and attitudes toward abortion were changed.

——, *A Girl Like Me*, Lippincott, 1966.
Cass gets pregnant and is shipped off to a home for unwed mothers by her family. Robin, her best friend, begins to search for her own mother, who may have been in the same situation as Cass.

Ann Head, *Mr. and Mrs. Bojo Jones*, NAL, 1973.
Two young people have to get married but find that high school love and mature love are different. A TV movie.

Richard Peck, *Don't Look and It Won't Hurt*, Avon, 1973.
Seventeen-year-old Ellen leaves home to have a baby. Her fifteen-year-old sister, Carol, goes to Chicago to try to help her.

Jean Thompson, *The House of Tomorrow*, NAL, 1968.
The journal of Jean, a twenty-year-old college student, in a home for unwed mothers after she becomes pregnant by a married man.

5. Dealing with handicaps is important to adults and adolescents. Whether students are trying to overcome a personal handicap or know people who are, the following novels can lead the reader to some insights into physical or psychological handicaps:

Gunnel Bechman, *Admission to the Feast*, Holt, Rinehart & Winston, 1972.
A sixteen-year-old girl learns that she is dying of leukemia and writes a long letter to a friend.

Judy Blume, *Deenie*, Dell, 1974.
Deenie, just before she begins a modeling career, discovers she has curvature of the spine and will have to wear a back brace for four years.

John Branfield, *Why Me?*, Harper & Row, 1973.
Sarah, a young diabetic, comes to terms with her condition after many problems.

Beverly Butler, *Gift of Gold*, Pocket Books, 1973.
Cathy, blind since fourteen, is stunned when it is suggested she should not become a speech therapist.

Betsy Byars, *The Summer of the Swans*, Viking, 1970.
Sara is charged with the care of her mentally retarded younger brother. The story centers on her search for him when he disappears one afternoon.

Matt Christopher, *Long Shot*, Simon and Schuster, 1974.
A mentally retarded boy, after much practice and hard work, becomes a member of the basketball team.

Hannah Green, *I Never Promised You a Rose Garden*, NAL, 1973.
Deborah is committed to a mental institution at sixteen for schizophrenia. Story of her slow climb back to recovery. Excellent.

Mildred Lee, *The Skating Rink*, Dell, 1970.
Tuck, a stutterer, becomes an excellent roller skater, which does much for his self-esteem.

Jean Little, *Mine for Keeps*, Little, Brown, 1962.
Sal, a victim of cerebral palsy, leaves his protective environment and learns to function in the outside world.

John Nuefeld, *Lisa, Bright and Dark*, NAL, 1970.
Sixteen-year-old Lisa knows she is going insane. While her friends believe her, her parents do not.

Kin Platt, *The Boy Who Could Make Himself Disappear*, Dell, 1971.
Roger has a speech impediment and problems with his parents that cause him to become autistic.

_____, *Hey, Dummy*, Dell, 1971.
Twelve-year-old Neil and his relationship with Alan, a brain-damaged boy.

Veronica Robinson, *David in Silence*, Lippincott, 1965.
David and his friends get accustomed to his deafness. Realistic and interesting.

6. Students' problems with their parents, environment, peers, and school are a part of growing up. While hopefully most students do not have all the problems of the adolescents in the following novels, reading about them can be beneficial. Whether used as escape literature, as an opportunity to experience alternative life styles, or as part of the rite of initiation or empathy, there are many fine novels dealing with the theme of growing up troubled:

Judy Blume, *Are You There, God? It's Me, Margaret*, Dell, 1974.
Margaret is almost twelve and troubled by two cultures (big city and small town), two religions (Catholic and Jewish), and growing up.

Frank Bonham, *Cool Cat*, Dell, 1971.
Buddy and Little Pie are trying to stay straight in Dogtown, while many of their friends are getting involved in drugs and gangs.

____, *Durango Street*, Dell, 1972.
Rufus, on probation for auto theft, tries to escape the street gang world.

Bruce Cassiday, *The Wild One*, Pyramid, 1969.
Rick has a fight with his girl, trouble at school, and problems with the law over his motorcycle. How do you stay cool and solve these problems?

Alice Childress, *A Hero Ain't Nothing but a Sandwich*, Avon, 1974.
Benjie's story is told by him, his mother, his grandmother, and his friends as he begins to experiment with drugs.

John Donovan, *I'll Get There: It Better Be Worth the Trip*, Dell, 1969.
Thirteen-year-old Davy tells about his new school, new friends, success in sports, his alcoholic mother, and Fred, his dachshund.

Hal Ellson, *Tomboy*, Bantam, 1969.
Tomboy plans most of the capers for the guys in the Harps street gang. Pretty tame, but controversial when published in 1950.

Jeannette Eyerly, *Escape from Nowhere*, Berkeley, 1970.
Carla has an upwardly mobile father, a drinking mother, and a sister in college. Overweight and shy, she drifts into drugs before coming to terms with herself.

Nat Hentoff, *I'm Really Dragged but Nothing Gets Me Down*, Dell, 1968.
Jeremy, a high school senior, does not want to go to war. Does he go to Canada or stay? Dated, but excellent.

S. E. Hinton, *That Was Then, This Is Now*, Dell, 1971.
Gang wars, drugs, and everyday teenage existence in a slum are parts of this story.

____, *The Outsiders*, Dell, 1968.
Ponyboy learns the senselessness of gang wars and the meaning of tragedy. Single most popular adolescent novel.

M. E. Kerr, *Dinky Hocker Shoots Smack*, Harper & Row, 1972.
Dinky has a weight problem. Her mother has no sympathy until Dinky gets her attention.

____, *If I Love You, Am I Trapped Forever?*, Dell, 1974.
An honest look at divorce, a boy's attraction to an older woman, and growing up.

____, *The Son of Someone Famous*, Ballantine, 1975.
Adam lives in the shadow of his father, a presidential adviser. Brenda fights her mother's concept of what a woman should be.

Lee Kingman, *The Peter Pan Bag*, Dell, 1971.
Wendy runs away and gets in with Boston's drug culture.

Glendon Swarthout, *Bless the Beasts and Children*, Pocket Books, 1973.
Six misfit boys at an Arizona summer camp for rich, unwanted kids try to stop the annual buffalo hunt.

Robin S. Wagner, *Sarah T.—Portrait of a Teenage Alcoholic*, Balantine, 1975.
The story begins when Sarah is fifteen and already a heavy drinker for two years. A TV movie.

Barbara Wersba, *Run Softly, Go Fast*, Bantam, 1972.
Davy is nineteen and living with a girl in Greenwich Village. He knows that he is obsessed by a hatred for his father that grew from disappointment in his father for not being a hero.

Anonymous, *Go Ask Alice*, Avon, 1972.
A normal fifteen-year-old girl turns on to drugs. Mature.

SCIENCE FICTION

1. Divide students into groups of four and have them interview ten people who are younger, ten the same age, ten older (parents' age), and ten much older (grandparents' age). Have students ask all interviewees what they think the world will be like in the year 2000. Share the results with the class. Are there any generalizations to be made about the different age groups and their visions of the future? Compare the results with novels set in the future.

2. Research the life and writing of one science-fiction author and give an oral and/or written report.

3. Design a community of the year 2077. What will it be like? Housing, transportation, schools, shopping, medicine, and government should be considered. This is often a good assignment for groups. When designs are compared, you should have several alternative views of the future. They can also be compared with future societies in novels.

4. After reading a vintage science-fiction novel (Burroughs, Verne, Wells), discuss those things written about as science fiction that are now common. What were the writers wrong about? What is likely to occur that is prophesied in a novel you are now reading?

5. You have invented a rocket ship capable of supporting eight lives until you find a new planet. A catastrophe occurs. Since you can only take seven people with you, who will they be? Justify your choices. This assignment can be done on three levels: (1) people you know of; (2) people you know; and (3) kinds of people—farmer, doctor, astrologer, and so on.

6. If any of your TV stations show reruns of science-fiction-based series—"Outer Limits," "Twilight Zone," etc.—or old science-fiction movies—*The Day the Earth Stood Still, 1984, The Invisible Man, Soylent Green,* or made-for-television movies—try to find out ahead of time and assign them to the class. Often television schedules are made up months in advance. If a novel-based movie is listed as coming up, it can be assigned to the class along with a reading.

7. Because they write of the future or the unknown, science-fiction novelists cannot describe setting, scene, and characters in the same way other novelists do. Consequently, *similes* (direct comparisons) or *metaphors* (implied comparisons) are used more frequently. Find descriptive passages in your novel that use metaphors and similes. Do they present a mental picture of what is described?

8. Dystopias (antiutopias) are a common theme in science fiction. An interesting unit can be developed by using three dystopian science-fiction novels that vary in reading difficulty. Aldous Huxley's *Brave New World*, Harper & Row, 1969 (difficult); Eugene Zamiatin's *We*, Bantam, 1972 (average); and John Neufeld's *Sleep Two, Three, Four*, Avon, 1972 (easy) would be good choices. All deal with carefully controlled societies of the future that are questioned, with serious consequences, by the protagonists.

9. A major feature of Arthur Clarke's *Childhood's End*, Ballantine, 1972, is the modern conception of the devil, overlord Karellen. Compare it with other fic-

tional conceptions: Benét's *The Devil and Daniel Webster*, Levin's *Rosemary's Baby*, and Blatty's *The Exorcist*.

10. The problem of overpopulation is a serious one discussed by scientists and science-fiction writers alike. Possible solutions are offered in the following novels:

T. J. Bass, *Half Past Human*, Ballantine, 1975.
  What happens when population gets completely out of control?

John Brunner, *Stand on Zanzibar*, Ballentine, 1976.
  Long but excellent novel. Hugo Award winner.

Lester Del Rey, *The Eleventh Commandment*, Regency, 1968.
  "Be fruitful and multiply."

Harry Harrison, *Make Room, Make Room*, out of print.
  The movie *Soylent Green* is based on this novel. Overpopulation in a big city.

Robert Silverberg, *The World Inside*, NAL, 1974.
  Most people live in mile-high skyscrapers and the floor number denotes social class. Some savages live outside as in *Brave New World*.

11. Science fiction is mainly a male-chauvinist genre. Some novels have broken from the mold.

Suzy McKee Charnas, *Walk to the End of the World*, Ballantine.
  Set in an antifeminist society of the future.

Sylvia Louise Engdahl, *Enchantress from the Stars*, Atheneum, 1972.
  Elana saves a primitive planet from destruction.

Robert Heinlein, *Podkayne of Mars*, Berkeley, 1974.
  Girl abandons her dreams to old stereotypes.

Ursula Le Guin, *The Left Hand of Darkness*, Ace Books, 1976.
  The people of Gethen are both male and female.

Robert C. O'Brien, *Z For Zachariah*, Atheneum, 1977.
  Sixteen-year-old Ann Borden thinks she is the only survivor until she sees a campfire.

Theodore Sturgeon, *Venus Plus X*, Pyramid, out of print.
  Another one-sex world.

12. Nuclear holocaust is on the minds of many people. Several good science-fiction novels deal with this theme, with a variety of conclusions.

Leigh Brackett, *The Long Tomorrow*, Ballantine, 1975.
  Life after the holocaust.

Lester Del Rey, *Nerves*, Ballantine, out of print.
  Story of a catastrophe in a nuclear plant of the future.

Pat Frank, *Alas, Babylon*, Bantam, 1976.
  Survivors of a nuclear holocaust try to hold on to life.

A. M. Lightner, *The Day of the Drones*, Bantam, 1970.
  "Black" people think they are the only survivors but set out looking for others.

Walter M. Miller, Jr., *A Canticle for Leibowitz*, Bantam, 1961.
  People revolt against leaders held responsible for nuclear tragedy, revert to the Dark Ages, then reemerge. Excellent.

George R. Stewart, *Earth Abides,* Fawcett World, 1976.
Ish sets out to build new world for few survivors.

13. The achievements of modern medicine can have social repercussions. Science fiction emphasizes the social problems inherent in medical advances.

Robert Heinlein, *I Will Fear No Evil,* Berkeley, 1971.
Death is vanquished through brain transplant.

Aldous Huxley, *Brave New World,* Harper & Row, 1969.
Medical science is able to control intelligence in test-tube babies.

Daniel Keyes, *Flowers for Algernon,* Bantam, 1970.
Retarded hero has operation increasing brain power threefold. The movie *Charlie.*

H. G. Wells, *The Invisible Man,* Scholastic, 1972.
Being invisible is not as much fun as you would think.

MULTIETHNIC NOVELS

General

1. Unless you teach in a school that is predominantly black, Mexican American, or native American, students will have to read novels about their heritage individually. Note the various multiethnic resources in the Suggested Resources.

2. The following annotated bibliographies deal with native Americans, blacks, and Mexican Americans. If your students are predominantly members of one of these groups, the novels can be read as part of a unit on ethnic heritage. If students are of other groups, the novels can be read for ethnic awareness. The lists include books written both by and about members of the ethnic groups. The native American group is divided into units: "Indians in White Society," "The Conflict between White and Indian Society," and "A Doomed Way of Life." The black American group is also divided into units: "Growing Up Black (Urban)," "Growing Up Black (Rural)," "Black and White," and "Making It." Many of the novels are also suitable for individual reading or bibliotherapy.

Mexican American

Oscar Zeta Acosta, *The Revolt of the Cockroach People,* Bantam, 1973.
Mexican Americans in Los Angeles fight the white-dominated churches, courts, and government. For mature readers.

Rudolfo A. Anaya, *Bless Me, Ultima,* Quinto Sol, 1972.
Called by some the best Mexican American novel yet written, Anaya's work captures the many conflicts of a young man growing up in New Mexico.

Raymond Barrio, *The Plum Plum Pickers,* Harper & Row, 1969.
The lives and living conditions of Mexican migrant laborers and their battle with a major grower. Excellent.

Hila Colman, *Chicano Girl*, Morrow, 1973.
A Mexican American girl leaves her small-town Arizona home only to become bitter and disillusioned.

William R. Cox, *Chicano Cruz*, Bantam, 1972.
Four high school students—two white, one black, one Mexican American—learn to live and play together. Good sports-oriented novel.

Carol Laklen, *Migrant Girl*, McGraw-Hill, 1970.
Truthful study of the way many Americans live and Dacey's attempt to better her people's living conditions.

Scott O'Dell, *Child of Fire*, Houghton Mifflin, 1974.
Good novel about Mexican Americans seen through the eyes of a parole officer and two gang leaders.

James Summers, *You Can't Make It by Bus*, Westminster, 1969.
Paul is torn between his conservative father and his revolutionary friends.

Richard Vasquez, *Chicano*, Avon, 1971.
The Sandoval family moves from Mexico to Los Angeles in search of the good life. An epic novel spanning several generations.

Edmund Villasenor, *Macho!*, Bantam, 1973.
Roberto enters the United States illegally in search of a better life. Hard portrayal of the life of the migrant worker.

Bob and Jan Young, *Across the Tracks*, Julian Messner, 1958.
Betty Ochoa finds herself torn between white high school friends and her Mexican American heritage.

Growing Up Black (Urban)

Ralph Ellison, *Invisible Man*, Random House, 1959.
A rural black goes to Harlem after being expelled from college. He gets involved with communists and takes refuge underground. Good serious fiction.

Ronald L. Fair, *We Can't Breathe*, Harper & Row, 1972.
Story of growing up and attempting to survive in Chicago during the 1930s and 1940s.

Rosa Guy, *The Friends*, Bantam, 1973.
The story of two black girls in New York, one struggling to find her identity, the other trying to cope with it.

Virginia Hamilton, *The Planet of Junior Brown*, Macmillan, 1971.
Buddy has no family and lives with other runaways in a cooperative system. Junior, a three-hundred-pound musical prodigy, joins him. Excellent for junior high students.

Louise Meriwether, *Daddy Was a Number Runner*, Pyramid, 1971.
A twelve-year-old girl growing up in Harlem. A fine story.

Warren Miller, *The Cool World*, Fawcett World, 1969.
Frank and bitter novel of growing up in Harlem. Mature fiction.

Growing Up Black (Rural)

William Armstrong, *Sounder*, Harper & Row, 1972.
The story of a black sharecropper family in the South, told by a young son. A good film.

Ernest J. Gaines, *The Autobiography of Miss Jane Pittman*, Bantam, 1972.
Traces the life of a slave girl from the Civil War to the 1960s. Excellent film.

Barbara Glasser and Ellen Blustein, *Bongo Bradley*, Hawthorn, 1973.
A kid from Harlem spends the summer with relatives in North Carolina. He learns about himself and his heritage.

Virginia Hamilton, *M. C. Higgins the Great*, Macmillan, 1974.
Life in a strip-mine area. M. C. finds out he can be the master of his own fate. Good for junior high.

Toni Morrison, *Sula*, Knopf, 1974.
Two friends, Sula and Nel, live in the country until Sula leaves for ten years. She returns to break up Nel's marriage.

Gordon Parks, *The Learning Tree*, Fawcett World, 1974.
An autobiographical novel of a young black man growing up in rural Kansas.

Black and White

Betty Baum, *Patricia Crosses Town*, Knopf, 1965.
This is probably the first novel dealing with school busing. Told from a black student's point of view.

Judy Blume, *Iggies's House*, Bradbury, 1970.
Novel about the first black family in a neighborhood. Told from a white girl's point of view.

Natalie Savage Carlson, *Marchers for the Dream*, Harper & Row, 1969
Story of a black family's attempt to get housing under the Fair Housing Law.

Robert Cole, *Saving Face*, Dell, 1972.
Whites overreact when busing starts. Seen through the eyes of Andy, a policeman's son.

Molly Cone, *The Other Side of the Fence*, Houghton Mifflin, 1967.
Another novel about the first black family on the block.

Lorenz Graham, *South Town*, NAL, 1966.
A well-done account of the struggle of a black family in the South before the Civil Rights movement. Excellent.

Marilyn Harris, *The Peppersalt Land*, Four Winds, 1970.
Two girls, one black and one white, are friends until they realize their differences. A story of the strengthening of their friendship.

Nat Hentoff, *Jazz Country*, Harper & Row, 1965.
Story of Tom Curtis, a young white boy, who tries to live in the black world because of his interest in jazz.

Melissa Mather, *One Summer in Between*, Avon, 1971.
In diary form, the story tells of a black college student from South Carolina who moves in for one summer with a white family in Vermont to study Caucasians.

Ester Weis, *Easy Does It*, Vanguard, 1965.
Two new families, one black and one white, move to a new neighborhood. The story of their adjustment.

David Westheimer, *My Sweet Charlie*, NAL, 1966.
Two people on the run, a northern black intellectual and an uneducated southern white girl, meet. Story moves from hate to trust to love. Excellent TV movie.

Making It

Frank Bonham, *The Nitty Gritty*, Dell, 1968.
Charlie is a hustling young black trying to escape the ghetto. Humorous, good junior novel.

Claude Brown, *Manchild in the Promised Land*, NAL, 1971.
An autobiographical novel of a black man breaking out of the ghetto. Mature fiction.

Kristin Hunter, *The Soul Brothers and Sister Lou*, Avon, 1969.
Louretta Hawkins decides there is more to life than the ghetto, and she and her friends start a musical group.

Jessie Jackson, *Tessie*, Dell, 1968.
Young girl from Harlem gets a scholarship to an exclusive private school. Story of Tessie's struggles, disappointments, and successes. Excellent.

Robert Lipsyte, *The Contender*, Bantam, 1969.
Young black attempts literally to fight his way out of the ghetto as a professional boxer. Excellent.

Native Americans: Indians in White Society

Jay Bennett, *The Deadly Gift*, Hawthorn, 1969.
The moral dilemma of a young Mohawk living in New York City who finds ten thousand dollars.

Dale Fife, *Ride the Crooked Wind*, Coward McCann, 1973.
Story of Po Three Feathers's successful adaptation to white society while retaining his ethnic heritage.

Dorothy Hamilton, *Jim Musco*, Herald Press, 1972.
Jim, a Delaware Indian, prefers to stay on an Indiana farm rather than move west with his tribe.

Mitchell F. Jayne, *Old Fish Hawk*, Pocket Books, 1971.
The town drunk decides to regain his pride and return to the wilderness. Good adventure.

Florence Crannel Means, *Our Cup Is Broken*, Houghton Mifflin, 1969.
Sarah moves from her Hopi village to a white middle-class family. After high school she returns to the reservation.

N. Scott Momaday, *House Made of Dawn*, NAL, 1969.
Torn from his culture by the Anglo American war and the lure of Anglo American values, the main character gradually begins to lose his soul. A Pulitzer Prize winning novel.

James Welch, *Winter in the Blood*, Bantam, 1974.
The main character fights to control his existence, to survive in a world that seems beyond his control.

The Conflict between White and Indian Society

Nathaniel Benchley, *Only Earth and Sky Last Forever*, Harper & Row, 1972.
A young warrior leaves the reservation to join Crazy Horse, even though he knows the cause is doomed.

Thomas Berger, *Little Big Man*, Fawcett World, 1974.
   The only white survivor of Little Big Horn is adopted by the Indians. The story of his life in both cultures.

Hal Borland, *When the Legends Die*, Bantam, 1972.
   Tom Black Bull goes from the new life (reservation) to the old, back to the new, and finally returns to the old. An exciting story of initiation.

Molly Cone, *Number Four*, Houghton Mifflin, 1972.
   Benjamin Turner is only the fourth Indian to graduate from the local high school in many years. A story of his return to ethnic pride and the problems it causes.

Edwin Corle, *Fig Tree John*, Pocket Books, 1972.
   First published in 1935, the story of the white man's move into the Salton Sea area of California. The hero's wife is killed, and his son is attracted to white culture.

Mel Ellis, *Sidewalk Indian*, Holt, Rinehart & Winston, 1974.
   Charley Nightwind must leave Milwaukee after being falsely accused of killing a policeman. His flight leads to a discovery of his heritage.

Thomas Fall, *The Ordeal of Running Standing*, Bantam, 1971.
   A young Indian couple splits when she remains on the reservation and he leaves for the white man's world. After being cheated by the whites, Running Standing wants revenge.

Frank Herbert, *Soul Catcher*, Bantam, 1973.
   A thirteen-year-old white boy is kidnapped by a militant Indian seeking revenge for past injustice. They both learn from the experience. Excellent.

Marion Lawson, *Maggies Flying Bird*, Morrow, 1974.
   A half-breed woman lives alternately in both cultures in nineteenth-century Wisconsin.

Patrick Smith, *Forever Island*, Dell, 1973.
   Eighty-six-year-old Charlie Jumper's way of life is threatened for the second time by the white man.

Frank Waters, *The Man Who Killed the Deer*, Pocket Books, 1971.
   Martiniano is caught between his white education and the laws of his tribe.

A Doomed Way of Life

Betty Baker, *And One Was a Wooden Indian*, Macmillan, 1970.
   Struggle for survival of a small band of Apaches living a doomed way of life. Best for junior high readers.

John Craig, *Zach*, Coward, McCann, 1972.
   Zach travels through much of the country searching for his cultural roots.

James Foreman, *People of the Dream*, Dell, 1974.
   Chief Joseph leads his people out of Oregon in a struggle to remain free. Excellent.

Christie Harris, *Raven's Cay*, Atheneum, 1966.
   The decline and fall of the British Columbia Haidas, as told by three generations of chiefs.

Scott O'Dell, *Sing Down the Moon*, Houghton Mifflin, 1970.
   A story of the historic Long Walk told through the eyes of Bright Morning, a fifteen-year-old Navajo girl.

Thomas Sanchez, *Rabbit Boss*, Ballantine, 1973.
   Four generations of the Washo Indians in Nevada. Long, mature fiction.

CLASSICS

The activities for teaching classic novels are considerably different from those for teaching adolescent, science fiction, or multiethnic novels. First, the activities all refer to specific novels rather than to types of novel or theme. Many of the activities, however, can be used with other serious fiction. Second, an approach to teaching the novels is suggested.

The selection of novels for intensive study was somewhat arbitrary, although they all appear on the list of suggested classics on page 103. Of the eight, four are English and four are American: *Pride and Prejudice, Jane Eyre, Great Expectations, The Mayor of Casterbridge, The Scarlet Letter, Moby Dick, Huckleberry Finn*, and *The Red Badge of Courage. Pride and Prejudice* and *Jane Eyre* are not only two of the finest novels ever written but also were created by two of the world's finest women writers. *The Mayor of Casterbridge* is included because it is representative of Hardy's finest work, has strong male characters to balance Austen and Brontë, and is easier to read than *Jude the Obscure* or *The Return of the Native*. A Dickens novel should certainly be included in the literature program. *Great Expectations* was chosen over other good Dickens novels—*Bleak House, A Tale of Two Cities, Dombey and Son*—because it is more representative of Dickens than *A Tale of Two Cities* and is a little easier to read than others. All four choices are commonly taught in high school.

The four American novels were somewhat easier to choose. *Moby Dick, The Scarlet Letter*, and *Huckleberry Finn* would appear on almost everyone's list of great American novels. In fact, when the authors surveyed many English teachers and American literature scholars to find out what four novels they would teach in high school, these three appeared on every list. *The Red Badge of Courage* appears because it is short, excellent, and a stylistic departure from the others. Again, all four are often taught in high school.

Several activities are listed for each novel. While they refer to specific selections, slight modifications can make them suitable for other novels discussed here or any other serious fiction. Questions of theme, point of view, character, literary devices, and form are often universally applicable.

Classics are usually not taught the same way as less difficult novels. While adolescent, science-fiction, and multiethnic novels are often related to student need, interest, and ability, the classics are read for themselves. While other novels are read for escape, bibliotherapy, enjoyment, social problems, or interest, the classics are read for aesthetic reasons. The reading difficulty of many classics usually means they should be read intensively, except by more able readers who can read them individually or as supplementary material.

To do justice to a classic, it should be studied for at least three or four weeks. This time investment usually means that only two or three can be read intensively. While most novels should not be read in class chapter by chapter, the classics probably can be. A typical approach might be to begin by reading aloud the first day until ten minutes or so before the period ends. This time can be used to discuss what has been read and to assign fifteen, twenty, or thirty pages to be read at home. The number of pages read at home will depend on two things: the difficulty of the text and natural stopping points. The next day begins with a discussion of what was read at home, then proceeds to more oral reading and concludes with the next day's assignment. This approach can be followed until the novel is completed. Culminating activities could include writing assignments (many of the activities can be writing assignments), a film version of the novel, and a discussion of related works.

Reading the novel with the class assures that everyone will benefit from in-class reading and follow-up discussions on reading done at home. More able students will be able to continue with outside reading of other books.

Pride and Prejudice

1. Although published in 1813, *Pride and Prejudice* is set at the time of the American Revolution. From your knowledge of American history and a reading of the novel, what are the differences in the English and American character? Possible points of difference might be: the role of women, social class, the landed gentry, and old versus new money.

2. Which female characters in *Pride and Prejudice* would best fit in the last half of the twentieth century? Why? Which male characters?

3. *Pride and Prejudice* has been called a satire. What is Jane Austen satirizing? Is it successful? What do you think her contemporaries thought about the satire?

4. Novels have been titled after characters—*Jane Eyre, Tess of the D'Urbervilles, Billy Budd;* symbols—*The Red Badge of Courage, The Scarlet Letter;* places—*Wuthering Heights, A Tale of Two Cities.* What is the meaning of *Pride and Prejudice?*

5. The world of *Pride and Prejudice* is foreign to us today. Why is it still read? That is, what are the basic human characteristics and emotions the novel is concerned with?

6. What social customs govern our behavior? How do they differ from the social customs described in *Pride and Prejudice?*

7. Much of the satire in *Pride and Prejudice* is covered by irony. The real is expressed in words and actions which carry the opposite meaning. This sophisticated literary technique is used in developing Lydia, Lady Catherine, and Mrs. Bennett. Find examples and describe the author's intent.

8. Discuss the dichotomy drawn between married and unmarried women in *Pride and Prejudice.*

9. Lionel Stevenson, in *The English Novel,* writes, "Egoism is in her [Jane Austen's] view the dominant vice of human beings, because an intelligent person ought to realize that he is no more important than anyone else."[9] What characters in *Pride and Prejudice* exhibit egoism? How does the author show she disapproves? What is the result of the characters' egoism?

10. Students are often surprised that people in Jane Austen's time were as concerned about finding mates, and as apt to experience the generation gap, as they are: What are the differences in these problems between then and now?

11. Irony is a major literary device in *Pride and Prejudice.* When does Jane Austen use it, and to what effect?

9. Lionel Stevenson, *The English Novel* (Boston: Houghton Mifflin, 1960).

12. Read as many criticisms of *Pride and Prejudice* as you can. (As an alternative, several students can be assigned to read one criticism.) Compare the criticism written when the novel was published with later criticism and modern criticism as an indication of changing or unchanging tastes.

13. *Pride and Prejudice* is in many ways autobiographical. Compare it with Austen's life as presented by a biographer.

Jane Eyre

1. Though published in 1847, *Jane Eyre* concerns a heroine much in tune with the feminist movement of today. She is both strong-willed and talented. Point out scenes in which her feminism is displayed. Are there any in which she appears antifeminist? In the context of the times, was her personality unusual?

2. Charlotte Brontë makes use of dreams, visions, and voices in *Jane Eyre*. Do they detract from the novel? Given the world of the novel and its characters, are they out of place?

3. *Jane Eyre* is a first-person narrative, and consequently we see the world through Jane's eyes. Are there any characters whom you feel were treated badly by Jane's view? How would an omniscient narrator have treated them?

4. Using the chart for differentiating between romance and realism, how would you classify *Jane Eyre?* Why?

5. Charlotte Brontë was raised in the harsh north of England in genteel poverty. Before publishing *Jane Eyre* at the age of thirty-one, she lived through the deaths of her mother, sisters, and brother; she lived with an eccentric minister father who delighted in telling his children ghost stories; and she lacked the companionship of people her own age (with the exception of sisters and brothers). How are these facts reflected in the novel?

6. Kathleen Tillotson, in *Novels of the Eighteen Forties*, writes, "This novel *[Jane Eyre]* makes its appeal first and last to the unchanging human heart."[10] Do you agree? Does this account for its status as a classic?

7. Contemporary readers were shocked that Rochester was rewarded for an immoral life by a happy marriage. Were you? Why were Brontë's contemporaries shocked?

8. Charlotte Brontë is masterful at creating atmosphere. Her experience as a poet trained her to create impressions with words. Find especially powerful details in *Jane Eyre*, noting the use of simile and connotative words.

9. *Jane Eyre* is in many ways autobiographical. Compare it with Brontë's life as presented by a biographer.

10. If possible, see the film after reading the novel. Was it faithful to the book? Did it help explain the novel?

---

10. Kathleen Tillotson, *Novels of the Eighteen Forties* (Oxford: Clarendon Press, 1954).

Great Expectations

1. Critics have argued about the major theme of *Great Expectations.* One group feels the novel is a study of guilt, corruption, and redemption. Others think it is a study of the corrupting influence of money and social class. What do you think? Support your decision from the text.

2. What is the meaning of the title *Great Expectations?*

3. Dickens is known for his use of symbols. Some that are used in *Great Expectations* are insects, chains, and light. What do these symbolize? Find others in the text and explain their significance.

4. *Great Expectations* can be read as a novel of character development. Trace Pip's development throughout the novel.

5. *Great Expectations* contains many "parasitic" relationships. What are some of them?

6. For much of the novel Pip was what we now call a juvenile delinquent. What does this term mean to you? What are the causes of juvenile delinquency? Do they apply to Pip?

7. While much of *Great Expectations* is sad and tragic, it is also a story of love. How do the characters Pip, Estella, Miss Havisham, and Joe react to love? How do they express love?

8. Unlike many writers we study as great novelists, Dickens was an immensely popular figure in both England and America. It is reported that he made $200,000 one year by giving readings in America. Why do you think he was so popular in his own time? Why is *Great Expectations* still read while most best-sellers are soon forgotten?

9. Dickens, through Pip, criticizes aspects of his society. What is he criticizing? What is his view of the class system? The courts? Wealth?

10. Dickens wrote two endings to *Great Expectations.* One is the more popular happy ending. The other is ambivalent. Estella's brutal husband dies, and she marries a ne'er-do-well doctor. Pip has a talk with her on the street, and they both go their own way. Which ending is more true to the novel? Why?

The Mayor of Casterbridge

1. *The Mayor of Casterbridge* can be read as an allegory for Hardy's view of history as cyclical. In the novel, both Henchard and Farfrae follow a pattern of the creation of authority, the consolidation of power, its weakening, and its collapse. Give examples of these four gradations in the novel.

2. Hardy complained that many of the plot Incidents in *The Mayor of Casterbridge* were forced on him because the novel was serialized. What incidents seem to be contrived?

3. *The Mayor of Casterbridge* has been compared with Greek and Shakespearean tragedies. Do you agree? Is Henchard a tragic hero? What is his "tragic flaw"?

4. Henchard has violated the moral order by selling Susan—an immoral act in Western culture. How is he made to pay for his crime? How many "minor" tragedies does he face that lead to total collapse?

5. How are Henchard and Lucetta alike? What is her immoral act?

6. Hardy places Henchard and Farfrae in opposition. How does one epitomize passion and the other reason? The rugged individualist and the organization man? Primitive and modern?

7. Hardy abounds in symbols. Three important ones are rain, the name Abel, and Mixen Lane. Try to explain them and their significance.

8. At the furmity women's trial she reveals Henchard's secret and says, "It proves that he's no better than I, and has no right to sit there in judgement of me." Do you agree? Can you think of any modern instances of this attitude either in literature or life?

9. What is your assessment of Susan? Elizabeth-Jane? Do you like them? Are they real? Do they symbolize anything?

10. Hardy's philosophy of life is clearly reflected in his novels. What does ne think about the human condition? Is he a pessimist or an optimist?

The Scarlet Letter

1. The four major characters in the novel are Hester, Pearl, Dimmesdale, and Chillingworth. To what extent is Puritan society a fifth major character?

2. *The Scarlet Letter* is written from an omniscient point of view. How different would it be if narrated by Hester, Pearl, Dimmesdale, or Chillingworth?

3. It has been said in reference to the novel that Hawthorne loves the sinner but hates the sin. Explain.

4. The novel abounds in symbols: the letter *A*, the scaffold, Dimmesdale's gesture of hand over heart, and so on. What do they symbolize? What nature symbols are used? To what effect?

5. What was the effect of the sin of adultery on Hester? Chillingworth? Dimmesdale?

6. Compare the character growth of Hester with the character disintegration of Chillingworth and Dimmesdale.

7. Pearl has been called "otherworldly." What manifestations of abnormalities are there in the novel? What is the purpose of portraying her as different?

8. Many believe that Chillingworth's major sin is "severing himself from humanity." Do you agree?

9. Chillingworth was upset at Hester and Dimmesdale's sin at two levels, the physical and the philosophical. On the philosophical level, what did the sin represent to him?

10. David W. Noble, in *The Eternal Adam and the New World Garden*, writes, "Dimmesdale is the most beloved minister in the community precisely because he

admits inwardly that he is a sinner."[11] What does this mean? How is it manifested in the novel?

11. What in Puritan society is Hawthorne criticizing? Perry Miller's *The Puritan Writers* might be a good source for insights into the Puritan mind.

Moby Dick

1. Father Mapple said in his sermon, "If we obey God, we must disobey ourselves, and it is this disobeying ourselves, wherein the hardness of obeying God consists." In the context of the novel, what does this mean?

2. Contrast Queequeg's behavior to that of the rest of the crew. Why is he different?

3. What is Melville criticizing through his portrayal of Bildad and Peleg? Give examples.

4. Why does Ishmael survive? Why do you think Melville allowed it? Why not Starbuck?

5. The majority of critics have agreed that the sin that led to Ahab's downfall was pride. Find examples of it.

6. Early in the book, when Ishmael and Queequeg spend the night in the inn, Ishmael says, "And what is the will of God?—to do to my fellow man what I would have my fellow man do to me—that is the will of God." Does Ishmael follow this rule? Queequeg? Ahab?

7. Critics have said that the three mates, Starbuck, Stubb, and Flask, symbolize the three parts of the psyche: reason, impulsive passion, and blind will. Do they? Give examples from the text.

8. What does the white whale symbolize for Ahab? Ishmael?

9. D. H. Lawrence, in *The Symbolic Meaning*, writes, "Melville is a master of violent, chaotic physical motion, he can keep up a whole wild chase without flaw. He is as perfect at creating stillness."[12] Find examples of what you think Lawrence is praising.

10. *Moby Dick* is an extended allegory replete with symbolism. To interpret the allegorical meaning of the novel, the frequent use of symbols should be studied. The names Ahab, Ishmael, and Peter Coffin are symbols, as is the international makeup of the crew. What do they all symbolize? What are some other symbols? What is your allegorical interpretation of the novel?

11. *Moby Dick* is a stylistic treasure. Melville uses biblical and mythical references, foreshadowing, expert detail, humor, simile, metaphor, and alliteration, among other devices. Find examples as you study the text.

11. David W. Noble, *The Eternal Adam and the New World Garden* (New York: Grosset & Dunlap), p. 29.

12. D. H. Lawrence, *The Symbolic Meaning* (New York: Viking, 1962), p. 221.

The Adventures of Huckleberry Finn

1. Underlying Huck's story is Twain's criticism of taste, manners, morals, white supremacy, slavery, and monarchy. What are some examples of these criticisms? What literary devices does Twain use to criticize?

2. Irony is used throughout the novel. Find examples of it. What is its effect?

3. Like many novels, *Huckleberry Finn* is a story of the main character's inner growth. Trace Huck's inner growth.

4. Is the journey of Huck and Jim an escape from the real world or an escape from slavery to freedom within the real world? Defend your choice.

5. A major theme of the novel is the conflict of romance and realism, with Tom embodying romance and Huck realism. What other examples can you find? Which does Twain favor?

6. Twain makes a sharp distinction between two kinds of cruelty—the deliberate cruelty of the hardhearted and the unintentional cruelty of the usually kind-hearted. Find examples of each.

7. Huck is forced into several moral choices in the novel. What are they? Are you happy with his choices?

8. Throughout the novel Huck is made to feel guilty by his actions. Does he make the right choices? Why do they trouble him?

9. If you have read *Great Expectations*, how are Huck and Pip alike? Why do they choose different routes at the end?

10. On one level, the novel is the story of a teenager's conflict with the adult world. Have you read other novels with the same theme? Why has *Huckleberry Finn* endured?

The Red Badge of Courage

1. There is a marked contrast between the dialogue and exposition of the novel. That is, the dialogue is harsh, dialectical, and often foolish, while the exposition is written in flowering prose. Why does Crane do this?

2. The novel has been called a heightened treatment of common subjects. Do you agree? Why?

3. What are the major symbols of the novel? What do they symbolize?

4. Part of Crane's artistry is his ability to transfer clear pictures of emotional states into words. Find examples in the text.

5. V. S. Prichett, in *The Living Novel,* has observed that Crane "does not look mildly into the blank expressionless features of death; but dramatically with face half-averted."[13] Find examples of this contention in the text.

---

13. V. S. Pritchett, *The Living Novel* (New York: Reynal & Hitchcock, 1947), p. 173.

6. The first half of the novel is a study of fear and cowardice, the second of courage and heroism. Where, in your opinion, does the second half begin? How is it different from the first half?

7. How do veterans and raw recruits differ in the way they face battle? Is there a difference between courage and foolishness? If so, what is it?

✓ 8. David W. Noble writes, "*The Red Badge of Courage* is the story of initiation of one young man, Henry Fleming, into the awful truth that even in America the eternal environment for man is war."[14] Do you agree? Is the novel an antiwar novel? Why?

SUGGESTED RESOURCES

Print:

"Adolescent Literature Revisited After Four Years." *Arizona English Bulletin.* Champaign, Ill.: NCTE.

The April 1976 issue of the bulletin is a 248-page single-spaced issue devoted to the teaching of adolescent literature. If you have only one source, this should be it.

Aquino, John. *Science Fiction As Literature.* New York: NEA, 1976.

A short introduction to teaching science fiction as literature. Includes methods and media appropriate to the topic. Also, a good defense for using science fiction in the classroom.

The Ballantine Teacher's Guide to Science Fiction. New York: Ballantine, 1975.

Includes a description of the various types of science fiction and projects and ideas for discussion and reports. In-depth analysis of several popular novels—*Fahrenheit 451, Childhood's End,* etc. Excellent source.

Bone, Robert. *The Negro Novel in America.* New Haven, Conn.: Yale Univ. Press, 1958.

An excellent chronological survey of black novels through the 1950s. Bone divides the works into historical periods: 1890–1920, 1920–1930, 1930–1940, 1940–1952, and Postscript. Should be read by every teacher of black literature.

Boulton, Marjorie. *The Anatomy of the Novel.* London: Routledge & Kegan Paul, 1975.

Good short work on the structure of the novel. Boulton covers point of view, plot, character, and theme. Many examples are used from both American and English literature, classical and modern. A source for the teacher not very experienced with the novel or the high school student who wants to learn more.

Chase, Richard. *The American Novel and Its Tradition.* New York: Doubleday.

A scholarly work exploring main currents in American fiction from Cooper to Faulkner.

Fiedler, Leslie A. *Love and Death in the American Novel.* New York: Dell, 1966.

Fiedler's thesis is that American literature has failed to deal with adult sexuality and is obsessed with death. In the process he discusses every major American novel.

Forster, E. M. *Aspects of the Novel.* New York: Harcourt Brace Jovanovich, 1954.

An indispensable guide to different ways of considering the novel.

Friend, Beverly. *Science Fiction: The Classroom in Orbit.* Educational Impact, 1974.

Subtitled a "mini-course text," and it is. Suggests many units and activites in science fiction. A wider range but not as specific as Ballantine's guide to science fiction.

Gordon, Caroline. *How to Read a Novel.* New York: Viking, 1964.

An excellent guide, written by a novelist, that attempts to answer two questions: What is a novel? How should it be read? Both are answered. An excellent resource for teachers and students interested in the novel form.

Individualized Literature Program. New York: American Book Company.

Free catalogue. Over 200 titles in series, ranging from adolescent literature *(My Darling My Ham-*

---

14. David W. Noble, *The Eternal Adam,* p. 121.

burger, *The Outsiders*), to science fiction *(Planet of the Apes, Fahrenheit 451)*, to classics *(Wuthering Heights, Great Expectations)*. Good prices on the novels (most under $1.00) plus Teacher-Student Package for each book, including a teacher's guide, ten student guides, a 2-page trial test, and 3-page mastery test.

Lever, Katherine. *The Novel and the Reader*. New York: Appleton-Century-Crofts, 1961.

In the author's words, "a handbook for students who seriously want to learn how to tell a good novel from a bad." Not really appropriate for secondary students but a must for English teachers, especially those interested in serious fiction.

Meade, Richard A., and Small, Robert, Jr., eds. *Literature for Adolescents: Selection and Use*. Columbus, Ohio: Charles E. Merrill, 1973.

A book of readings dealing with adolescent literature. Articles defending the use of adolescent literature as well as selection. Good source if you cannot get the *Arizona English Bulletin* issue.

Moskowitz, Sam. *Strange Horizons: The Spectrum of Science Fiction*. New York: Scribner's, 1976.

Explores the major themes of science fiction: religion, civil rights, anti-Semitism, women's liberation, birth control, crime, psychiatry, and unexplained phenomena, with many examples. For the teacher seriously interested in science fiction.

Noble, David W. *The Eternal Adam and the New World Garden*. New York: Grossett & Dunlap, 1968.

A historian writing about literature. His thesis is that the great drama of American intellectual history has been the hope of the immigrants in coming to the New World. Deals with almost every major American novel. A rich source.

Ryan, Margaret. *Teaching the Novel in Paperback*. New York: Macmillan, 1963.

The first book emphasizing the importance of paperbacks in the classroom. Several plans and study guides for frequently taught novels with an emphasis on middle-brow classics.

Shefter, Harry, ed. *Teaching Aids for Forty Enriched Classics*. New York: Washington Square Press, 1975.

If you teach the classics, this book will be worth the price even if you use it only once a year. Objective tests, ideas for discussion, reports, writing assignments, and vocabulary exercises for forty commonly taught classics. A real time saver.

Tanner, Tony. *City of Words*. New York: Harper & Row, 1971.

Study of the work of some 25 American novelists from 1950 to 1970. Excellent for contemporary fiction.

Nonprint:

Many fine films are available on or about novels. A list of university film libraries is in Appendix B. Catalogues may be obtained on request.

The American Experience in Literature: Five Modern Novelists. Encyclopaedia Britannica Corp.

Series of five sound filmstrips, sixteen minutes long, on Lewis, Fitzgerald, Steinbeck, Hemingway, and Faulkner. Available for preview.

Literature and Film. Audio Brandon Films.

Presents films in the Audio Brandon catalogue from works of literature. Includes a teaching manual for each film. Novels in the series include: *The Old Man and the Sea, The Pearl, Lilies of the Field, Lord Jim, Lord of the Flies, Of Human Bondage, Great Expectations, Wuthering Heights*, and *Jane Eyre*.

What Is Science Fiction? Guidance Associates.

Sound filmstrip program of two filmstrips and two cassettes or records. Part I examines the use of scientific fact and realistic description in plot, character, and setting. Part II explores several basic themes: the future of science and technology, the future of society, and the universe and man's relation to it. Available for preview.

5

Teaching Poetry

"How am I to teach poetry if I don't even enjoy it myself?"
—student teacher

"Oh, I can't wait until spring comes—then I can teach poetry."
—teacher with fifteen years' experience

I always recall these two comments primarily because they represent two attitudes that have an important bearing upon the decision to teach poetry. My initial reaction to the first comment bordered on incredulity: How could anyone be an English major, plan to become an English teacher, and still not like—nay—*love* poetry? But whether I am justified in my dismay or just plain naive, I do realize that many English teachers do not like all aspects of literature and that this variation in preference is quite natural for human beings. Such a teacher has essentially two options. One is to swear never to teach poetry to students. This may not be sacrilegious, for teachers communicate their feelings very easily to students, whether they intend to or not. So the teacher who hates poetry may present it in a dull, mechanical fashion that tells students, "Poetry is hard or strange or something only scholars or weird people enjoy. But I have to teach it, and you have to learn it, so let's make the best of it." Hopefully, you do not feel that way, but if you do, this chapter is designed to provide a variety of approaches to teaching poetry. Some are analytic by nature, but if they do not appeal to you, pick the ones that do appeal. If you enjoy the exercise, your students will probably respond more positively than they would if they sensed your dislike.

The second comment quoted above bothers me more than the first, for it tells me that the teacher has a very narrow concept of why poets write and what the nature of poetry is. A friend of mine, walking down the aisle of a theater in El Paso many years ago, pointed to a cute child and said, "Now, that's a poem." Well, allowing for the extension of the metaphor, I had to agree, but, by the same extension, the spilled popcorn, worn seats, and gray, splattered chewing gum were poems as well. Poetry is not just pretty words, not just pleasant subjects, and certainly not just for springtime. Poetry relates to all aspects of life and death. Asked why they write poems, few, if any, professional writers would claim that they wanted to convey beautiful thoughts or even that they wanted to convince anyone of a

127

particular philosophical viewpoint. Poets write because they enjoy putting words together and finding out how the poem will turn out. A poem is essentially an experience—with words, with images, with all the feelings and connotations that those words and images may convey. And that sense of experience, of seeing some aspect of the world in an entirely new light, is what we as teachers have to convey to students and what we have to involve them with.

Should a teacher present students with the analytic terms associated with poetry, terms such as "image," "metaphor," "symbol," "sonnet," and "eye rhyme"? The answer is no—and then yes. First the teacher has to involve students with the poetic experience, enable the students to realize that poems—not all poetry, but many poems—do have something to offer each of us. This is another aspect of developing student response to poetry. If the Poets-in-the-Schools projects around the country have meant anything, it is that students enjoy writing poetry when poetry becomes an enjoyable experience—when students play with words and sounds, when they write poetry themselves. Introducing students to poetry by analyzing poetic technique only convinces students that poetry is difficult, much like diagramming sentences without ever writing. Once students have become involved in poetry as a creative experience, then they can be given analytic terms, for then the terms will have meaning for them.

When I was a student teacher, filled with the scholarly knowledge of the "New Critics," I observed a teacher presenting "General William Booth Enters Heaven" to her class. These were not parent-motivated, college-bound students, but a group of kids who were there because the law said they had to be, and, besides, what else was there to do? The teacher led the class in a—horror of horrors—choral reading of the poem. She told them to take out their key chains, coins, anything that would make noise, and then she orchestrated the entire production, quickly. What I observed appalled me. As they read—shouted, really, out loud—they banged on the desks to the rhythm of the poem, rattled chains, stomped on the floor, and had one good, all-around go at the poem. Scholarly? No. Did they learn to scan the poem? I don't know. I hope not. For that group at that moment, "General William Booth Enters Heaven" was a true experience and that poem was alive. Teachers cannot bang and rattle and shout their way through all poems, but they can find ways to make poems real experiences for students. (It took me a couple of years to realize this fully, to break out of my commitment to total scholarly analysis. I think the great turning point occurred when one of my classes joined me—quite spontaneously—in shouting out the refrain to Kipling's "Boots.")

The activities in this chapter are designed to:

A. Provide the teacher with ways of involving students personally with poetry, of developing honest student response, and of creating positive attitudes toward poetry.

B. Present varied approaches to the learning of analytic terms so that those terms become meaningful to the student, not merely facts one learns in English class.

C. Develop approaches to teaching poetry as a form of creative writing.

PERFORMANCE OBJECTIVES

As a result of the learning experiences in this chapter, students should be able to:
1. Write a variety of metaphors, similes, images, and poetic forms.
2. Recognize and evaluate metaphor, simile, and imagery as they are found in poetry and in prose.
3. Indicate their appreciation for techniques employed in specific poems by discussing whether or not those techniques appeal to them.
4. Identify and evaluate poetic techniques in nonpoetry contexts, such as advertisements and everyday language.
5. Understand the voice and tone embodied in specific poems.
6. Recognize and be able to explain symbols in their own words.

One of the unnecessary built-in problems many teachers face is the feeling that poetry is created only for the English class. Poetry is everywhere—in advertisements, songs, and children's games; in insults, nicknames, and puns; and in the very rhythm of the many dialects of English. For the teacher, this vast, natural poetic resource makes teaching poetry much simpler. For the students, it reveals that their lives are involved with poetry more than they may realize. For this chapter, the exercises make abundant use of the poetry available within and without.

DECIDING HOW TO TEACH POETRY

One of the basic curricular choices the teacher must make is how to incorporate poetry into the total class structure. Several choices are available.

1. Teach poetry as a genre unit in poetry. Advantages of this approach are:

   a. The class can concentrate upon poetry as a form, comparing and contrasting the elements of poetry as they are employed from poem to poem and from poet to poet.

   b. Because of the brevity of most poetry, the class can concentrate upon only one poem or upon several poems at once, thus broadening their awareness of the poet's craft.

   c. By employing inductive strategies, the teacher can stimulate students to discover for themselves the many vital aspects of poetry, and the unit on poetry provides time for this approach.

   Disadvantages of this approach include the following:

   a. By extensive study of poetry, students may begin to tire of poetry and react negatively to it. A poem is an extremely concentrated experience. To expect students to maintain a high level of involvement throughout a number of poetic experiences may be expecting too much.

   b. By isolating poetry from other forms of literature, the teacher may indicate to students that it is a form so unique that it has little relationship to anything else.

2. Teach poetry as part of a thematic unit. Include a variety of genres relating to a central theme. Advantages of this approach are:

   a. The poetry becomes a unique experience which adds variety to the study of literature.

   b. Because the poetry relates to a central theme, both teacher and student are more likely to pay attention to what the poet says, rather than how the poet says it, thus avoiding the possible pitfalls of concentrated analysis.

   c. Students can view poetry as another way of dealing with a real issue in life, the poet having structured his experience in a very special way.

   d. By comparing the poetry with the short stories, novels, or essays in the unit, the students can begin to grasp the value of the concentrated language of poetry.

   Disadvantages of this approach include:

   a. By concentrating upon what the poet says more than how the poet says it, the teacher may never enable students to appreciate the poet's craft.

   b. Because poems are usually short, compared with short stories or essays, their concentrated language may cause some students to view poetry as hard or cryptic, and to turn away from poetry to more easily grasped prose.

   c. The brevity of a poem might indicate to students that the poem is less important than the longer prose selection, sheer volume being misconstrued as quality.

3. Read poems incidentally, that is, read a poem when the mood of the class seems right, to provide a break in what might otherwise be a tedious routine, or simply because you feel like it. Advantages of this approach include:

   a. Poetry becomes a special experience, not something that must be taught and learned. The reader is enthusiastic, and this enthusiasm may be transmitted to others.

   b. Students can be encouraged to do the same thing, thus validating their right to read poetry if and when they feel like it.

   c. Most adults do not sit down and purposefully read great quantities of poetry. They read poetry occasionally, because they happen to come across a poem in a magazine or newspaper, or because they simply feel like it. This approach replicates what is a realistic phenomenon in adult reading.

   Among the disadvantages of incidental reading are:

   a. Students may not consider the poetry experience to be a legitimate learning experience in the classroom if the teacher treats the poetry casually.

   b. Simply hearing a poem read does not enable students to develop an awareness of the poet's craft.

c. Unless students are encouraged to try their hand at poetry, they may always view it as a strange way of writing.

Successful teachers of poetry often mix these methods. They want to teach the aspects of the poet's craft, but at the same time, they consider the nature of each of their classes and how ready they are for any particular approach. Involving the students means making the experience of poetry meaningful to them. Clearly, the more mature the reader, the more able he or she is to approach poetry in depth.

LEARNING EXPERIENCES

INVOLVING STUDENTS WITH POETRY

This is the most important objective of the teacher, for unless students respond to poetry in personal terms, unless what the poet says and possibly how the poet says it relates to their lives, poetry becomes one more mechanical process that goes on in English classes, a process about as valuable as Reed and Kellogg sentence diagrams.

The most direct way to involve students with poetry is to cause them to become poets, to write poetry, to think poetically. I have found that my best students in classes that involve the literary study of poetry have been those who have written poetry themselves, whether as part of a class or entirely on their own. Those students know what it is to have to search out the particular metaphor that fits, to have to follow a tight structure, to arrive at that special insight that says, "Yes, that is it—that says what I feel, what I want to say."

If the teacher has students who have elected a course on poetry writing, then the teacher does not have to worry too much about motivation, for it is already there. In such an instance, the teacher might want to structure the poetic experiences so that the students are forced to experiment with forms that they might not normally attempt. The exercises might be relatively difficult, designed to challenge the creative abilities of the students.

If, as is more likely to be the case, the students are in the English class because they have to be, then the teacher must find ways to involve students in being poets without feeling punished or forced. Poetry can be fun. It can add to the generally good feeling that pervades an English class where learning is relaxed and natural. The exercises in Part 1 are intended for any class where the teacher wants students to enjoy poetry, not just know facts about poetry. For further examples of techniques to use in such a class, the teacher ought to read such works as Doug Anderson's *My Sister Looks Like a Pear* and Kenneth Koch's *Wishes, Lies and Dreams.*[1]

1. Have students create "concrete poetry." Concrete poetry is created by arranging words to form pictures upon the page. The actual sound of the poetry does not matter, but the visual impact does. Sometimes single words can be used:

---

1. Douglas Anderson, *My Sister Looks Like a Pear: Awakening the Poetry in Young People* (New York: Hart, 1974), and Kenneth Koch, *Wishes, Lies and Dreams: Teaching Children to Write Poetry* (New York: Random House, 1971).

Or sometimes the same word can be arranged in special formats:

For more examples of such poetry, see Emmett Williams's *Anthology of Concrete Poems* and Eugene Wildman's *Anthology of Concretism.*[2] This exercise could be an excellent way of convincing students that they can play with words, for that is what poets do.

2. Have students create "typographical poetry." Typographical poetry is created by typing or printing the words of a poem in ways that force the reader to look closely at the poem, perhaps breaking up words with other words. Following e. e. cummings's example, in R-P-O-P-H-E-S-S-A-G-R one student created:

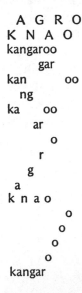

3. Found poetry is created by taking some form of the printed word and cutting out and rearranging parts in such a way that some new meaning is created. Give students a pile of old newspapers, magazines, and catalogues. Let them cut and paste until they have made some new sense out of what they find on one page. For a

2. Emmett Williams, *Anthology of Concrete Poems* (New York: Something Else Press, 1976), and Eugene Wildman, *Anthology of Concretism* (Chicago: Swallow, 1969).

variety, give them copies of the morning announcements. The easiest way to teach the technique would be to introduce it one day when the blackboard is covered with writing. Erase bits of it, perhaps at random or by design. See if the remaining parts fit together in new and surprising ways. The students can rearrange the words, phrases, and sentences that they find to look like a poem. Perhaps, having all the word groups begin directly underneath each other, the end result can have the physical appearance of a poem. Sometimes students find words that rhyme. Other times they repeat for effect. The object is to produce a result that is funny, ironic, or sad, and somehow not what the original author intended. The following found poem was developed from a political campaign leaflet:

For the Governor

record of performance
guess
guess
major achievements
guess
guess
worth billions
expending thousands
organic life   relicted and exposed
hue and cry   morally wrong
upheld the right   to heinous crimes
reclaimed . . . recovered . . . fought for . . .
opposed . . . exposed
giving the people
guess
guess
Enclosed is my campaign contribution for
guess
guess

4. Have students create telegrams to practice the compression of language and thought contained in poetry. Find a long statement that the students can turn into telegrams. The object is to use the fewest number of words while maintaining the maximum amount of meaning. Make a game out of this exercise: See which student can still communicate the original message in the fewest words. Discuss with the class which of the telegrams still maintains the most of the original message. Which of the telegrams has destroyed most of the original meaning? Which words are absolutely essential to maintain the meaning?

5. Try rhythm rhyming with the class to begin a day's work on poetry. Ask one of the students to start clapping a regular rhythm and then have the class join in with the regular rhythm. Decide upon a word to be rhymed before you start. Then one student gives that word. At the end of each segment of rhythm, the next student must state a word that rhymes, but not a word that has already been given. See how many rhymes can be created before the class runs out of rhymes. Or, pit two teams against each other, scoring points for the number of times each team rhymes with a word that the other team gives it.

6. On special occasions, have the class write "occasional poetry." Occasional poetry is just what its name implies—poetry written for occasions. Poems can be written for special holidays, such as Christmas or George Washington's birthday, or to commemorate special events, such as the winning of the football championship or the occasion of the teacher's having a cold. If students have a hard time getting started, suggest particular poems or structures that the students could copy. Limericks work well for funny poems. Other forms might be better for more serious poetry. Ballads will fit virtually any occasion.

7. Create a class ballad. After deciding upon a particular topic, have each student create one stanza. Put the entire poem together either by drawing the stanzas at random (the result may be hilarious), by appointing a committee to do so, or by printing all the stanzas on one or two sheets of paper and trying various organizations that the individual students devise.

8. Forced format poems, such as cinquains and diamantes, are easy ways to enable students to follow strict structures without discouraging them. The teacher can create the structure or can ask students to create the structure that they will follow. Several examples follow:

A

line 1: your name

line 2: two words describing you

line 3: three words telling how you feel

line 4: two words giving your favorite colors

line 5: your nickname

B

line 1: a place

line 2: two sounds from that place

line 3: three items at or in the place

line 4: two smells or sensations in that place

line 5: one word telling how one feels there

C

line 1: a noun

line 2: two adjectives describing the noun

line 3: three participles describing the noun

line 4: four prepositional phrases related to the nouns at the beginning and at the end

line 5: three participles describing the noun at the end

line 6: two adjectives describing the noun at the end

line 7: a noun that is opposite the noun at the top

After trying a few fixed-format poems, let the students suggest what sorts of things could go in each line. Let the class decide upon the number of lines that they would like the next fixed-format poem to contain and then provide a series of containers, one for each line. Have the students write down their suggestions for what should go in each line. Perhaps a group could work on line one, another group on line two, and so on. Then, from each container, draw out one of the suggestions, creating your fixed-format poem as you proceed. The class could then write any number of variations on the fixed-format poem.

9. Have students parody poetic formats that are obvious. One possibility is to use nursery rhymes as the bases of the parodies. Consider the following example, based upon "Hickory Dickory Dock":

> Grammar Oh Grammar's a crock
> Our teacher wastes her chalk
> The lesson's no fun
> The students are dumb
> Grammar Oh Grammar's a crock

If you have any students who think this is a juvenile exercise, introduce them to Frederick Winsor and Marian Parry's *The Space Child's Mother Goose*, which contains such parodies as:

> Flappity, Floppity, Flip!
> The Mouse on the Möbius Strip.
>   The Strip revolved
>   The Mouse dissolved
> In a chronodimensional skip.[3]

For a wide variety of sources of nursery rhymes, investigate William S. and Ceil Baring-Gould's *The Annotated Mother Goose*.[4]

10. The process of definition by metaphor is a common one used by poets. Creating definition poems is a way of developing poetry with direct, brief metaphoric impact, often more effective than long, descriptive efforts. You can, if you wish, provide your students with the example of Ezra Pound's "In a Station of the Metro." The directions to the students can be as follows: "On the first line state your topic, followed by a colon. On the second line write an image that the topic in line one reminds you of." The students need not rhyme their efforts, as:

> The end of the football game:
> Peas spilled on a plate.

Or they may want to rhyme, as:

> The first day of school:
> The surface of a calm, dark pool.

---

3. From *The Space Child's Mother Goose* by Frederick Winsor and Marian Parry. Copyright 1956, 1957, 1958 by Frederick Winsor and Marian Parry. Reprinted by permission of Simon and Schuster, Inc.

4. William S. and Ceil Baring-Gould, *The Annotated Mother Goose* (New York: Bramhall, 1962).

Other definition techniques come to mind as we read poetry. Consider, for example, Emily Dickinson's

> Exultation is the going
> Of an inland soul to sea[5]

Or present the students with a list of definitions of the same item, poetically defined by a variety of poets:

> Time is a kind friend, he will make us old.
> —*Sara Teasdale*

> Old Time is a liar! We're twenty tonight!
> —*Oliver Wendell Holmes*

> Time's a peddler deals in dust.
> —*Robert Underwood Johnson*

> Time is a sort of river of passing events.
> —*Marcus Aurelius*

> Time is a sandpile we run our fingers in.
> —*Carl Sandburg*

> Time is but the stream I go a-fishing in.
> —*Henry David Thoreau*

And ask them to define the same term in a new way. (By the way, finding such metaphors need not be a major task. I consulted Bartlett's *Familiar Quotations* to gather the ones on Time.) Abstract terms often make the best words to define metaphorically. Look how far Charles Schultz has gotten with such definitions as "Happiness is a warm puppy." And while not all definitions are comfortable thoughts, they stay with us because of their impact:

> Man is thy most awful instrument
> —*William Wordsworth,*
>   "Ode, Imagination Ne'er Before Content," IV

Or because of their unique perceptions:

> . . . africa is a baby to be
> tossed about and disciplined and loved
> and neglected and bitten on its bottom
> —*Nikki Giovanni*[6]

11. A simple game to get students into the poetic defining technique is the following: Ask your students to write on slips of paper nouns or noun phrases or structures such as an adjective describing a noun followed by a prepositional phrase or a

---

5. Reprinted by permission of the publishers and the Trustees of Amherst College from *The Poems of Emily Dickinson*, edited by Thomas H. Johnson, Cambridge, Mass.: The Belknap Press of Harvard University Press, Copyright © 1951, 1955 by the President and Fellows of Harvard College.

6. From "Afrika II," *My House* by Nikki Giovanni. Copyright 1972 by Nikki Giovanni. By permission of William Morrow and Co.

participial phrase (e.g., black holes in space, or merry spider dancing in my hair). Collect all the slips of paper. Then decide upon an abstract noun to define. Write the abstract noun on the board, followed by the words *is a* or *is the*. Then draw the slips of paper at random and read them. Some may be humorous, others nonsensical, and others quite revealing. Discuss with the class which they enjoyed the most, which provided the greatest insight into life, or which they might want to include in a poem. For a variation upon this exercise, substitute an action for the abstract noun or a place or person. While the metaphors the students create may be quite unplanned and haphazard, this technique is simple, fun, and direct. You might even ask students if any of the results can be improved, thereby leading them to evaluate the effectiveness, the appropriateness, or even the sound of metaphors.

12. The catalogue technique has been used successfully by many poets, most notably, perhaps, by Walt Whitman:

> I hear the bravuras of birds, bustle of growing wheat, gossip of flames,
>   clack of sticks cooking my meals,
> I hear the sound I love, the sound of the human voice,
> I hear all sounds running together, combined, fused or following,
> Sounds of the city and sounds out of the city, sounds of the day and night,
> Talkative young ones to those that like them, the loud laugh of
>   work-people at their meals,
> The angry bass of disjointed friendship, the faint tones of the sick,
> The judge with hands tight to the desk, his pallid lips pronouncing
>   a death-sentence. . . .[7]

Or Carl Sandburg:

> They have yarns
> Of a skyscraper so tall they had to put hinges
> On the two top stories so to let the moon go by,
> Of one corn crop in Missouri when the roots
> Went so deep and drew off so much water
> The Mississippi riverbed that year was dry,
> Of pancakes so thin they had only one side,
> Of "a fog so thick we shingled the barn and six feet out on the fog,"
> Of Pecos Pete straddling a cyclone in Texas and riding it to the
>   west coast where "it rained out under him,"
> Of the man who drove a swarm of bees across the Rocky Mountains
>   and the Desert "and didn't lose a bee,"
> Of. . . .[8]

Give your students copies of these poems and ask them if they can add to the catalogues. (What sounds has Whitman not used? What tall tales has Sandburg left out?) Then ask them to create their own catalogues. They can pick a subject and list as many things as possible about that subject. You might want to start them with suggestions such as:

7. From "Song of Myself," page 26, lines 3–9 by Walt Whitman.
8. From "They Have Yarns," *The People, Yes* by Carl Sandburg. By permission of Harcourt Brace Jovanovich.

Schools are the places where . . .
or
People who watch television . . .
or
Christmas is the time that . . .

Or your directions could tell them to describe something, such as all the motions that a football player makes sitting on the bench or all the facial expressions a woman makes while putting on makeup or all the ways to cheat on a test or in life. There is an interesting discussion by Philip Booth of his own catalogue poem, "Crossing," in Stephen Dunning and Allan B. Howes's *Literature for Adolescents.*[9] Is such a list poetry? Sometimes. Again, ask students to look at the effect of the total list. Is the way it is worded unique? Does it create a special feeling in us? Does it add some insight about life? Such questions enable students to evaluate poetry clearly and honestly. Don't try to force your opinions on the students. If some of them say that they don't think Walt Whitman is a poet, they will have some critics who will support them.

13. Haiku is a form of poetry that many teachers have used with success. Its compressed form leads to interesting discussions about what the poet is trying to say—if anything. Since haiku in its original form depended upon Japanese characters for its effect, we cannot say that there is any one haiku format. Nevertheless, a workable format for haiku is the following:

> one sentence
> perhaps with a dash or colon dividing it in the middle
> written in three lines.

Some teachers insist that the haiku have seventeen syllables (or thirteen or fourteen), but that is not necessary. The compressed language will be difficult enough for the students. The easiest way to explain haiku would be to give the students a number of examples of the form. Let this become an inductive learning experience: Ask them to decide what the form is that is being used. Then let them practice writing haiku. The main thing to accomplish with the haiku is the development of a special view of the world. A simple tendency for students who do not write much poetry is to slip into a trite statement:

> A baby plays
> On the green grass:
> Love's proof.

For most of your students, if you get a haiku out of them, you will probably be pleased. But don't stop there. Try to find—brainstorm with the class—images that are unusual, images that force new realizations out of the students. Juxtapose those images with other images to arrive at new conclusions. You might even want to have one half of the class write the part of the haiku before the colon or dash and the other half of the class write the last line. Then put them together, either at random (with its resulting revelations and frustrations), or through careful discussion and selection by the students. The results may surprise everyone:

---

9. Stephen Dunning and Allan B. Howes, *Literature for Adolescents* (Glenview, Ill.: Scott, Foresman, 1975).

Wet sponges
soaking in the white enamel sink—
Thanksgiving ends.
or
Skis slip down the slopes
on hard crust:
the wind listens.

Some of the most effective haiku are those that concentrate on specific images and do not attempt to convey messages. The images often convey to the readers more than the poet ever intended.

14. Occasionally ask your students to draw the images they receive while reading a poem. This is a good way to get a discussion going or to force the students to look carefully at the poet's words. But it is also a way to give students something to write about. Save the drawings and then ask the students to write poems about the drawings without knowing what the original poem was.

15. To develop a kinesthetic feel for poetic rhythm, lead the class in unison clapping of the various traditional rhythms of poetry.

iamb—clap-CLAP-clap-CLAP-clap-CLAP
anapest—clap-clap-CLAP-clap-clap-CLAP
trochee—CLAP-clap-CLAP-clap-CLAP-clap
dactyl—CLAP-clap-clap-CLAP-clap-clap
pyrrhic—clap-clap—clap-clap—clap-clap
spondee—CLAP-CLAP—CLAP-CLAP—CLAP-CLAP

When you do this, do not tell your students what the traditional name for the rhythm is. Your purpose is not to teach them scansion but to give them a feel for the rhythms of poetry and of their language. After each clapping exercise, ask the students what images entered their minds as they listened to the rhythm. Ask them how they felt when they heard the rhythm. Ask them what they would like to do when they hear that rhythm. Have them describe in writing what images or ideas the rhythm creates and then discuss their writings with the class. Which might make good topics for poems? Contrast the responses students have when they hear both the iamb and the anapest or the trochee and the dactyl. Is one more serious than the other? Are the images the students have after clapping the rhythms different? Can the images that came to them from hearing the iambic or the anapestic rhythm be categorized? If so, are there differences between those categories? What are they? Having gone through this exercise, varying the pace of the clapping to see if that changes any of the responses, present examples of poems that employ those rhythms and discuss with the class whether the poems fit the categories the students developed earlier in the clapping exercise. A Shakespearean sonnet *usually* fits the iambic pattern, and the students will find it to be reasonably serious. "Hiawatha," by Longfellow, is written mostly in trochees. Ogden Nash has fun with anapests and dactyls, but usually writes in no traditional rhythm. As you read examples of poems to the students, they may realize that the rhythms are not consistent. That in itself is an important conclusion. A poem may be mostly iambic, but, if it were always iambic, in oral reading the tendency would be to fall into a singsong pattern. Ask the students to try writing a poetic line according to the pattern they have just been clapping and discussing. Discuss the results. How easy is it to write a line entirely of pyrrhic or spondiac feet? Indeed, is it even possible? Through such discussions of the rhythm of their language, students may gain greater insights into the purpose of rhythm in poetry (in addition to the traditional reason that it is an aid to memorization). Remember, your purpose as teacher is not to teach the students analytic terms but to make rhythm a living reality for them, a tool that they can use. If they ask for names, you might as well tell them, but do not make the name the important part of the lesson.

16. Creating "beastiaries" has intrigued poets through the ages. Ask your students to write brief poems about animals after they have seen some examples, such as Ogden Nash's "The Kipper," "The Redcap," "The Emmet," "The Clam," "The Shrimp," "The Dog," "The Armadillo," "The Carcajou and the Kincajou," and "The Oxolotl," in *Everyone but Thee and Me.*[10]

    Betsy B. Kaufman has collected several ideas for teaching poetry in "EJ Workshop: Teaching Poetry,"[11] including such ideas as having students read the title and discuss what they believe the poem will be about before reading the poem and having them illustrate a narrative poem in comic-book style. In fact, this issue devotes over twenty pages to creative ways of teaching poetry: games, student anthologies, poetry fairs, and more.

17. The letter poem is a form that has traditional roots but that has received increased interest from modern poets. The form employs language that is concise but that still reads much like a letter. Ask your students to write one to a friend or to pretend that they are another person, such as a historical figure, writing to yet another person, such as another historical figure. Another option is for them to pretend that they are authors writing to one of their characters or that the person speaking in the poem is a character writing to the author. For examples of letter poems, see Richard Hugo's letters in Stephen Berg and Robert Neezey's *The New Naked Poetry* or Charles Olson's "Letter for Melville 1951."[12] The heritage of the letter poem may easily be found in the many poems beginning "To. . . ." See, for example, Marvell's "To His Coy Mistress," Herrick's "To Electra," Poe's "To Helen," Henley's "To A. D.," and Frost's "To E. T."

18. Provide a list of types of poems students may want to identify (see Reproduction Page 19). Ask the students to add to the examples of types of poems as they read poetry in class. By doing so, a student can have a collection of poetry titles in a notebook that can be referred to later.

19. Hand out a sheet of basic poetic terms (see Reproduction Page 20) to which students may refer. Encourage the students to use the terms once they become familiar with them.

20. Keep on hand as a general reference work *The Complete Rhyming Dictionary,* edited by Clement Wood.[13] In addition to lists of words that rhyme, the book

10. Ogden Nash, *Everyone but Thee and Me* (Boston: Little, Brown, 1962).

11. Betsy B. Kaufman, "EJ Workshop: Teaching Poetry," *English Journal* 64 (1975), 64.

12. Stephen Berg and Robert Neezey, eds., *The New Naked Poetry* (Indianapolis: Bobbs-Merrill, 1976), and Charles Olson, *The Distances* (New York: Grove Press, 1959).

13. Clement Wood, ed., *The Complete Rhyming Dictionary* (Garden City, N.Y.: Blue Ribbon, 1936).

TYPES OF POEMS

    I. Lyric—an imaginative, melodic poem that conveys subjective feelings
        A. Songs
        B. Sonnets
        C. Elegies and epitaphs
        D. Epigrams
        E. Dramatic poems

   II. Narrative—a poem that tells a story
        A. Epics
        B. Ballads
        C. Fables
        D. Metrical romances

POETRY TERMS

Alliteration— the repetition of sounds in words that are close to each other (usually initial sounds).
    ex.: "*M*any a *momm*y has clothing to *m*end."

Assonance—the repetition of vowel sounds.
    ex.: "The b*a*d c*a*t stole my h*a*t and r*a*n."

Consonance—the repetition of consonant sounds.
    ex.: "The *s*nake his*s*ed and *sl*ithered *sl*owly through the gra*ss*."

Cliché—a word or phrase that has been used so many times that it has lost its original impact and is now stereotyped and too familiar.
    ex.: red as a rose, tried and true, happy as a lark

Figure of speech—a changing of the word order or meaning of words in order to gain greater impact upon the meaning. Some figures of speech are similes, metaphors, metonymies, personifications, and synechdoches.

Imagery—the use of words to represent sensations. Images may be literal ("The sun was hot-yellow") or imaginary ("The sun's stare turned me into jello").

Lyric—the use of words so that the sounds are melodic, or "sing."

Metaphor—an implied comparison; one item may be given the characteristics of another or may be described in terms of the other.
    ex.: "My car is my friend—he takes me where I want."

Metonymy—a figure of speech in which an object is referred to by a term closely associated with it.
    ex.: "We are waiting to hear from the White House." *White House* is a metonymy for the president or his associates.

Onomatopoeia—the suggestion of a particular sound by means of a word.
    ex.: the bee *buzzed*, her dress *swishes*, the saw *whined*

Personification—giving an inanimate object the characteristics of an animate object.
    ex.: "The door complained when I opened it."

Refrain—lines that are repeated at the ends of different stanzas.

Rhyme—the repetition of like sounds in different words, especially in the last syllables and when the words are physically near one another.

Simile—a direct comparison using the words *like* or *as*.
    ex.: "He is as constant as the tide."
         "Her hair is like coarse wire."

Stanza—a group of lines repeated in similar groups throughout a poem.

Symbol—an object, person, or event that stands for something in addition to itself.
    ex.: The American flag stands for the United States.
         A handshake is symbolic of friendship.

Synechdoche—a figure of speech in which part of an object is used to represent the entire object.
    ex.: "hired hands" "set the table"

Verse—a single line of poetry; or poetry in general, usually poetry that has rhythm and rhyme.

contains an excellent poet's craft section that provides a vast amount of information on such aspects of poetry as verse forms, meter, and types of poetry. Ask advanced students to learn one new type of poetry a week and write a poem according to that form, or divide the forms among the students in your class and have them report to the class on each type of poem.

21. To introduce students to poetry in nonpoetic contexts, ask them to read the following selection from Edgar Allan Poe's "The Fall of the House of Usher" and find the answers to the questions that follow (see Reproduction Page 21).

REPRODUCTION PAGE 21

POETIC TECHNIQUES IN PROSE

Directions: *Edgar Allan Poe began his short story, "The Fall of the House of Usher," with a paragraph that is very poetic. Read this paragraph and answer the questions below it. As you read, pay particular attention to the sounds the words make, to the comparisons the author makes, and to places where Poe tells you how he feels.*

During the whole of a dull, dark, and soundless day in the autumn of the year, when the clouds hung oppressively low in the heavens, I had been passing alone, on horseback, through a singularly dreary tract of country; and at length I found myself, as the shades of evening drew on, within view of the melancholy House of Usher. I know not how it was—but, with the first glimpse of the building, a sense of insufferable gloom pervaded my spirit. I say insufferable; for the feeling was unrelieved by any of that half-pleasurable, because poetic, sentiment, with which the mind usually receives even the sternest natural images of the desolate or terrible. I looked upon scene before me—upon the mere house, and the simple landscape features of the domain—upon a few rank sedges—and upon a few white trunks of decayed trees—with an utter depression of soul which I can compare to no earthly sensation more properly than to the after-dream of the reveler upon opium—the bitter lapse into everyday life—the hideous dropping off of the veil. There was an iciness, a sinking, a sickening of the heart—an unredeemed dreariness of thought which no goading of the imagination could torture into aught of the sublime. What was it—I paused to think—what was it that so unnerved me in the contemplation of the House of Usher? It was a mystery all insoluble; nor could I grapple with the shadowy fancies that crowded upon me as I pondered. I was forced to fall back upon the unsatisfactory conclusion that while, beyond doubt, there are combinations of very simple natural objects which have the power of thus affecting us, still the analysis of this power lies among considerations beyond our depth. It was possible, I reflected, that a mere different arrangement of the particulars of the scene, of the details of the picture, would be sufficient to modify, or perhaps to annihilate, its capacity for sorrowful impression; and, acting upon this idea, I reined my horse to the precipitous brink of a black and lurid tarn that lay in unruffled lustre by the dwelling, and gazed down—but with a shudder even more thrilling than before—upon the remodeled and inverted images of the gray sedge, and the ghastly tree-stems, and the vacant and eye-like windows.

1. List all the examples of alliteration that you can find in this selection. What types of sound are they? How do they make you feel?

2. List all the metaphors that Poe employs. What is the purpose of each metaphor?

3. Underline all the places where Poe tells you how he feels rather than where he describes the scene to let you determine how he feels. Now circle all places where Poe describes rather than tells. Which occurs more often? Do you think this is good or bad? Why?

4. What aspects of the house has Poe selected to describe or tell about? What other things could he have talked about? What does this indicate about his purpose in writing this passage?

5. Look at the sentence beginning with "There was an iciness. . . ." Does Poe repeat the idea of iciness with other words or images? Or does he change from iciness to some other image? What is his purpose?

6. What colors does Poe talk about? Why did he select those particular colors? Could he have used any other colors to convey the same mood?

7. Try to arrange this selection into the form of a poem. You may have to leave some words out, but try to use as much of the original version as possible. Which version do you think conveys the mood better, yours or Poe's?

---

22. To give more practice to finding poetic elements in prose, have your students look at the selection on Reproduction Page 22 and list the poetic techniques they find, commenting on the purpose and effectiveness of those techniques in those places.

REPRODUCTION PAGE 22

MELVILLE AS A POET

Directions: *The following is Herman Melville's description of a whale's head. As you read it, note how he compares an object (the head) that you may never have seen with objects that may be familiar to you. Underline these comparisons. Then list the poetic techniques that the author uses. How well does he use those techniques? Do they make his description clearer or more confusing? Explain.*

Crossing the deck, let us now have a good long look at the Right Whale's head.

As in general shape the noble Sperm Whale's head may be compared to a Roman war-chariot (especially the front, where it is so broadly rounded); so at a broad view, the Right Whale's head bears a rather inelegant resemblance to a gigantic galliot-toed shoe. Two hundred years ago an old Dutch voyager likened its shape to that of a shoemaker's last. And in this same last or shoe, that old woman of the nursery tale, with the swarming brood, might very comfortably be lodged, she and all her progeny.

But as you come nearer to this great head it begins to assume different aspects, according to your point of view. If you stand on its summit and look at these two f-shaped spout-holes, you would take the whole head for an enormous bass-viol, and the spiracles, the apertures in its sounding-board. Then, again, if you fix your eye upon this strange, crested, comb-like incrustation of the top of the mass—this green, barnacled thing, which the Greenlanders call the "crown," and the Southern fishers the "bonnet" of the Right Whale; fixing your eyes solely on this, you would take the head for the trunk of some huge oak, with a bird's nest in its crotch. At any rate, when you watch those live crabs that nestle here on this bonnet, such an idea will be almost sure to occur to you; unless, indeed, your fancy has been fixed by the technical term "crown" also bestowed upon it; in which case you will take great interest in thinking how this mighty monster is actually a diademed king of the sea, whose green crown has been put together for him in this marvelous manner. But if this whale be a king, he is a very sulky looking fellow to grace a diadem. Look at that hanging lower lip! what a huge sulk and pout is there! a sulk and pout, by carpenter's measurement, about twenty feet long and five feet deep; a sulk and pout that will yield you some 500 gallons of oil and more.

Herman Melville
Moby-Dick: or, *The Whale*

TEACHING THE TERMINOLOGY OF POETRY

Analysis is the quickest means of understanding poetic terminology. Before employing such an approach, however, the teacher must consider what the purpose of teaching poetry is. If the teacher believes that students must understand poetic terminology in order to talk about poetry, then the classroom approach must consider the nature of the students. Students who are not personally involved with poetry may not become any more involved after learning terminology.

The approaches suggested below range from extremely traditional techniques to extremely experimental. The teacher should consider all of them before deciding upon the approaches that will best accomplish the objectives for the class.

Metaphors and Similes

Metaphors and similes are the heart of poetry, the physical proof of the mental leaps poets make in creating their works. The two are essentially the same, one (the simile) employing *like* or *as* in making a connection between two seemingly dissimilar things, and the other (metaphor) making a direct comparison and not using *like* or *as*. One option available to the teacher is to have students memorize two definitions and have them repeat them on a test or quiz. That might serve as a means of testing the students' memories, but it does not involve the student with the process of metaphoring and it does not help the students "get into" a poem, connect with the mind of the poet, or experience metaphor (or simile) as a meaningful mental process. The activities suggested in the following list are designed to help students know a metaphor, not just know what metaphor is.

1. To develop students' abilities to think in terms of similes, have the class play the following game: One student leaves the room while the rest of the class selects one of its members to be *it*. When the student who left the room returns, he or she must guess which of the other students is *it* by asking questions using similes. For example:

   Is this person more like Sweden or Italy?

   Is this person like spaghetti or like steak?

   Is this person like blue or like brown?

   Is this person like a truck or a car?

   Is this person like a small foreign car or a large American car?

   Is this person like a banana or an orange?

   The student who asks the questions must think of them—the class is not to provide them. When the student thinks he or she knows who is *it*, the student guesses. Each student who is asking the questions has three chances to guess the right person. Then, another person has a turn to ask the questions.

2. One way to develop the ability of students to create similes is to ask students to note similarities between two very dissimilar things. For example:

   • How is a clock like a chair? Possible answers: If not set in motion, they will both just sit there. They both have arms. They can both be sprung.

   • How is a teacher like a horn? Possible answers: Unless turned off, they will both run on without stopping. Hot air, in the form of noise, comes out of both of them.

   • How is chalk dust like a rug? Possible answers: One carpets a house while the other carpets your clothes. They each manage to get into corners.

   Allow the wildest possible comparisons and the wildest possible answers. The object is to force students to think in terms of creative likenesses. The class could be divided into teams that compete against each other, or the class could just try to list as many answers as possible.

3. Solving riddles enables students to develop an understanding of extended metaphors. Some Anglo-Saxon riddles are in the form of poems. Encourage students to bring in riddles when they find new ones. Even some of the old ones can have new, creative answers. For example, what is black and white and red all over? One old answer was: a newspaper. A newer answer is: an embarrassed zebra. Some of your students might create answers no one has thought of, such as: an integrated school filled with communists.

4. To encourage students to create and to be aware of similes and metaphors that are not trite, give them a list of similes and metaphors that are clichés and ask them

to create better ones. For example, given the simile "as red as a rose," the students might respond:

as red as a bloody nose

as red as a tomato in fall

as red as a student whose teacher catches her kissing her boyfriend

as red as brake fluid on snow

For some expressions that are now trite, they might suggest substitutes that vary greatly from the original. For example, given "smart as a whip," some of the students might think of regional variations such as "slick as spit on a doorknob." Or they might create new ones, such as:

right as a computer

bright as a teacher with the answer key in his book

as quick thinking as a man stepping accidentally on a rattlesnake.

Give the students the following list of similes and metaphors and challenge them to develop as many new versions as possible:

mad as a wet hen	black as night
scared to death	sure as shootin'
as right as rain	pleased as punch
rock-hard	tickled to death

Let the students suggest other worn-out similes and metaphors.

5. Examine the metaphors and similes of a poem to determine how accurate they are. Ask students to think about what the poet means exactly. For example, Emily Dickinson's poem, number 986[14] (see Reproduction Page 23).

6. Ask your students to define words in metaphoric ways. First discuss with them such poetic efforts as:

> Freedom's just another word for nothing left to lose
> —*Kris Kristofferson and Fred Foster*

> Happiness is a warm puppy
> —*Charles Schultz*

> Exultation is the going
> Of an inland soul to sea
> —*Emily Dickinson*[14]

You might want to ask your students to define one of the above words in a new way. Many students have fun with the "Happiness is . . ." definition. Either have each student write a new definition or pass around a sheet of paper folded like an

---

EMILY DICKINSON'S USE OF WORDS

Directions: *Read Emily Dickinson's poem. Read it again. Think about the specific words she uses to describe her subject. Then answer the questions that follow.*

A narrow Fellow in the Grass
Occasionally rides—
You may have met Him—did you not
His notice sudden is—

The Grass divides as with a Comb—
A spotted shaft is seen—
And then it closes at your feet
And opens further on—

He likes a Boggy Acre
A Floor too cool for Corn—
Yet when a Boy, and Barefoot—
I more than once at Noon
Have passed, I thought, a Whip lash
Unbraiding in the Sun
When stooping to secure it
It wrinkled, and was gone—

Several of Nature's People
I know, and they know me—
I feel for them a transport
Of cordiality

But never met this Fellow
Attended, or alone
Without a tighter breathing
And Zero at the Bone—

Explain why you think Dickinson chose the following metaphors:

1. Why *narrow* (1.1)? Why not *thin*? Or *skinny*?

2. Why *rides* (1.2)? Why not *travels*? Or *slithers*? Or *slinks*?

3. Explain the image of the grass dividing "as with a Comb—" (1.5). Is that what happens when a snake moves through grass?

4. Why *shaft* (1.6)? Why not *rope*? How does a snake move?

5. Draw or explain "a Whip lash/Unbraiding in the Sun." What is the snake doing here?

6. Why does Dickinson use the word *wrinkled* (1.16)? Are there more accurate metaphors possible, such as *unwound*?

7. What is another way of saying "Zero at the Bone—"? What is a cliché that many people use to mean the same thing as "Zero at the Bone—"? (List as many responses as possible on the board and then ask if any are better—some may be. Substitute them at the end of this poem and determine with the class whether these other versions are better or not and why.)

---

accordian with the word to be defined written at the top. Each student writes his definition and then folds the paper so that the next student cannot read the definitions already written. The paper is passed around the room until all students have had a chance to write a metaphoric definition, and then the entire sheet is read to the class. In order to keep all students involved, the teacher might want to have several sheets passed around the room at once, each with a different word or concept to define. Begin with easy words such as *gloom* or *victory* and then move to possibly more difficult ones such as *intimidation* or *politics*. You might even want them to read such a clever definer as Ambrose Bierce, who defined "happiness" in *The Devil's Dictionary* as "An agreeable sensation arising from contemplating the misery of another." Eventually, students should realize that many poems are themselves complete definitions, such as David Wagoner's "The Bad Fisherman."

7. A game to involve students in creating metaphors follows this format: While a

student steps outside the room, the class decides upon something or someone to be *it*. Specific ground rules might state that the *it* has to be in the room or in the school or perhaps anywhere in the entire world. Then the student comes back into the room and proceeds to ask a series of questions the class must answer with metaphors. Further rules can specify the exact number of questions (the old twenty questions format is quite serviceable). When the student thinks he or she knows what *it* is, the student can guess. Another rule might state the number of guesses allowed (three has always been traditional but certainly has no basis in law). Here are examples of the types of question the students might ask and the types of answer the class might provide:

> Q: If it were a building, what would it be?
> A: a library
> Q: If it were a person, who would it be?
> A: Noah Webster
> Q: If it were a poet, who would it be?
> A: Wordsworth
> Possible answer: the class dictionary

8. To enable students to practice using extended metaphors or similes, provide similes or metaphors for the students (or, better still, have them create some themselves or choose some from the poetry they have read) and require that they write essays using the metaphor or simile as their thesis statement. Students could use self-developed similes or metaphors such as "A person's face is a book," or "A good football coach is like a cook." Or they could use literary metaphors or similes such as: "There is a garden in her face," or "Life is a short summer," or "Education should be gradual as the moonrise." The students need not be required to speak in metaphor throughout their essays, but they should be asked to stick as closely to the main metaphor or simile as possible. The extensions of the metaphoric process will sometimes delight and surprise. Pick parts of the essays and display them on the bulletin board. Talk about them from time to time.

9. Study poems in groups that have related metaphors. By doing so, students will be enabled to see the many varied ways that poets can manipulate the same images, ideas, or words and arrive at vastly different results. The following poems exemplify what can be done with "stones": "Stone," by Charles Simic; "The Stone," by Wilfrid Wilson Gibson; and "Mending Wall," by Robert Frost.[15]

10. Force students to describe something from an entirely new perspective. For example, have the entire class describe their school, but have each student use a point of view different from that of the other students. They might choose to describe the school from the point of view of a book, a pencil sharpener, a specimen in the biology lab, a locker, the door to the principal's office, a mouse, the public address system, the gym, and other things the students themselves could suggest. Brainstorm ideas with the class.

11. Students need to realize that language is extremely metaphorical, that metaphor weaves its way through all our thoughts, and that metaphor is something they use

---

15. Charles Simic, "Stone," in *What the Grass Says* (Santa Cruz, Cal.: Kayak, 1967); Wilfred Wilson Gibson, "The Stone," in *Collected Poems* (St. Clair Shores, Mich.: Scholarly Press, 1971); Robert Frost, "Mending Wall," in *Robert Frost: Poetry and Prose* edited by Edward C. Lathem and Lawrence Thompson (New York: Holt, Rinehart & Winston, 1972).

every day. Introduce students to metaphors they are familiar with. Consider the names of various teams in sports:

San Diego *Chargers*	New Orleans *Saints*
San Francisco *Giants*	New England *Patriots*

Some of the students might argue that these names are actually symbols, and they would be right. Discuss the similarity of symbols and metaphors. The Stars and Stripes is a symbol of the United States. At the same time, use "Stars and Stripes" metaphorically when referring to the United States or the influence and power of the United States. Ask students to list metaphor-symbols that are commonly used.

12. Notice with students the brand names of commercial goods. What do the following automobile names bring to mind:

Pinto	Granada	F10	Lil Hustler
Colt	Monaco	280Z	Ranger
Maverick	Seville	XJ6C	Scout
Thunderbird	Le Sabre	Mark IV	Explorer
Mustang	Coupe De Ville	LTD	Blazer
Impala	Le Mans	B210	Land Cruiser

Or the following tires:

Tru Trac

Campack

Norseman

Sure-Grip

Or the names of cereals, cigarettes, nonprescription drugs, even models of homes. Have your students collect metaphoric names and create more names to go along with current trends.

13. Study the metaphor of slang. Slang is always changing but is extremely metaphorical. Consider formal, informal, and slang terms for the same concept; for example, intoxicated (formal), drunk (informal), and bombed, smashed, gooned, planked, zonked, snockered, high, zapped, feeling no pain, and the like. Point out how such slang is often adopted for other concepts, such as drug use. Discuss each slang term with the students. What does each bring to mind? Why are slang terms often used more than formal or informal terms? Which is more accurate—formal, informal, or slang terms? Why does slang change so rapidly and die out so quickly?

14. Consider how certain metaphors become ordinary words in our language, words we no longer consider metaphors. For instance, *grueling* may have come from the practice of using gruel as punishment. Have students trace the etymology of many words. *The Oxford English Dictionary* is a prime source, as are such works as Alfred H. Holt's *Phrase and Word Origins.*[16] Consider how words transfer their

---

16. J. A. Murray *et al.*, eds. *The Oxford English Dictionary* (Oxford: Oxford Univ. Press, 1961), and Alfred H. Holt, *Phrase and Word Origins* (New York: Dover, 1961).

meanings from one item to others, such as the parts of the body. In how many ways is *foot* used? *Foot* of the mountain, *foot* of the tree, *foot* of the bed, to *foot* the bill, or to put one's *foot* in it are only some of the ways. What other parts of the body become metaphorically transferred? Can the students use the same words in new metaphoric ways? Ask the class to create a new meaning for an old word and transfer the metaphor, such as, perhaps, *testfooter:* one who *foots* a test. Have them use the word around school without telling others why. How long will it take for the word to catch on?

Voice and Tone

1. Students often have a difficult time determining what the tone of a poem is. If they are unable to determine the tone, they may misinterpret the meaning entirely. Rather than telling the students that "tone" is the author's attitude toward his or her subject and then asking them to describe the tone, try asking the students to tell you who is speaking in the poem, or what the voice is. Many students believe that the poet is always the one who is speaking the poem, but this is most often not the case. Providing autobiographical information about the poet may only strengthen this predilection. Once the students can tell you who or what type of person is speaking, then you can ask them what the speaker's attitude is. When you have determined the speaker's attitude, ask the students to determine whether the poet feels the same way as the speaker, if the speaker is not actually the poet. If they believe that the poet does not have the same attitude as the speaker, ask them to prove it by finding clues in the poem itself. Sometimes it is not possible to determine the poet's attitude. If that is the case, do not push the students to create one. Their ability to state the voice should give them the insight they need to understand the poem at their level.

2. To stress the fact that the voice, persona, or speaker in the poem is not always the poet, present your students poems in which the speakers refer to themselves as "I." Ask the students to state what the "I" person is actually like, and how they know. Poems that will work well in this exercise include:

   Robert Browning's "My Last Duchess"

   Emily Dickinson's "There's been a death in the opposite house"

   Gwendolyn Brooks's "We Real Cool"

   Thomas Hardy's "Channel Firing"

   Philip Booth's "Convoy"

   More difficult selections might include:

   T. S. Eliot's "The Love Song of J. Alfred Prufrock"

   Henry Reed's "Naming of Parts"

3. Ask students to pretend that they are the speaker in a particular poem and that they are writing their autobiography. A poem has often been called a "slice of life." Rightly or wrongly, the term does indicate that a poem seldom re-creates a person's entire life. But if students have to do this after reading the snatch of life

the poem presents, it will force them to think about the nature of the speaker and what may have caused that speaker to say the things he or she does say.

4. If the speaker in a poem is different from the author, give students imaginative writing exercises that stress that difference. For instance, have them pretend to be the author writing a letter to the speaker, or vice versa. Or let them write a play script in which the speaker goes to the poet for advice about some difficulty revealed by the poem. Or have them write about what the poet would do if that poet were in the same place as the speaker in the poet's poem.

5. Let students act out poems. If you have been working with creative dramatics in your classroom, this activity will fit right in. If not, find someone in the class who would like to act before the class. Finally, barring that, ask the drama teacher to allow some drama students to carry out this assignment for your class. Dramatic monologues are particularly effective in this assignment. Poems such as Browning's "Soliloquy of the Spanish Cloister" (which might require more than one speaker, but which works better with only one), Tennyson's "Ulysses," and Robert Graves's "The Traveler's Curse after Misdirection" provide enough for good acting or just plain hamming it up. One student might read the poem while another pantomimes the action. Don't worry if the students make fun of the poem while they act it out. If they are able to do that, then they probably understand it.

6. To see how an individual's reading might possibly influence the impression one gets of the speaker, voice, or persona, have students individually tape a reading of a poem without hearing the other students reading. For fun, find a poem that has been recorded by a professional actor. Slip that on to the tape also. Discuss with the students which reading they preferred and why. For an even greater revelation, find a poem that has been recorded by the poet. Often poets are the worst readers of their own poetry. Let students decide and discover that they are capable of better interpretations.

7. Ballads, both old and new, provide an easy way for students to grasp the idea of who is speaking. Have one of your students sing one of them for the class or have the entire class join in on a group singing of a ballad. Traditional ballads that reveal the nature of the speaker fairly easily include: "Lord Randal," "Get Up and Bar the Door," and the western "Oh, Bury Me Not on the Lone Prairie." Poets have taken the traditional ballads and made the language more concise (and usually, as a result, more difficult to understand). Examples of literary ballads include: William Schwenk Gilbert's "The Yarn of the Nancy Bell," W. H. Auden's "As I Walked Out One Evening," and John Davidson's "A Ballad of Hell." Sometimes authors make fun of other authors' ballads, as Lewis Carroll's "Father William" does of Robert Southey's "The Old Man's Comforts." When students read such parodies, students learn that the author clearly is not always the speaker.

8. Let students write parodies of famous poems, especially poems where the speaker is clear. What might result if a student parodied Browning's "My Last Duchess" with his own version called "My Last Teacher"? If students have a hard time getting started, you might suggest some possibilities:

Elizabeth Barret Browning's "How Do I Love Thee?"

　　("How Do I Loathe Thee?"; "How Am I Lovely?")

Robert Frost's "Mending Wall"

("Erasing Blackboards"; "Writing Essays"; "Doing Pushups")

William Shakespeare's "Shall I Compare Thee to a Summer's Day"

("Shall I Compare Thee to a Football Game"; ". . . a Winter's Night")

9. The tone of a poem is often determined by noting the poet's use of sound. Are the consonantal sounds soft, the vowel sounds drawn out? Or are the consonantal sounds harsh, the vowel sounds short? Encourage students to read poems aloud, to listen to the sounds the words make. Do not spend much time analyzing the sounds with students who do not read poetry voluntarily, for then you may destroy the complete impact that brief exposure to a poem may have. For example, read the poem "Dulce et Decorum Est" by Wilfred Owen. What kind of sounds are revealed when the poem is read aloud? How do the sounds reflect what is happening in the poem? How does this compare with the last lines in the poem, "Dulce et decorum est/Pro patria mori"? What does the answer to that last question reveal about Owen's attitude toward his topic? For contrast, read with the class John Masefield's "Sea-Fever." What kinds of sound are conveyed by Masefield's words? How and what does Masefield feel about the sea? The ways that Masefield and Owen feel are revealed by a combination of their subjects, the meanings of their words, and the sounds of their words. Ask students to pick other poems and read them for the class so that the sound reflects the sense.

Imagery

1. To enable students to discuss the appropriateness of imagery in poetry, substitute images in well-known poetry and ask the students to discuss which is better. Much of the poetry of the Romantic age lends itself to this approach. Have the students consider the effect of this line:

> My pulse skips a beat when I behold
> A storm cloud in the sky:
> (*based on Wordsworth's "My Heart*
> *Leaps Up When I Behold"*)

or this:

> It is a worn-out sailor
> And he stoppeth one of three.
> "By thy dirty beard and dreary eye,
> Now wherefore stopp'st thou me?"
> (*based on Coleridge's "The Rime*
> *of the Ancient Mariner"*)

or this:

> Ah, cheery, cheery tree limbs! that can't drop
>   Your leaves, nor ever tell the Spring good bye;
> And, cheery horn blower, unpooped,
>   For always blowing songs like a sigh;
>   (*based on Keats's "Ode on a Grecian Urn"*)

2   Extended metaphors rely upon poets' abilities to sustain an image by developing relevant aspects of the image. Ask students to read poems with extended metaphors and to pick out the images that help sustain the metaphor. Examples of poems that would work for this exercise include Shakespeare's Sonnets 18 and 73 and Donne's "The Flea."

3.   Imagery is the technique of using words to represent the impressions of the senses: sight, sound, taste, smell, and touch. Some images are recognized and used by most of us. For instance, if we want to say that we are cold, we could say that we feel icy, that our bones are chilled, that our breath is foggy, that our teeth are chattering, that our ears are about to drop off, or that our hands have turned blue. All of these descriptions rely upon images, words that convey to the listener or reader exactly what we mean. We do not have to tell the reader or listener that we are cold, for the image means that. What are ways that we tell people that a person is shrewd or sly? Brainstorm expressions with students, such as "As slick as spit on a doorknob," "Sly as a fox," "Cagey," and "Quick as a whip," writing these on the blackboard or using an overhead projector. How could we tell people that we are scared? (Again, list the students' suggestions.) Angry? (After listing various images on the board, you might want to consider with the class which are the most unusual, which convey the idea best, and when each might be appropriate.) (See Reproduction Page 24.) Finally, to see whether students understand the concept of *imagery,* have them turn to a poem in the books and pick out the imagery.

REPRODUCTION PAGE 24

EVALUATING IMAGES

Directions: *Consider the following images that are intended to describe women. Which is the best image? Which is the worst? Why? If you were a woman being described this way, how would you feel? If you were a man whose wife was being described this way, how would you feel? Why? If you think the way you would feel depends upon the situation, explain what the possible situations might be and then answer the questions above.*

A. She was a phantom of delight

B. O my luve is like a red, red rose

C.   the youthful hue
Sits on thy skin like morning dew

D. She walks in beauty, like the night

E. O Helen fair, beyond compare!

F. Her face is like the milky way i' the sky

G. Was ever book containing such vile matter
So fairly bound?

H. 36–24–36

---

4. If students have difficulty perceiving the imagery of a poem, find pictures that illustrate the poem. Or, better still, prepare slides that capture the mood created by the imagery. The imagery of much poetry does not require this, but some poems are much more difficult. Consider, for example, Robert Herrick's "Upon Julia's Clothes." What image is conjured up by these lines?

> Whenas in silks my Julia goes,
> Then, then, methinks, how sweetly flows
> The liquefaction of her clothes.

How many students can picture what *liquefaction* means? Is it a good image? Is it actually an image? How can it be communicated?

5. Encourage students to create slide and tape shows of particular poems. If they cannot find scenes to photograph in their community, scenes that capture the imagery of the poem, have them look for pictures in magazines and newspapers that they can copy with a close-up lens. Provide magazines for them. Have students conduct a magazine drive in their neighborhood. Keep files of pictures around for them to use.

6. Videotape commercials on television. Play the sound track of commercials for the students and ask them to describe the scenes. Since many students may know these commercials by heart, try to find unusual ones or save them on videotape from year to year so that the commercials are forgotten by the time you bring them out in class. Ask the students to explain how they knew what images accompanied the sound. If they were wrong, why? If they were right, why? Were the images stereotyped? What do the images reveal about the purposes of the creators of the commercials? Then have students consider the imagery in poetry they are reading. Are the images stereotyped there? How unusual are the images? How common are they? Have the poets used common images in unusual ways? Are the images the best images, or could the poets have selected better (have the students define what they mean by *better*) ones?

7. If you have students who are creative dancers, encourage them to re-create a poem for the students in the class. Other students might be involved in the process by asking them to suggest music that would be appropriate for a given poem.

8. Find a recording that evokes mental images, such as "Peter and the Wolf," without narration of lyrics. Play the record, asking students to record their impressions of what is happening. Compare and discuss the results. Lead the discussion, if it does not naturally flow there, to the relationship of sound and rhythm imagery.

Symbolism

1. In order to begin understanding symbols, students must understand that all content words are symbols, that words are not the things they represent, but are, in fact, symbols for those things. Yet, words can be very powerful. They carry emotional overtones that influence the way people react to them. In order to develop the concept of words as symbols, ask your students to write what the following words mean to them:

   mother

   United States

   communism

   death

   love

   earth

   baby

   Each student will probably have a slightly different meaning for each word. Compare and discuss the differences with the class. Are there any common meanings or attitudes toward those words? Consider with the class the idea that each word is a symbol of something to each person and that the same words may mean different things to different people. Then ask the class what makes a good symbol. What characteristics must a symbol have to be meaningful?

2. To stress the symbolic effect of words, ask your students to discuss the difference between the following:

   mother

   mama

   old lady

   my father's wife

   Do these represent different things to us? Which are positive? Negative? Neutral? Then, to show how these ideas relate to poetry, you might want them to read Theodore Roethke's "My Papa's Waltz." How does his use of the word *papa* instead of *father* or *old man* indicate the speaker's attitude toward the father? Has Roethke specifically chosen to use that word because it symbolizes something?

3. Ask your students to explain what the following symbols stand for:

   "Old Glory"

   "The White House"

   a cross (perhaps several types of cross might be drawn on the board)

   the color white

   Then ask them to list other symbols they might ordinarily see or read about. When they have indicated that they are familiar with common symbols, introduce the idea that poets often create symbols so that they can communicate their attitudes more effectively. Read such poems as Amy Lowell's "Patterns," Coleridge's "The Rime of the Ancient Mariner," Frost's "Mending Wall," and Dorothy Parker's "One Perfect Rose." In these poems, the symbols move from being more to less obvious; in the Parker poem, the symbol is given a twist to make the poem funny. If students are unable to perceive that twist, they may interpret the poem incorrectly.

4. In teaching symbols, provide students with the following information: A symbol is something that means more than what it actually is. For instance, consider the name "Snow White." What type of person is Snow White? (Discuss the characteristics of Snow White with the class.) If one says that the governor's record in office has been snow white, what does he mean? If he says that one cannot expect every person to be Snow White, what does he mean? Snow White has become a symbol, a name that means something more than just a color. Much language is symbolic. Consider insults. If someone called you a "coyote," what would he mean? What would these terms mean if they were applied to people: dog, cat, mouse, tiger, bull, pig, snake, worm, old crow? The animals' names become symbols when they are used in a special way—in this case, when they are applied to people. Can you think of any other animals' names that are symbols for something other than what they are? (Here, if the students do not, you might want to note the bald eagle as a symbol of the United States or the shark as a symbol of something frightening—in fact, quite fearful.)

5. To show students that many authors use the same object to symbolize different things, have students compare poems in which that occurs. Examples include: Emily Dickinson's "A narrow Fellow in the Grass" and D. H. Lawrence's "Snake." The rose is employed in several ways in the following: Herrick's "How Roses Came Red"; Blake's "The Sick Rose"; Burns's "A Red, Red Rose"; Christina Rossetti's "Hope Is Like a Harebell"; and, for a bit of fun after digging through those, Robert Frost's "The Rose Family."

6. To stress the idea that a symbol can only be a symbol in a given context, ask your students to define the word *run*. If they work at it, they will have come up with a number of different definitions. In fact, were they to look the word up in a dictionary, they might well find over forty definitions for the word. Ask them which is the "right" definition. If they decide that one cannot tell which is the "right" definition, ask them how they would know what the word meant if they encountered it in print. At this point the idea of context should come out. Then, using a symbol in one of their poems, discuss how they know that it is a symbol in that context and how the meaning of the same symbol might be changed in other contexts. Consider, for example, Shelley's "Ozymandias." What is the statue a symbol of? After many people have read "Ozymandias," what does the name become a symbol of? Ask the students to imagine the statue in different settings, such as in a museum, in front of their school, in the middle of the Roman Forum. Do those locations change the way people might view the symbol? What other locations could Shelley have selected for the statue that would have given the symbol the same power? After this discussion, return to the poem and ask the students to consider whether Ozymandias in fact has been forgotten, as Shelley would have us believe, or whether Ozymandias is actually still remembered as a

result of Shelley's having made him a symbol. As an optional exercise, have students compile lists of poems in which the poet has created a symbol that is still remembered for what it symbolizes.

7. Ask students to compile anthologies of poems that employ the same symbol or manipulate the same symbol. They might want to explain the poems or write an introduction to the anthology in which they try to tie the poems together somehow or even write an introductory poem of their own about the symbol, using the symbol in some unique way.

8. Using an overhead projector, place a number of small objects on the glass (perhaps one type of object, such as paper clips, or a variety of objects). Ask a student to arrange the objects so that they form a recognizable pattern. Then have the students guess what the pattern is. You could make a contest of this by having one student put the pattern together piece by piece until the class finally guesses what it is. Then ask the class how they knew what the pattern represented. Ask them if the pattern was the thing itself. When they have told you that of course it isn't, then tell them that the pattern has become a symbol of something, just as a symbol represents something it actually is not.

SUGGESTED RESOURCES FOR THE TEACHER

The following materials are helpful for the teacher thinking through the issues involved in teaching poetry and planning the specific lessons:

Print

Anderson, Douglas. *My Sister Looks Like a Pear: Awakening the Poetry in Young People.* New York: Hart, 1974.
Anderson discusses his experiences in "The Poets in the Schools" projects and provides valuable insights into how the writing of poetry increases students' awarenesses of poetry as an art form.

Brooks, Cleanth, and Warren, Robert Penn. *Understanding Poetry* 3rd ed. New York: Holt, Rinehart & Winston.
Brooks and Warren provide clear insights into the close analysis of poetry.

Chicorel, Marietta, ed. *Index to Poetry in Collections: Poetry in Print.* New York: Chicorel Library Publishing.
This reference work is a collection of numerous poems organized by title, author, first line, editor, translator, and collection title.

Ciardi, John, and Williams, Miller. *How Does a Poem Mean?* 2nd ed. Boston: Houghton Mifflin.
This work should be considered essential reading by every teacher of poetry. It contains poems, explanations of how the elements relate, exercises in understanding poetic techniques in relation to the poet's purposes, and a poet's advice on evaluating poetry.

Drew, Elizabeth. *Poetry, A Modern Guide to Its Understanding and Enjoyment.* New York: Dell.
Drew emphasizes the relationship of meaning to form and clearly discusses the poet's craft.

Hadel, Max, and Sherror, Jr., Arthur. *A Poetry Handbook.* Woodbury, N.Y.: Bardon's Educational Series.
This handbook presents types of poetry, poetic technique, and poetic terminology. The work contains examples and discussion questions. It is intended for advanced students.

Henderson, Harold G. *Haiku in English.* Prepared for the Japan Society of New York. Champaign, Ill.: NCTE.
For the many teachers who believe in teaching haiku, this book provides good ideas for both the teaching and writing of haiku.

Koch, Kenneth. *Rose, Where Did You Get That Red?: Teaching Children Great Poetry.* New York: Vintage

This book continues where Koch's *Wishes, Lies, and Dreams* ended, giving the teacher many new ideas for directly involving students with poetry.

Lusk, Daniel. *Homemade Poems: A Handbook.* Hermosa, S. D.: Lame Johnny Press.
This is a how-to book on how to get your students to create poetry. It is based upon a program in South Dakota.

Petitt, Dorothy, ed. *Poetry in the Classroom.* Champaign, Ill.: NCTE.
Twenty-two poems for twenty-two separate class periods are discussed in the collected articles.

Shaw, John, and Dyer, Prudence. *Working with Poetry.* Cambridge: Educator's Publishing Service, 1968.
Focuses on the various aspects and techniques of poetry. Chapters on words, images, rhythm, rhetorical devices, and the process of analysis. Many examples with numerous activities for students.

Solt, Mary Ellen, ed. *Concrete Poetry.* Bloomington, Ind.: Indiana Univ. Press.
The book treats concrete poetry through theoretical considerations, historical background, biographical information, and a collection of concrete poetry.

True, Michael. *Poets in the Schools: A Handbook.* Champaign, Ill.: NCTE.
This is a guidebook for teachers who would like to have poets in their classrooms. It explains how to request participation in a "Poets in the Schools" project, tells how to plan for it, and contains an annotated list of contemporary poetry.

White, Gertrude M., and Rosen, Joan G. *A Moment's Monument: The Development of the Sonnet.* New York: Scribner's.
Historical development of the sonnet. Examples from all the masters of this form along with essays on its development. Excellent source for those interested in poetry.

Whitman, Ruth, and Feinberg, Harriet, eds. *Poemmaking: Poets in Classrooms.* Lawrence, Mass.: Massachusetts Council of Teachers of English.
This collection of fifteen essays is designed to help creative teachers find ways to involve themselves and their students with the poetic process. The poets who wrote them present varied ways to enable students to respond honestly and teach while they learn.

Nonprint: Films and Film Strips for Poetry in the Classroom

The following selected films and filmstrips provide a varied approach to the study of poetry. The annotations indicate some possible applications for each.

"University libraries" refers to the state university libraries most likely to have these inexpensive rental films. See Appendix B for complete list.

American Experience in Literature: Poets of the Twentieth Century. Encyclopaedia Britannica Educational Corp.
Series of five sound filmstrips on Frost, Moore, Cummings, Hughes, and Sandburg, with teacher's guide.

Black Poems, Black Images. Schloat Productions. Six color sound filmstrips, 95 frames each, record or cassette.
These filmstrips trace the history of black poetry and the black experience as revealed by black poets, past and present. The visual images are photographs taken in Harlem, Watts, and the South. $120 w/record; $138 w/cassette.

Concrete Poetry. Pyramid; color, 12 min.
This film is an adaptation of nine poems in Emmett Williams's *An Anthology of Concrete Poetry* (New York: Something Else Press, 1967). The words and images interrelate by moving across the screen. Use it to give students ideas on how to understand and create concrete poetry.

Great British Narrative Poems. Encyclopaedia Britannica Educational Corp. Series of six sound filmstrips of about fifteen minutes each.
Includes "The Rime of the Ancient Mariner," "The Deserted Village," "The Eve of St. Agnes," "The Prisoner of Chillon," "The Pied Piper of Hamelin," and "The Lady of Shalott."

Greek Lyric Poetry (The Humanities Series). Encyclopaedia Britannica Educational Corp.; color, 28 min.
This film explains the Greek lyric poetry, with a dramatization of a Greek chorus. After viewing the film, some students might want to dramatize a reading from one of the Greek plays. Others might want to try choral reading.

Haiku. ACI Films; color, 18 min.
This film may be used as an introduction to haiku, or, better still, after students have had a chance to practice writing haiku and have developed some feel for the form. It discusses the history and origins of haiku, presenting works

from masters Matsuo Basho, Yosa Buson, and Kobayashi Issa.

Harlem Renaissance: The Black Poets. Carousel Films; color, 20 min.

This film portrays the emergence of black writers in the 1920s and 1930s. Selections of the poetry of Countee Cullen, Fenton Johnson, W. E. B. Du Bois, and Langston Hughes are presented. After students view the film, have them read poetry by non-Anglo American writers. Some might choose to compare those poems with the poetry of Anglo American writers. What is different, and what is similar?

How to Kill. Benchmark Films; color, 11 min.

This film illustrates six poems by the English poet Keith Douglas. The film and poems recreate the experiences of Douglas prior to his death in 1944. Use the film to encourage students to find other poems about the experience of war or to give students an example of how they might illustrate through film, videotape, or slides poetry of their choosing.

Jabberwocky. Western Woods; color, 14 min.

This is a strong interpretation of Carroll's poem. Discuss the poem with students before showing it, for the fine film version may be so powerful that it limits students' ability to understand the poem at many levels.

Lament. Contemporary Films—McGraw Hill Textfilms; b/w, 20 min.

Have your students read Federico Garcia-Lorca's poem, "Lament for Ignacio Sanchez Mejias." Ask them to draw the setting that they would create if they were to create a film about this poem. Then show them this film, which interprets the poem through modern dance. Discuss with them how accurate they believe the interpretation to be.

Literature Appreciation: How to Read Poetry. University libraries; b/w, 11 min.

Good introductory film for students inexperienced in reading poetry. A bit formal for some teachers.

Making Haiku. University libraries; color, 9 min.

This will get the student involved in the poetic process. An excellent film if you want students to produce poetry.

Man and Earth: The Poet's View. Schloat Productions; two color sound filmstrips, 106 frames each, record or cassette.

By presenting works about nature from such poets as Shakespeare, Wordsworth, Hopkins, Frost, Ferlinghetti, and Langston Hughes, this set

follows a young man as he leaves nature, considers his alienation from nature, and develops a greater awareness of the power of nature. $42 w/record; $48 w/cassette.

Plethora of Poets/The Best of Poetry International, A. Center for Internationalizing English; color, 49 min.

This film features the works of such poets as Sylvia Plath, Louis Simpson, W. H. Auden, Petru Poescu, and Josif Brodsky. It is a quick way of introducing students to a breadth of modern poetry.

Poems Are Fun. University libraries, b/w, 11 min.

A good film to balance the often ponderous tones of poetry introductions. Emphasis on light verse.

Poet. University libraries; b/w, 29 min.

An interview with three American poets to discover why they write poetry. Opinions offered concerning the poet's function, what motivates the choice of subject, and why some contemporary poetry seems incomprehensible.

Poetic Experience, The. Guidance Associates.

Sound filmstrip program of two filmstrips and two cassettes or records produced specifically to help junior high school students understand the techniques and objectives of poetry. Uses works of both classical and modern poetry.

Poetry; An Introduction. William Sullivan. Holyoke, Mass.: Scott Graphics.

This is a set of twenty-three base transparencies, nineteen overlays, and a teacher's guide. The transparencies treat the purpose of poetry, the nature of the poet, imagery, abstract and concrete language, musical devices, and response to poetry.

Poetry: Commitment and Alienation. Schloat Productions, two color sound filmstrips, ninety frames each, record or cassette.

This filmstrip set attempts to encourage students to respond to poetry through visual images related to the poetry. The two underlying strands are the quest for identity and commitment based upon personal values and beliefs. $44 w/record; $50 w/cassette.

Poetry for Fun: Dares and Dreams. University libraries; color, 13 min.

A good film for junior high school students. Emphasizes light poetry and student involvement.

Poetry for Fun: Poems about Animals. University libraries; color, 13 min.

A good film for junior high school students.

Poetry: The World's Voice. Univ. of Iowa; color, 22 min.

This film, directed by Paul Engle, presents samples of poetry read in their native language and then in English. Have students listen to the poems to determine how the sound of the language reflects the meaning of the poem. If some students know a language other than English, give an optional assignment of translating a poem into English.

Poetry to Grow On. Grove Press; color, 18 min.

This film is designed to encourage student responses through group and individual projects. View the film yourself or show it to your students to give them ideas on how to read poetry in the classroom.

Uppity Albert McGuire. Learning Corporation of America; color, 10 min.

This is an animation of a poem written by two high school students, the film created by the students. It is a good example of using media to illustrate and actually be poetry.

What Is Poetry? BFA Educational Media; color, 9 min.

Two ways of reporting the same incident are contrasted in this film: the news report and the poem. The poem is Karl Sharpiro's "The Auto Wreck." After discussing the film and the poem, students might try their hand at translating a poem into another format, such as a newspaper article, a play, or a short story.

6

Teaching Nonfiction Prose

Nonfiction prose often appears to be the poor stepchild of the literature program, taught, if at all, because anthologies contain it. Yet it remains the form that all of us must deal with most in our lives, the form that conveys most of our cultures' ideas, facts, and opinions. It is the typical form teachers ask our students to use, and so that is the most compelling reason for its study.

One of the problems teachers face in teaching nonfiction prose is defining it. Clearly, teachers see biography and autobiography fitting into this area, but what do they do with that amorphous beast called "the essay"? In its classic format, there is that highly adult form, sophisticated in concept and execution, referred to in traditional textbooks as "an attempt," and related to Montaigne. The writers who have descended from that school, writers such as E. B. White and Arnold Toynbee, appeal mostly to the educated adult, and then only the adult who has developed a taste for the interplay of words and wit. To find essays that are literature and yet are written at a level most secondary students can appreciate seems an almost stupefying task. Some have concluded that the form should not be taught.

However, two reasons justify our teaching nonfiction prose. The weaker reason explains that it appears in our anthologies. But anthologies include nonfiction because teachers indicate to publishers that they expect it to be there. Thus, we have a vicious circle. Recently, some publishers have eliminated the rather artificial categories that separated, for example, biography and autobiography from essay. Is there a difference between a highly personal, informal essay and an autobiographical account? Perhaps a professional rhetorician can distinguish one from the other, but for the teacher's purposes, and certainly for those of the students, such classifications seem useless.

The stronger reason does not rely upon convoluted argument for its basis. The most popular form of reading in the United States today is nonfiction. Some might argue that it is the task of the shop teacher to teach students to read the auto mechanics book, the home economics teacher to teach how to read a cookbook, the history teacher to teach how to read the history book, and so on *ad nauseam*. While I heartily support that practice, it does not seem to be universally practiced today. And wise teachers, recognizing the needs of adults, have begun teaching students to read insurance forms, fishing regulations, sales contracts, job application forms, and other nonliterary types of prose that also fall within the boundaries of nonfiction. But beyond the study of types, is there also not the need to consider the quality of nonfiction, the aesthetic appeal? Some sections of cookbooks are beautifully written. And can one distinguish the creative historian from the creative historical novelist? If so, then it can be taught, and I would much rather that a qualified English teacher did so than an uninterested teacher in some other field.

PERFORMANCE OBJECTIVES

As a result of the learning experiences in this chapter, students should be able to:
1. Identify the characteristics of different types of biography and autobiography.
2. Evaluate the degree of objectivity in biographies.
3. Recognize fictional devices employed by biographers.
4. Respond to a particular work in terms of their own experiences, values, and beliefs.
5. Evaluate the sources of a particular writer.
6. Evaluate the purpose and content of magazines.
7. Select material to read that will be valuable to them personally.
8. Analyze and evaluate language and language strategies employed in political speeches and literature, advertising, and other forms of nonliterary prose.

LEARNING ACTIVITIES

BIOGRAPHY AND AUTOBIOGRAPHY

Biography and autobiography can be treated jointly because the distinction between them is so simple: one is written by someone other than the subject; the other is written by the subject. More subtle distinctions will be revealed by the activities that follow:

1. Before beginning the biographical unit, send your students to the library to find biographies there. Have them skim the books and write summaries for other students to read so that they can choose those that appeal most to them. Do this as part of a unit on advertising, having the students write advertising blurbs for each. Run off copies of the student productions for the entire class.

2. While each student reads a book-length biography, use the biographical selections in your anthology to teach the characteristics of biography and evaluative criteria.

3. Ask your school librarian to select specific biographies and autobiographies that match the age level, reading level, and interests of your students. (Note the reading interest inventories in Chapter 8.)

4. Biography and autobiography serve as a direct way to introduce students to other cultures. Read biographies and autobiographies of people from ethnic groups different from those of your students as a way of convincing them that other peoples have similar fears, loves, and other emotions.

5. If you have students from different ethnic groups in your classes, encourage them to read biographies and autobiographies written about and by members of their own ethnic groups. Check with your librarian to determine that such books are available. Junior high school students in particular need role models, regardless of their ethnic group. (Note the suggested bibliographies in Chapter 8.)

6. Immature readers often assume that everything that is written has to be true. When students approach biographies, this attitude can be particularly misleading. To make students aware of the possible subjectivity of biographies, have them read several biographies about the same person. To guide their comparative reading, ask them to determine which events the authors choose to emphasize and which to ignore. Speculate with them why this might be. In preparing for this task, have the students compile a basic list of facts about the subject's life from each book and then contrast the lists to note differences.

7. If a biographical film is available, have students view the film after reading the biography and note the differences in interpretations.

8. Discuss the following comments made by director Joseph Sargent about the film *MacArthur* in a prerelease report written by Vernon Scott for United Press International:

> . . . Sargent fretted that his negative bias might creep into the film. By the end of the production, like (Gregory) Peck, he had come to admire MacArthur. . . .
>
> "On any biographical picture it's difficult not to become empathetic toward the principal character.
>
> "If you don't like the leading character, neither will the audience. And if the audience is unsympathetic toward the lead, it also becomes unsympathetic to the picture. . . .
>
> "The first problem was to prevent the picture from being an historical documentary and to involve the audience with MacArthur, the man."[1]

Ask students whether these comments reveal anything about the possible objectivity or subjectivity of biographical films, and of biographies in general.

9. To develop students' criteria for judging biographies and autobiographies, have them read several brief biographical sketches. Then discuss the sketches: Which presented the subject in the best light? In the worst light? Which were most interesting? Why? Which presented the most facts about the subject? Do you know if you can believe the facts? Which involved you emotionally with the subject? How did they do this? As students answer such general questions, list their criteria on the board. Then have them group the criteria into categories and copy them down so that they may apply them to other biographies and autobiographies.

10. To make students aware of the ways biographers work and to provide a base for judging the objectivity of biographers, have students list, as they read, the sources that biographers use. They will discover that some biographers cite their sources quite clearly in footnotes or in the body of the work, while others never tell where

---

1. From *The Salt Lake Tribune*, Salt Lake City, Utah. December 30, 1976. Reprinted by permission of United Press International.

they gathered their information. When all students have completed this assignment, compile a list with the class of all possible sources a biographer might use.

11. To gain greater insight into the techniques a biographer might employ, the purposeful selection of details to accomplish the biographer's purpose, and also the accuracy of biography, have students select one prominent incident from the life of a well-known person and research that incident as much as they can: by reading histories which recount the incident; by reading other biographies of the same person; perhaps by reading an autobiography if one exists; and, if possible, by going to original sources. Ask the students to note discrepancies they may find. After discussing everyone's findings, you might have the students consider whether a biographer can possibly be accurate, and, if so, whether the biography would be interesting reading.

12. When students read the literature of a particular period, have them conduct research to find anecdotes about people and events of the period. The students can report the anecdotes to the class orally, as the literature is studied, or in writing. Perhaps, as an introduction to the period for other classes and as a review of the period for this class, the students might want to tape a radio program pretending to have originated at that time, reporting news and gossip. Some might even want to videotape their version of such a program.

13. Even while they study other types of literature, encourage students to read biographies of authors (but do not emphasize biographical data very much yourself). If students recognize something in the literature that might relate to the life of an author, fine.

14. Organize biography study in thematic units. In that way, you deemphasize the study of structure and analysis of style (which destroys biography for younger readers), and you give the biography and autobiography an interesting context. Such units take many appealing forms, such as "Brave Women," "Men and Women Who Shaped the Future," "Famous Black Inventors," or "Five Who Changed the World."

15. When working with junior high school students, be sure to pick biographies that are filled with action and dialogue. Your aim with these students is not so much to teach them the characteristics of biography as it is to involve them with the form as enjoyable literature.

16. To distinguish the possible fictional techniques a biographer might employ (meetings that never actually occurred, dialogue that no one ever recorded, etc.), have students keep a list of events and conversations recorded by the biographer. After finishing the biographies, have students compare their lists, and then, as a class, develop a list of guidelines to alert readers to aspects of biographies that might not be authentic.

17. For older students, develop their ability to recognize different types of biography: scholarly biographies, biographies that are basically catalogues of facts, popular biographies, biographical novels, historical novels, documentaries. Consider whether these distinctions are always clear. While Antonia Fraser's *Cromwell the Lord Protector* and Fawn Brodie's *Thomas Jefferson* are considered quite

scholarly, they are also popular, enjoyable reading. At what point does a historical novel such as Doctorow's *Ragtime* cease being history and become pure novel?

18. Have the class prepare a library display of the men and women most admired by the class. If you keep a record of this over the years, it will be interesting to note how student tastes change or remain the same.

19. Have the class prepare a "Who's Who" based upon their biographical readings throughout the year. Add to the selections as each student reads a new biography. A card file makes a flexible format for future additions, with each card noting the source or sources used for the basic information. If the students want a book format, photo albums or loose-leaf binders make good systems for changing entries.

20. After students read and discuss biographies and autobiographies, encourage them to write autobiographies or biographies of their friends. Teach them interviewing techniques to help them learn how to gather information. Brainstorm key questions for interviewers.

21. If students seem hesitant or unable to write autobiographies, have them keep a daily diary or journal that they write in for five or ten minutes daily. At the end of a month or grading period, have them reread their entries and then write autobiographies for that period of their lives.

22. As students investigate autobiography, note the difference between memoir and autobiography. In autobiography, writers concentrate upon themselves. In memoir, writers emphasize the people and events they have seen or been involved with. If students seem self-conscious about writing autobiographies, have them write memoirs.

23. To emphasize artistic interpretation of a person's life, find poems and short stories that are about the people whose lives have been recorded in biographies. After students have read the biographies and the poetic or fictional interpretations, ask them to consider whether the artistic interpretations add any insights. Does the artist twist the facts as we know them? Is the artist's purpose to be objective? If not, what is the particular writer's purpose?

24. Encourage your students to write "family biographies." To do so, they might have to collect old letters, photos, and mementos; interview relatives; possibly search public records for birth certificates, deeds, and death notices; and write to distant relatives. Such a project involves a multitude of language skills. Michael Cochran began such a project on his own in junior high school, continued it through high school, college, and a military career, and managed to trace his ancestors back to sixteenth-century Europe.

25. To capture the essence of a person whose biography a student has just read, have your students write epitaphs for the subjects of the biographies.

26. As an alternative to writing epitaphs, have students write obituaries for people whose biographies they have just read. These can also serve to introduce future students to the possible biographies they could read.

27. Take a field trip to a local cemetery. Have your students find the names of people on tombstones, people who might interest them, and then proceed to find out all they can about those people: interview people who might have known them when alive; look through newspapers for information; check with the county historical society. Caution them not to interfere with people who prefer to maintain their right to privacy. Trips to cemeteries often result in exciting finds. While a freshman in high school, I discovered the grave of John Honeyman, the spy who gave Washington the information he needed to attack Trenton. One of my major reports that year was a biography of Honeyman.

28. To illustrate their reports on people in the community, students can, where permitted, make tombstone rubbings. All they need is some rice paper, some masking tape to hold the paper to the stone, a stamp pad and ink, and a piece of wadded cloth to rub ink across the paper on the tombstone. Hang these rubbings around the room, in the library, or in safe locations in the school halls.

29. As an alternative to students' writing biographies, assign them to pick some house in the community and write a biography of the house. Inevitably homes are tied to people. As an imaginative variation, allow some students to write what they discover in autobiographical form, pretending that they are the home.

30. Encourage students to audiotape sections of biographies they think would interest other students. Use the tapes to motivate future classes to read the biographies.

31. Provide the students with a selected, limited list of biographies of well-known people. After the students each have read one of the biographies, play a game of twenty questions to see if the class can guess who the biographee was. As a variation upon this, the student who read the biography can provide clues one by one until the biographee is guessed. If your class likes team games, divide the class into two teams, scoring points for the number of guesses it takes to identify each biographee.

32. To demonstrate their understanding of the subjects of their biographies, have each student act out the main person in the biography or autobiography or role-play a situation involving that person, using several students for different parts. (See Chapter 2 for role-playing suggestions.)

33. Assign several students to read biographies about the same person. For their report, let them role-play situations that happened in the person's life, with some of the students acting the parts of people who knew the biographee.

34. Allow students to submit slide and tape shows as their reports on biographies.

ARTICLES, COLUMNS, DEPARTMENTS, AND FEATURES: THE MODERN ESSAY

This section anticipates the casual reading most adolescents are likely to involve themselves with on their own time. Rather than the English class being a place where people read literature that they normally wouldn't, it can be a place where people learn more about the literature that they normally would read, the popular literature of magazines and newspapers. The person who possesses a liberal education today is still one whose tastes are eclectic, who reads widely in his or her specialty, whether it is auto mechanics, nursing, archaeology, or business, but who also takes time out to learn more about the world or just plain relax. For the involved person, newspapers and magazines are primary sources of reading when one does not have the time to read in depth. Since those two forms of journalism constitute a great portion of the adult's reading, the English class can provide experiences that make such reading more meaningful.

1. The editorial pages of a newspaper provide a wide variety of columnists and feature writers discussing many subjects. Encourage students to read widely and to become familiar with some of the writers whose works are found regularly.

2. Ask students to study one columnist in depth. Have them read everything the columnist has written for at least a month. What are his or her favorite subjects? Does the columnist have a particular political viewpoint? Can you determine what the columnist's philosophy toward life might be? Do not stick to the columnists who are found only on the editorial page. Throughout the paper are other regular writers: education specialists, gossip columnists, advice-to-the-lovelorn writers, cooking experts, sports writers, gardening advisers, and many more.

3. When the students have studied one columnist in depth, ask them to try to write a column using the style and attitudes of that writer. When possible, ask the students to comment on something the columnist has not written about but that he or she is likely to: an event current and controversial, a personal problem, an artificial story about an actor, and so on.

4. Have students find columnists whose viewpoints or political orientations differ. Consider which one supports his or her arguments best. Does the writer use many facts or only opinions? If the opinions are based on facts, does the writer manipulate facts so that only one opinion seems possible?

5. Encourage students to write to columnists expressing their viewpoints about a particular issue found in the columns. Writing to local columnists is more likely to stimulate responses than writing to nationally syndicated ones.

6. To allow students to educate each other in a wide variety of magazines, have each student study one magazine in depth. What types of articles appear in it? What regular columns are found in it? Does the magazine seem to attract a particular type of advertiser? Whom is the magazine intended for—what type of reader? Would you recommend it to anyone in this class? Who? Why? Have one magazine review a day in class.

7. Divide the class into groups and give each group a number of copies of one magazine. Have the group count the number of fiction and nonfiction articles. Ask them to determine if the types of nonfiction are somehow related—by subject matter, theme, political orientation, or possibly by style. What can they conclude about that magazine?

8. After the students have studied a number of magazines in depth, have them read the nonfiction selections in their anthologies. Then, for each selection, have them predict which magazine each selection would be likely to be found in. They must justify their selection.

9. Divide the class into groups of students who appear to have similar interests. Assign each group to create a magazine that would appeal to them, a magazine composed of articles, advertisements, and features they like. They may want to submit their productions in a loose-leaf binder. If you would like them to consider such aspects as layout and aesthetic appeal, you may want them to cut and paste everything until it fits into the page size they select. This may lead them to consider what factors cause a reader to read a specific article or feature. Invite students on the school newspaper staff to explain layout techniques to your class.

10. Assign students to find articles, newspaper accounts, editorials, and columns about one specific event currently in the news. Arrange an informal debate in the class in which people can speak only to an issue based upon something they have read and can cite. A competitive game can be devised in which points are given to either of two teams based upon specific facts cited.

11. After reading a particular writer, ask students to determine what the writer is like as a person. If time permits, read more selections by the same writer. Do the students change their opinions, or are their opinions reinforced?

12. Encourage students to find articles about their hobbies. Collect a variety of the articles and then report to the class: What are the best and worst articles? Why? What can a person learn from reading them? Are the authors experts? How do you know? Where can a person who is interested find these articles?

13. If students say that a nonfiction selection is "dumb" or "stupid," instead of simply asking them to explain why, give them these specific questions, which Mortimer Adler, in *How to Read a Book,* has suggested:

   A. Is the author uninformed? How?

   B. Is the author misinformed? How?

   C. Is the author illogical? How?

   D. Is the author's analysis or account incomplete? How?[2]

14. Give students "real" experiences to write about based upon the essays they read. For example, after they have read Wallace Stegner's "The Dump Ground," have them visit their local garbage dump and write imaginatively about the memories evoked there. Or, after reading Mario Suarez's account of life in the barrio of Tucson, "El Hoyo," challenge your students to capture the sights, sounds, smells, and emotional feelings of their neighborhood in a descriptive essay. Develop student responses that involve them personally with the nonfiction they read.

15. By providing nonfiction prose that concerns a current fad, you eliminate the problem of content motivation. But remember, a current fad on "death" or "the occult" may not be popular next year. Talk to students personally to find out what they are interested in.

16. Find a display area in school where students may display artifacts related to a topic that interests them as well as nonfiction prose that deals with the topic. Advertise the display in the morning announcements.

---

2. Mortimer Adler, *How to Read a Book* (New York: Simon & Schuster, 1967), p. 267.

17. John Simmons, Robert Shafer, and Gail West, in *Decisions about the Teaching of English*, suggest that nonfiction be used to teach basic reading skills:

    A. word attack skills, including abstract and technical terminology;

    B. identifying sequences, such as cause-effect relationships;

    C. finding important facts;

    D. finding main ideas, both expressed and implied;

    E. drawing inferences and making judgments;

    F. varying reading rate according to subject and purpose;

    G. finding the unifying ideas.[3]

18. Have students read a nonfiction prose selection without knowing the author. Then ask them to state what they can infer about the author: age, sex, ethnic group, economic class, political orientation. Vary the selections from the more obvious to the less obvious. Direct the students in considering the implications of such inferences.

19. Read difficult nonfiction prose (difficult in terms of word choice, ideas, logical development, metaphoric language, allusions, or strange subject matter) out loud and slowly to the students. Stop at particularly difficult points to determine whether the students have understood the point being made. Use this type of experience to develop reading and thinking skills.

20. Encourage students to read to the class nonfiction prose they have enjoyed. If students are hesitant, allow them to record the selection on tape.

21. Before having students read a particularly difficult selection silently, give them prereading exercises: Define predictably difficult words, give them background for the selection, ask them how they would respond to a circumstance similar to that discussed by the writer, or have them write an essay about the same topic before they read the selection.

22. As a homework assignment for a nonfiction prose work, ask each student to paraphrase one paragraph in the selection; then, the next day, instead of discussing the selection itself, have each student discuss the paraphrases. Have each student read his or her paraphrase in the order of the original paragraphs. An incorrect paraphrase will throw off the meaning and continuity of the selection.

23. If a nonfiction prose selection is particularly long, some students will not get through it. Therefore, give them a series of questions before they read the selection, encouraging them to scan the selection for basic information rather than trying to read every word.

24. Enable and encourage students to read quantities of nonfiction prose by providing class time for silent reading. Have each student keep a record of the material read during this time, perhaps by completing note cards that you can file at your desk.

---

3. John Simmons, Robert Shafer, and Gail West, *Decisions about the Teaching of English* (Boston: Allyn & Bacon, 1976), p. 88.

25. Develop a file of essays on selected topics that may appeal to your students. Know your individual students. If they have nothing to do, hand them a file on a subject that interests them, telling them that you think they would enjoy it.

26. As a follow-up to a particularly stimulating or controversial selection, ask your students to raise the topic with friends and relatives, reporting the results afterward. Perhaps a survey of attitudes will focus their investigation. In addition to finding out the opinions of those surveyed, they can classify the responses according to the answerers' age groups, education, areas where they were reared, and anything else the class decides is pertinent. An essay about politics, for instance, might be followed by a survey that also determines which political party, if any, the individuals consider themselves members of. Publish survey results on a bulletin board or in the school newspaper.

NONLITERARY PROSE

In one's daily life one constantly encounters prose forms that control one's thinking, one's major and minor decisions, one's very life. Yet most English classrooms have purposefully ignored these forms, teachers insisting that they were not true literature, often represented language abuse and misuse at its worst, and could be understood only after studying the basic principles of literature. A few voices have suggested that it is precisely because these forms *do* have such a major influence upon our lives that teachers must study them and involve their students with them. In "English in the Real World: The Uses of Non-Literature," F. Andre Favat argues that

> ... students pass through the English program trained to deal with the literary matters they will seldom have to deal with in the real world, and not trained to deal with the non-literary matters they will constantly encounter. ... It is essential that the rigor which characterizes our approach to literary matters must characterize as well our approach to the non-literary. ... It must be seen that the focus of study of non-literary materials is not their content, but their use of language and its strategies.[4]

Several things we do in treating nonliterary prose may destroy its value: (1) Teachers may apply the same standards to nonliterary prose that they would apply to literature; (2) they may treat its study as an interlude intended only as an intellectually relaxing break between the more serious studies of literature; (3) they may accentuate some students' belief that the English classroom is where one reads printed words that have little bearing upon life; (4) they may dwell upon the purely factual comprehension and recall which inhibit the students' abilities to critically judge what they read; and (5) they may slip into discussing the issues that nonliterary prose forms are concerned with rather than the methods of presentation and the manipulation of language revealed by study of each selection. Clearly, if teachers treat nonliterary prose forms with the seriousness they deserve, involving students with the manner as well as the content of each selection, and developing the students' abilities to evaluate what they read, then they will have made the English classroom perhaps the most important place for students to acquire the intellectual skills needed to survive successfully in the world.

---

4. F. Andre Farat, "English in the Real World: The Uses of Non-Literature," *English Journal* 65 (1976), 28–31.

1. Students can examine interviews to determine how specific types of questions influence and structure the nature of responses. Current magazines such as *Newsweek* and *Playboy* regularly publish interviews with well-known people, and newspapers occasionally print direct transcripts of interviews. Yet another source is the proceedings of various congressional investigating committees. Direct the class in answering such questions as: Are the questions so structured that only one reasonable response is possible? Do the questions allow the respondent to frame a well-considered, well-supported, honest response? Do the questions indicate a particular bias on the part of the interviewer? Does the interviewer indicate that he or she knows the person being interviewed and the subject of the interview? Additional interviews may be obtained by videotaping television interviews.

2. Have students examine the answers given in interviews: Do the replies to questions really answer them, or does the respondent somehow avoid the specific question? Does the respondent support her or his answer, qualifying as well as detailing? Does the respondent control the interviewer by moving the discussion in a direction desired by the respondent and not by the interviewer?

3. After they study the process of generalization, of inductive and deductive thinking, students can consider the following: Are answers in interviews structured according to induction or deduction? Are generalizations based upon the facts that are given?

4. Tape-record interviews on television or radio. Have students transcribe them for detailed study. Compare such interviews with those published in magazines and newspapers. Have the students determine whether the printed interviews are more structured than the "live" interviews. If so, what does that mean? Do newspaper and magazine interviews appear to be edited? If so, what might have been left out? Why? Which is more intellectually stimulating, a highly structured interview or a loose, open-ended interview? Which appears to be more accurate or to give greater insights into the person being interviewed?

5. If possible, find two different interviews of the same person. Have students compare them to determine whether the interview reveals more about the interviewer than about the interviewee. Does the person being interviewed adjust his or her answers to fit the interviewer, the nature of the publication, or the image he or she may wish to project at the moment? After studying interviewing techniques, have students improvise interview situations, the interviewee being either a famous person or someone the students can easily relate to, the interviewers being well-known news reporters or the students themselves.

6. Assign students to study the texts of political speeches, answering the following questions: At what point in a political campaign was the speech given? What were the characteristics of the audience (political persuasion, organizational membership, economic class, ethnic group, reason for gathering, etc.)? Did the speaker refer specifically to interests of the audience, or did the speaker avoid those interests? Was the speaker specific in supporting generalizations, or did the speaker avoid specifics? Did the speaker appear to have a specific theme, or was the speech a loose collection of topics? If the speaker's purpose was to convince, did he succeed? Why or why not?

7. Have students collect a chronological sequence of political speeches given by one person from the beginning of a campaign to its end. Direct them to answer the following questions: What themes appeared to run throughout the campaign? Did the candidate change views at any point? If so, can you determine why? Did the candidate say different things to different audiences, or was the candidate consistent throughout? Was the candidate able to move particular audiences emotionally? How? Was the candidate's emotional appeal (or lack of it) the result of what the candidate said or of the physical manner of presentation? By encouraging students to be present while speeches are given, you enable them to note nonverbal as well as verbal characteristics of a candidate's speeches.

8. Advanced students may profit from examining the logic a speaker employs. Pass out Reproduction Page 25, "Some Logical Fallacies." Many teachers have had great success using Max Shulman's "Love Is a Fallacy."

REPRODUCTION PAGE 25

SOME LOGICAL FALLACIES

"Logical Fallacies" are attempts, purposefully or accidentally, to persuade through incorrect thinking. They may be used on purpose to twist or cloud or hide the truth. If not used purposefully, they are examples of weak thinking.

ARGUMENT TO THE MAN (AD HOMINEM): Arguing against the person rather than the person's ideas: "How can you believe a convict?"

BANDWAGON: Arguing that something is right because it is popular: "Most people do this—they can't all be wrong."

BEGGING THE QUESTION: Assuming something is true before proven true: "High school students can't write because they watch too much television." (Is it true that they cannot write?) "You wouldn't want to hire a man who was arrested, would you?"

FALSE COMPARISON (FALSE ANALOGY): Comparing things that are not truly comparable: "If Abraham Lincoln became president of the United States, so can you."

EITHER/OR FALLACY (FALSE DILEMMA): Providing only two choices when many more may exist: "If you don't support me, then I'll know you're my enemy." "Work hard or you will never be happy."

HASTY GENERALIZATION: Coming to a conclusion without enough information: "These students did poorly on their first essays—their teachers didn't teach them anything." "I just failed the test—teachers sure are hard here!"

NON SEQUITUR: A conclusion that does not follow from the evidence: "Many lambs did not survive the winter—the coyote population must be increasing."

---

9. Purchase recordings of famous speakers, persons who were able to move their audiences, such as Martin Luther King, Jr.; John F. Kennedy; Winston Churchill; and Adolph Hitler. Direct students to listen to intonation patterns and syntactic structures as well as what the speaker says.

10. Students can examine speeches for the rhetorical devices employed by the speaker. How does the speaker begin a speech? Have students catalogue the techniques employed by a variety of speakers: anecdotes, shocking statements, statements of purpose, references to the audience, and so on. How does the speaker end a speech? Note whether the speaker ends with a call to action, an anecdote, an open-ended question, a restatement of the thesis of the speech, or possibly a weak statement that there is no more to be said. Examine the logical structure of the speech. Are each of the major points clearly specified? Is there a clear order of topics, and are they arranged according to some identifiable plan? Does the speaker use facts? Does the speaker specify tne sources of facts, or, if not, are the sources obvious?

11. Have students conduct a syntactic analysis of a speech. A brief series of sentences will serve to enable students to come to some conclusions. For guiding and tabulating their responses, a "Syntactic Analysis Sheet" is provided on Reproduction Page 26. To determine whether certain speakers can be characterized syntactically and whether speakers vary their syntactic structures according to their audiences, students can contrast their analyses of various speeches.

REPRODUCTION PAGE 26

SYNTACTIC ANALYSIS SHEET

Speaker or author's name:
Title of selection analyzed:
Additional data to identify source:

A.	no. of sentences analyzed ____	G.	av. no. of adjectives ____
B.	average sentence length (no. of words), or average t-unit length (main clause with all subordinate elements) ____	H.	av. no. of parallel single words ____
		I.	av. no. of parallel phrases ____
		J.	av. no. of parallel clauses ____
C.	average no. of subordinate clauses per sentence ____	K.	av. no. of transitional words or phrases ____
D.	av. no. subordinate clauses beginning sentence ____	L.	av. no. of similies or metaphors ____
E.	av. no. prepositional phrases ____	M.	av. no. of letters per word ____
		N.	av. no. of words with Latin or Greek roots ____
F.	av. no. prepositional phrases at beginning ____	O.	memorable word choices: maxims, metaphors, etc. ____

---

12. After students have analyzed the syntax and word choice of a particular selection, ask them to try to imitate the style of that selection.

13. Once students have analyzed and discussed a speech that was heard by many people, have them survey people who heard the speech to determine if they remember or interpret the speech similarly. Questions can be of the following types:

"Did Speaker A say that . . . ?"

"What did Speaker A say about X: A, B, or C?"

If only one point in the speech is being checked by the survey, then open-ended questions might provide the most interesting results:

"What was Speaker A's stand on X?"

14. Ask students to read letters to the editor in a local newspaper and answer the following questions:

A. What is the purpose of this letter?

B. Does the letter writer make only one point? Or is the letter writer arguing several points?

C. Does the writer offer any proof supporting his arguments?

D. What type of person is the author of the letter writing to? What is the assumed audience?

E. What can you tell about the writer of this leter: occupation, education, prejudices, values, and so on?

F. How well does the writer achieve his or her purpose?

15. Have your students collect a wide variety of materials designed to convince: advertisements, sermons, petitions, warnings, posters, flyers, and the like, and analyze them from the following questions:

A. What is assumed by the writer about the audience?

B. What are the arguments?

C. Are all the arguments logical?

D. Are the facts correct?

E. What is the tone of the piece?

F. How is the piece organized?

G. If there are illustrations, what is their purpose?

H. Does the piece convince you? Why or why not?

16. If feasible, have your students test the written claims of advertisers. After they actually try the product, determining whether what the advertisement says is true, they can write up their findings for the school newspaper or the local town newspaper.

17. To determine how popular opinion is shaped, students can follow the written history of an item from the first time it appears until it either becomes popular or definitely does not. For example, by collecting all the news releases on a specific movie from the time a producer announces plans to create the film through public relations releases about what happens on the set to the reviews in newspapers and magazines, students can consider how the public is convinced that a film is good or poor before they ever see it. Develop the same exercise with best-selling books, automobiles, political candidates, foods, fad diets, and clothing styles.

18. Assign students to follow the attempts of a major industry to convince the public that it does not harm the environment. What are the elements and characteristics of its news releases? Does the industry favor special types of legislation? Does it hand out propaganda to its employees? Does it sponsor special public events, such as sports events or charity drives? Does it issue environmental-impact statements? Have the students read the industry's stockholder reports. Are the reports consistent with its other public communications?

19. Bring in copies of legislative transcripts. Have students study the following:

A. What is contained in legislative records, such as the U.S. *Congressional Record?*

B. Is there an index to the contents of the record?

C. Does the record indicate other sources of information?

D. Is the material contained in the record comprehensible? Specify what you do not understand. How can you find out what it means?

20. Write to your legislature for copies of bills that have been introduced. With your students, read through a bill to try to understand it. Ask students each to take a separate bill and write a summary of it for other students. Reverse the process: Have each student read a summary written by another student and then read the bill to see if the other student's summary is accurate. Publish these summaries and send them home to parents, or offer them to community organizations such as the League of Women Voters.

21. Have students write for job descriptions and application forms and discuss with them what is expected on the forms. Invite people who evaluate such forms to talk to the students about what they look for. After having students fill out a sample form applying for a job, ask other teachers or personnel managers to evaluate the applications, perhaps ranking them. Discuss the results, developing guidelines for completing such forms.

22. Ask an economics teacher, business teacher, or tax consultant to help you teach your students how to understand an income tax form, including the instructions. Develop a sample statement of earnings and expenditures over a year and challenge your students to see who can save the most money on their income tax return. Develop vocabulary lists as your students question specific words. Ask your students to find examples of statements they cannot understand even though they know the meanings of the individual words. Make lists to be used in lessons on semantics or ambiguity.

23. To learn "about rhetorical stances, appeals, and in particular, the use of pithy epithet as persuasion," Conrad Geller recommends, in "The Rhetoric of Battle Creek," that students examine "T-shirt slogans, McDonald's advertising, and beer cans," but mostly cereal boxes. After studying the prose of cereal boxes, they can look at advertisements for the products and comments of consumer advocates on such advertising.[5]

24. Have your students write to the embassies of foreign countries, requesting information on the countries. They can obtain the embassy addresses from their nearest U.S. Government Federal Information Center. When the embassies have sent their magazines and information releases, have the students examine them for their propaganda techniques. What is the overall image the country wishes to communicate? What aspects of life in that country does the information emphasize? Is anything not said about the country? List and discuss all the adjectives that are applied to the country, its people, its government, and its products. How do photographs and illustrations reinforce the text? When students each have analyzed an individual country's propaganda, compare the results. What differences and similarities are contained in their publications? Acquire copies of similar propaganda publications sent out by United States embassies and conduct the same type of analysis. Write to tourist bureaus in the individual states of the United States and analyze them similarly. Continue the project with material from the Canadian provinces, chambers of commerce, public relations offices of major industries, and college admissions offices.

25. After students have studied varieties of propaganda, have them create their own

---

5. Conrad Geller, "The Rhetoric of Battle Creek," *English Journal* 65 (1976), 57.

country, state, community, college, or industry and produce a pamphlet which is designed to sell that institution's product to a group of potential consumers.

26. Direct your students to collect a number of advertisements for children's toys. Then have them survey younger children to determine which toys the children would want after reading or hearing the advertisements and to determine the children's reasons. Then create ads that will sell products aimed at those reasons.

27. Have students read and evaluate repair manuals. Request donations of old equipment that no one wants and have students tear them down using the repair manuals if they exist. A wide variety of machines would be appropriate: sewing machines, pocket calculators, electric lawn clippers, typewriters, and so on. Have students write to the manufacturers for equipment manuals. As students follow the directions, they can note the difficulties they encounter trying to follow the directions. Challenge them to write clearer directions.

28. Read *College English* 38 (April 1977). The issue is primarily devoted to "Mass Culture, Political Consciousness, & English Studies."

7

Rhetoric, Style, and Literature

This chapter considers the relationship of literature to style and the rhetorical process. Although composition, both oral and written, is essential in the English curriculum, the role of literature need not be diminished. Students can use literature to improve their writing rather than simply writing about literature.

Several seemingly disparate facts support the use of literature for writing and speaking models. Famous writers, such as Robert Louis Stevenson, have said that they tried to write in the styles of others when they were learning how to write. In learning their native language, young children copy and practice the language of adults. Many teachers feel that those students who write well are the ones who read widely. Could it not be, then, that good writers are those who store language models in their brains, calling upon them at will, whether their writing is elaborate and highly metaphoric or formal and objective?

If one of the teacher's purposes is to expose students to language in many contexts, then P. S. Doughty's statement that "Literature is a variety of varieties of English"[1] can help the teacher justify literature as a central component of the writing program. The activities in this book emphasize the need for students to respond to literature orally and in writing, and to do so in widely varying contexts. Hopefully, students will leave one's courses having learned, as Wayne C. Booth specified in "The Rhetorical Stance," the ability to select from available arguments those that best satisfy one's purpose, an awareness of the audience for whom one writes, and the need for a clear voice, or implied character of the writer.[2] Although the teacher cannot expect his students to be masters when they leave his courses, he can enable them to move closer to that mastery. Writing, as Robert Gorrel argued in *Rhetoric: Theories for Application*, is not a demonstration of previous truth: It is an act of discovery.[3] As students discover in literature, let us help them discover in their uses of

---

1. P. S. Doughty, *Linguistics and the Teaching of Literature* (London: Longmans, 1968), p. 25.
2. Wayne C. Booth, "The Rhetorical Stance," *Toward a New Rhetoric* (Champaign, Ill.: NCTE, 1963).
3. Robert Gorrel, *Rhetoric: Theories for Application* (Champaign, Ill.: NCTE, 1967).

language. In his compelling article, "Truth versus Beauty: Language and Literature in an Articulate Society," John H. Fisher maintained that "Literature is the foundation upon which language is built and not the other way around." What justifies teaching, he explained, is the conviction that "Language is a medium; literature is a form. Neither the form nor the medium is important in itself. Both are important only as they support human values, and . . . both language and literature are always as capable of being *mis*used, or *mis*leading, or *mis*informing, as they are of uttering the truth."[4]

PERFORMANCE OBJECTIVES

As a result of the learning experiences in this chapter, students should be able to:
1. Identify and categorize the rhetorical tools that a writer employs in a literary selection.
2. Evaluate a literary selection in terms of rhetorical strategies.
3. Employ a variety of rhetorical techniques that well-known writers have used.
4. Vary their writing according to their audience, their purpose, and the occasion.

LEARNING EXPERIENCES

STRATEGIES OF RHETORICAL MODELING

The following activities are examples of rhetorical modeling processes. Since the type of literature—poetry, drama, fiction, nonfiction—and the specific selections will vary, the teacher may have to adapt the exercises to the literature being studied at the moment. *Rhetoric* has a rather ponderous and scholarly connotation for many, but it should not. Richard Larson's definition is a broad enough definition for both junior high school and senior high school teachers to accept:

". . . . rhetoric is the art of adapting ideas, structure, and style of a piece of writing to the audience, occasion, and purpose for which the discourse is written."[5]

1. Assign students to copy, word for word, outstanding examples of good writing. Thus students are forced to write in styles that are not their own, but are, nevertheless, good writing. The way in which such an assignment is handled can vary and not appear to be a lesson in rhetoric. For instance, each day you could write a passage on the board and ask students to copy it into their notebooks (in doing so, you carry out the assignment yourself). Or each student could be asked to find a sample of writing that is enjoyable reading, copy it down, and explain

---

4. John H. Fisher, "Truth versus Beauty: Language and Literature in an Articulate Society," *English Journal* 62 (1973), 203–14.

5. Richard Larson, "Teaching Rhetoric in the High School: Some Proposals," *English Journal* 55 (1966), 1058–65.

why it is enjoyable. Afterward, the student could write the selection on the board for others to copy, each student putting one selection on the board each day.

2. To prepare students for sentence modeling and parody, have them imitate obvious poetry formats, such as the limerick and then the traditional ballad. As they become more adept at this, they may want to try imitating specific authors and works, such as Poe's "The Raven" or Longfellow's "Hiawatha."

3. Try sentence modeling. As you read specific selections with your classes, choose sentences from their readings that are the types that you would like to have your students write. For instance, if your junior high school students do not write sentences that begin with infinitive phrases, prepositional phrases, or subordinate clauses, find sentences in the selections they are currently reading. If your senior high school students do not write sentences with an occasional absolute construction or build sentences through parallel structure or modify main elements with many verb or noun clusters, find examples of sentences that do. Then ask them to write sentences that copy the original sentence syntax structure by syntax structure. This is sentence modeling. The results are often exciting and insightful. Discuss the results with the class. Using an overhead projector, compare and contrast the different versions. One of the major advantages of sentence modeling is that students do not have to know any grammatical terms to accomplish the assignment and to write more elaborate, inventive sentences. Limit the number of sentences modeled to one or at the most two per week. Do not run the risk of overkill.[6]

4. To encourage your students to employ the skill they have learned through sentence modeling, assign them to use the sentence model in their next assigned writing. Challenge them to try to disguise it in a way that you will not recognize but that still employs the exact syntax structures of the sentence they modeled.

5. After your students have mastered the technique of single-sentence modeling, have them model entire paragraphs. Through this procedure, they become more aware of the syntactic and semantic interrelations between sentences as well as within sentences. Type the original paragraph double- or triple-spaced, and duplicate it for all students. Discuss with the class what the author says as well as how he or she says it. Then have the class model the paragraph. Because of the complex nature of this task, students may have to try several subjects before finding one that can be encompassed by the entire paragraph. Thus they become more aware of the relationship between syntax structures and meaning.

6. Develop your students' ability to employ parody. Show them examples of famous parodies such as those contained in Oscar Williams's *The Silver Treasury of Light Verse*.[7] Remind them that it is usually the most famous works that are parodied and point out that the parody may actually prove the worth of the original. As Richard Armour wrote in *It All Started with Freshman English:*

---

6. For more information, read Raymond J. Rodrigues, "Sentence Modelling to Develop Syntactic Fluency," in Ouida Clapp, ed., *Teaching the Basics——Really!* (Champaign, Ill.: NCTE, 1977).
7. Oscar Williams, *The Silver Treasury of Light Verse* (New York: NAL, 1957).

Joyce Kilmer Revisited

I'd rather far have written "Trees"
Than all its thousand parodies.[8]

7. One step beyond parody is the use of the same style and technique of a famous work, the style itself being an allusion to the original work, and as such strengthening the student's point. Swift's *A Modest Proposal* is an excellent model for student satires; the work is so powerful that even today many teachers are not allowed to introduce it into the classroom. In studying the original, students can learn techniques of satire, such as diminution, and employ the same techniques in their own writing. Among strong "modest proposals" that my students have written in the past have been: "A Modest Proposal for Televising Public Executions," "A Modest Proposal for Eliminating Teachers," and one proposing that hall passes be stamped on students' posteriors, thus forcing them to "flash their passes" when requested.

8. Read Francis Christensen's *Notes Toward a New Rhetoric* to find strategies for helping students understand the specific techniques employed by a writer.[9] Christensen argues that rhetoric, specifically generative rhetoric, helps students "weave" their way through the "maze of complex literary style," and, as a result, understand and appreciate literature more. Use the strategies of generative rhetoric to teach one way of creating sentences.

9. Students can rewrite famous literary selections for either a different audience, occasion, or purpose. For instance, how would Browning's "My Last Duchess" have been written if the duke were explaining to his duchess why he was about to do away with her? What variations could be wrought if the poem were the dramatic monologue of a modern wife explaining why she divorced her husband? Could O. Henry's "The Ransom of Red Chief" be rewritten with a main character being a modern liberated young girl? What changes in Lincoln's "Gettysburg Address" would be necessary if it were written after the Vietnam War? Discuss an example with the class before assigning it. As a class project, work through one full example to show students how they might go about the assignment. Notice that this exercise might also be valuable when your students claim that a selection is dated or no longer relevant. Challenge them to undate the selection or make it relevant by rewriting it for a modern audience.

10. Using only one literary selection for the entire class, have each student rewrite the selection, but rewrite it for a different audience or purpose or occasion. For instance, after reading Huxley's "A Liberal Education," students could rewrite it for: a young child who has yet to enter school, a parent who wants to know what school is like these days, a teacher who thinks he or she knows what school is like, a classmate, a student in another country, and so on. (A typographical error in the previous sentence led to my typing "A Literal Education," which suggests even more assignments.)

---

8. Richard Armour, "Joyce Kilmer Revisited," *It All Started with Freshman English*. Copyright 1973. By permission of McGraw-Hill.
9. Francis Christensen, *Notes Toward a New Rhetoric* (New York: Harper & Row, 1967).

11. Encourage students to write the précis. In addition to forcing them to grasp the essence of a writer's point, it also compels students to use concise, accurate language.

12. Some successful writers have found the following exercise enabled them to master certain rhetorical models: Read, read, and reread a favorite passage, over and over. Then put it aside and try to re-create it. This exercise is somewhat like memorizing and is a process that many employ while memorizing. By writing the selection down before the memorization process is complete, the writer begins to internalize the rhetorical elements of the selection, as well as similar variations.

13. Have students paraphrase sentences they like or sentences that you believe are particularly effective. For example, given a sentence with a metaphor, can they translate the metaphor to a literal version or vice versa?

14. How many different versions of a well-wrought simple sentence can students write? Make a game out of this exercise: See which students can produce the most versions without losing the original meaning. The accuracy of the paraphrases can be determined by the students. Project the versions on an overhead screen and evaluate them with the class.

15. Both paraphrasing and writing versions of the same sentence can lead to questions of usage. For a historical perspective on usage, read Theodore M. Bernstein's *Miss Thistlebottom's Hobgoblins*.[10] For a rational discussion of current usage, read Robert C. Pooley's *The Teaching of English Usage*.[11] As a continuing exercise for students, have them collect examples of usage from their literature. Each student can accept as a long-range project the study of, say, the uses of *I* or *me* by different characters in literature. What conditions seem to determine the usage: age of character, setting of the occasion for use, education of the speaker, historical period presented, and date of publication of the book? Ask the students to come to some conclusions at the end of their study.

16. Employ oral interpretation exercises as much as possible. How many ways can a given selection be read without destroying its mood or the author's tone or the reader's (in this case, listener's) comprehension or appreciation of the piece? Rather than pit one student's reading against another's, which may cause some students embarrassment and lead to refusals or poor performance, ask one student to read a given selection in as many ways as possible. Tape the reading so that students can rehear the interpretations while they are discussing them afterward.

17. Have students translate a work from one genre to another. What rhetorical changes must be made? Make the assignment relatively brief, abstracting elements of long works, so that students do not adulterate their efforts by trying for quantitative, rather than qualitative, results.

18. Compare different writers' uses of one type of rhetorical device: a syntax structure, a poetic technique, a way of introducing or ending a selection, creative punctuation, or another device that you would like your students to manipulate

---

10. Theodore M. Bernstein, *Miss Thistlebottom's Hobgoblins* (New York: Farrar, Straus & Giroux, 1971).
11. Robert C. Pooley, *The Teaching of English Usage* (Urbana, Ill.: NCTE, 1974).

more. Have your students compile lists, indicating the specific contexts of use. Can some authors be identified by the way they use the rhetorical device studied? If a relatively limited number of techniques are identified, assign your students brief writing exercises in which they use each variation of the technique.

19. Encourage students to imitate famous writings. Challenge them to write a selection or sentence in the style of an author you are reading. Then show the class the student's sentence and the original author's sentence (or sentences), asking the class to determine which is the original and which is the imitation. Make a game out of this exercise, dividing the class into teams and scoring points when a team is able to recognize the imitation or counterfeit, possibly giving more points if the team is able to show stylistic factors that prove the imitation.

20. If your students know a language other than English, have them translate a selection from non-English-language literature into English, or vice versa. This exercise enables them to work in the natural rhythms of both languages. Have the students discuss their efforts with the class, noting places where translation was difficult and why.

RHETORICAL ANALYSIS OF LITERATURE

The following activities will necessarily have to be adapted to the ability levels of your particular class. You should not be deterred from approaching the exercises *at their level* if your students are in junior high school.

If you employ the inductive process of gathering quantitative data from literary selections and coming to some conclusions about the data, you may risk confusing students who do not know what to make of the data. This confusion may, in turn, lead to their frustration and viewing the task as tedious busy work. Leonora Woodman, in "A Linguistic Approach to Prose Style," advises that "we first begin with a hypothesis regarding narrative voice and only then do we count linguistic data to see if it verifies our hypothesis."[12] Unless students are first aware of an author's purpose, intended audience, and voice, they will not understand the results of rhetorical analysis.

1. Before beginning any rhetorical analyses, determine whether the students are aware of the author's purpose. To do so may involve discussions and activities related to "theme" (see Chapter 3, pp. 52–55) and "tone" (see Chapter 5, pp. 149–51).

2. If students can determine the author's intended audience, they possess a skill needed to understand and evaluate the particular selection. One activity to develop students' awareness of varying audiences involves letters to the editor from newspapers. Immature readers will actually assume that the letters *are* to the editor and therefore conclude that they would not accomplish any purpose. If your students believe this, tell them that the letters are really addressed to various audiences: for example, all the readers of the newspaper, everyone who smokes or

---

12.   Leonora Woodman, "A Linguistic Approach to Prose Style," *English Journal* 62 (1973), 587–603.

tolerates smoking, industrial polluters, the voters in a specific district, married women, church officials, the governor, and so on. Cut out letters to the editor, distribute one to each student, and assign each student to explain to the class the following day: (1) who the intended audience is, and (2) what the purpose of the letter is. For each, the students should be able to explain why. More advanced students may want to evaluate how well the writer accomplished the purpose. Less capable students may need more guidance. If after practicing in class students still cannot determine a letter writer's purpose, provide a list of key phrases:

to convince	to inform	to deny
to compliment	to complain	to explain
to correct	to ask	to make fun of

Some letter writers are satiric, the satire subtle, and the subtlety is missed by all but the most capable readers. Often letters allude to previous letters and events, leading uninformed readers to misunderstand or misjudge the writer's intent. A major advantage to this exercise is the brevity of such letters, so that students will readily be able to finish the assignment. In addition, the variety of letters, especially if you purposefully select them, will keep interest high. Letters to the editor provide a vehicle for teaching many reading skills.

3. To teach students to recognize voice, the intended character of the speaker or writer, you can ask students to speculate about the persons who write specific letters to the editor, their age, sex, occupation, education, and perhaps their religion and the area where they were raised. Often this exercise is an awareness exercise, for letters are typically brief, written in the heat of emotion, and clouded by a proclivity to cram in as much as possible about all aspects of an issue.

4. To make students aware of the possible *voices* in a given selection, read it aloud— read it as though you meant it. Find selections, such as Reed's "Naming of Parts," where there may be more than one voice. Ask students to suggest other possible voices when a work is read and to read the work with that assumed voice to prove themselves right. Humorous poetry, such as Parker's "One Perfect Rose," may not communicate anything to students unless they recognize the voice.

5. Students enjoy literature more when they recognize a voice operating behind the printed word. This may explain why the less capable readers prefer narrative poetry to highly imagistic poetry or drama to nonfiction prose. Remind students that all literature is essentially dramatic in nature, whether the literature is a soliloquy (the speaker speaking to himself); a monologue (the speaker speaking to someone else, but not expecting a response); or a dialogue (the speaker speaking to someone else and receiving a response). Emphasize activities that require the student to respond to the speaker, activities ranging from writing to the speaker to role playing a scene with the speaker—in short, any activities that involve the student with the person behind the words.

6. To draw students' attention to the arrangement an author employs, have them outline the selection. If the selection is a play, long narrative poem, or work of fiction, a plot outline will result. Ask students why the author chose to employ

the sequence they discovered. Suggest possible variations in sequence, always asking what the effect would be upon the work and, more importantly, the readers' understanding and interpretation of the work.

7. List on the board or use the overhead projector to list possible orders of arrangement an author might select. For example:

A. Spatial—moving from one area to another.

B. Chronological—moving from one time to another.

C. Cause and effect—moving from reasons to results.

D. Order of importance—ranking after evaluation.

E. Other classifications—such as descriptive categories, purposes, and internally suggested categories.

Tell students that authors may vary strategies within their arrangements and combine aspects of each. Ask students to give examples illustrating when each arrangement might be appropriate or to suggest examples from their readings that represent each organizational pattern. Assign writing that naturally causes students to employ these arrangement patterns. That is, rather than assign students to write a paper using spatial arrangement, have them describe a trip they once took or tell someone about the design of their school.

8. Encourage students to study the techniques writers use to begin their writings. Is a particular writer direct, moving right into the plot or development of theme? If so, why? Does the writer intend to have a particular effect upon a particular type of reader? Other than simply stating a thesis, what technique does the writer use—a proverb or aphorism, a word or partial phrase that jolts the reader, a question, or some other device? Or is the writer indirect, employing some method such as an explanation of what the writing will not discuss, a description of setting, an anecdote, a personal or historical background, a dramatic incident, a series of questions, or a shocking statement? If so, what is the writer's reason for doing so? After studying a particular beginning technique, students can write a brief attempt using the same technique.

9. Have your students collect as many first sentences as they can from their readings. List them in class and have the class decide which sentences they prefer and why. To encourage more discussion, inform the class that they must reach a consensus. If they do not do so themselves, suggest that they establish standards, such as: Which sentence would compel me to read further? Which sentence conveys the promise of exciting reading? Which sentence puzzles me most? When the class has selected its favorite sentence, ask them to model a sentence upon it (see activity 3 in "Strategies of Rhetorical Modeling") and write a brief paragraph using the resulting sentence as the opening sentence. Compare and discuss the results in class.

10. Examine famous opening lines from literature, such as in *Moby Dick, The Bridge of San Luis Rey,* and *A Tale of Two Cities.* Explore with the class possible reasons for their being memorable: unique word choice, shock value, an intriguing hint of what may follow, an unusual syntactic construction, or other reasons that seem

justified. Ask your students to create similarly good opening lines to novels that have yet to be written.

11. Study the ways that authors end their writings. If nonfiction, do the authors summarize, having followed a deductive pattern? Do they reach a conclusion, having employed an inductive pattern? Do they leave the conclusion to the reader? If fiction, is the ending neat, tying all together; or is it open-ended, leaving the reader wondering? Do narrative poems employ the same techniques as fiction? Have your students create a list of ending techniques they could employ in their own writing. Practice the techniques with the class.

12. Have your students note the transitions that an author uses in a selection long enough to be discussable and short enough to be encompassed in one lesson. Direct them to consider why specific transitions are used. What is the writer trying to do: Involve the reader emotionally? Change the reader's attitude? Explain something clearly? Force the reader to agree with the writer's conclusion? Substitute other transitions for those the author employed. What happens? Then have the students eliminate all the transitions a writer employs and discuss the results.

13. Assign students to determine all the ways that an author develops his selection: comparisons and contrasts, lists of causes, consequences, denials, descriptions, examples, illustrations, repetitions, statistics, quotations, and others they can find. Does the author move sequentially from one point to another, or do all the points seem to be of equal importance? After the students compile the lists of techniques, they can determine whether they can recognize an author by the strategies of development the author employs.

14. Have students study the ways that authors add emphasis in their writings. Possible techniques include: repetition of the same word; unique placement of a word in a sentence; shift in diction (perhaps moving from Standard English to colloquial English); special use of typography (such as underlining or CAPITALS); or specific hints to the reader, such as might be included in transitions. Direct the students to practice using these techniques in their writing.

15. Lead the students in studying the types of sentence that various authors use. Although it might simplify discussions, students do not have to know detailed grammatical terminology. If they have trouble naming a structure, give them the name after they have isolated the structure themselves. An important question to ask in this exercise is: Does the author use specific types of sentence for specific purposes? Have the class consider:

   A. Sentence length: Does the author use sentences of the same length or vary them? Are short sentences always related to topics involving action? Long sentences to scholarly topics or description? Are the sentences always complete, or are some partial?

   B. Position of sentence: Where does the author place specific types of sentence in a paragraph, if one can generalize at all?

   C. Sentence style: Does the author change style within a given paragraph? Why? Can a reader recognize a sentence written by a well-known author? If not a sentence, then a paragraph? Consider syntax structures, word choice, poetic techniques, sentence length, and subject matter.

With advanced students, you might suggest that they try writing in the style of a particular author.

16. Assign students to examine the ways that authors structure their paragraphs. Do all paragraphs have topic sentences, stated or implied? Read Arthur A. Stern's "When Is a Paragraph?" for some revealing thoughts.[13] Lead the students to consider how the purpose of a paragraph may determine the structure of the paragraph. Have them group a set of paragraphs according to structure and then group the same set according to purpose. Perhaps dividing the task between two separate groups would lead to more impressive results. Then compare the results of the two groupings. Discuss why some paragraphs were together in both results and why some were not.

17. Identify writers in your community who are willing to talk to your students about how they write and why they make the rhetorical choices they do. Before they come to class, have your students study their writings, analyze the rhetoric employed, and develop a list of questions to ask the writers about their work. (It would be a kind gesture to inform the writers of this list beforehand—some may not want to answer the questions and others may want to prepare for them.) One thing your students may discover is that many or most writers are not conscious of the techniques they employ. (I remember a conversation with W. D. Snodgrass some years ago. One of his students had asked him why he included wrists and elbows so much in his poetry. He had not realized that he did, but when he checked, he discovered he was right. He still did not know why.)

18. Highly inventive modern writing may prohibit rhetorical analysis based upon traditional concepts. In "Analogy as an Approach to Rhetorical Theory," William F. Irmscher employs a paradigm from drama for studying the art of writing: ". . . the interaction, both verbal and nonverbal, of Agent, Purpose, and Audience in terms of the choices made in creating the Act within a specific Scene."[14] When attempting to guide students through a particularly difficult piece of writing, consider employing analogies to help them understand how the writer operates: architecture, music, painting, football, television directing, military strategy—in short, anything that will communicate the rhetorical stance and enable students to develop their own.

19. For students to realize that poetic techniques provide rhetorical tools for the prose writer, direct your students to study a particular writing as though it were poetry. (Some writers, such as Rachel Carson, provide perfect selections for this exercise.) How does the writer manipulate rhythm and sound, employ metaphors, suggest symbols, and create images? Select a specific passage to illustrate these points for students: employ some of the activities in the poetry chapter to help students respond to the techniques; and have students write passages using the tools they have studied.

13. Arthur A. Stern, "When Is a Paragraph?" *College Composition and Communication* 27 (October 1976), 253–57.

14. William F. Irmscher, "Analogy as an Approach to Rhetorical Theory," *College Composition and Communication* 27 (1976), 350–54.

20. As students identify and categorize rhetorical tools, compare selections of literature that ostensibly have the same purpose. Ask students to determine which selection demonstrates a better use of rhetorical tools in accomplishing its task. When you first employ this exercise, direct students to concentrate upon the use of one rhetorical technique only. Gradually build the evaluative exercises until students are able to judge an entire work.

21. Have students evaluate the rhetorical techniques in the writing of their peers. Divide the class into small groups, each group to read the writings of students in other groups. Each group picks which paper they consider best, reads it to the entire class, and explains the decision.

22. Select literature to exemplify the problems of communicating. Read, for example, Robert Plank's "Communication in Science Fiction" in S. I. Hayakawa's *The Use and Misuse of Language*.[15] Use literature for the data bank in a unit on semantics. For more ideas, read:

Dieterich, Daniel, ed. *Teaching about Doublespeak*. Urbana, Ill.: NCTE, 1976.

Malmstrom, Jean, and Lee, Janice. *Teaching English Linguistically*. New York: Appleton-Century-Crofts, 1971.

---

15. Robert Plank, "Communication in Science Fiction," in S. I. Hayakawa, ed., *The Use and Misuse of Language* (Greenwich, Conn.: Fawcett, 1962), pp. 143–49.

8

Planning to Teach Literature

This final chapter is designed to help the English teacher begin. Ultimately, only the teacher can decide what approach is best for a given class. The purposeful eclecticism of the earlier chapters results from the truism that individuals do not learn in identical ways. The human brain, with its myriad synapses, interposes itself between experiencing literature and communicating a response based upon that experience. The teacher must somehow structure experiences that produce the best synaptic connections in the greatest number of diverse brains.

```
PERFORMANCE OBJECTIVES FOR THE TEACHER

As a result of reading this chapter and trying some of the suggestions, the teacher
should be able to:
1. Develop a unit plan that includes parameters, justifications, resources, objectives,
   skills, motivating activities, learning activities, evaluative techniques, and options.
2. Prepare for potential censorship problems, planning precautionary steps with
   other English teachers.
3. Experiment with varying methods of teaching literature in actual classroom
   conditions.
```

UNIT PLANNING

The key to good teaching is good planning. Like a road map, a unit plan lets the teacher know how to get where he is going. While serendipity may sometimes lead to a pleasant ending, the odds are greater that the teacher will reach his destination if he plans the trip.

Planning not only gives direction to teaching but also simplifies it, minimizing the frantic scurrying for materials or resources, and that desperate question, "What shall I do on Monday?" This long-range planning can be especially useful if you plan to use films, guest speakers, field trips, or the school's one class set of a particular book.

Good planning is flexible. If a plan is too rigid, the teacher loses the opportunity to exploit interesting teaching situations. A particular class may become so excited about a particular short story—for whatever reason—that worthwhile, stimulating discussion may go on for three days. The next year, with a different class, one day may be enough. If one allotted three days for the story based upon the previous year's experience, he could spend two days pulling hair and teeth. Another example: You are teaching a science-fiction unit when a spate of supposed UFO sightings is reported in your area. If your plan is flexible, an exciting few days can be spent discussing the UFO phenomenon, reading short stories dealing with alien landings, or reading reports of other sightings. With an inflexible plan, you still have to get to that story about ecology even though the students are talking UFO and more UFO.

The unit plan guides not only the teacher but also the students. If we discuss the plan with them, except for those parts that may rely upon discovery for their effect, the students know what is to come and why. Occasionally students may be able to add to the plan by suggesting alternate reading selections, mentioning a community resource that you may not be aware of, or finding a guest speaker.

Several components seem necessary to a good plan: parameters, justifications or rationale, resources, objectives, skills, motivating activities, learning activities, evaluative techniques, and options.

Parameters

In beginning, three things are essential. You must decide on a topic or title for the unit, know your students, and determine the time limits. These factors prepare you to select literary works and activities for a given audience in a given time allotment.

Titles can be perfunctory—"Early American Literature"—or catchy—"Where It's At." The catchy title has the advantage of appealing to the student's curiosity; the perfunctory lets the student know what the concern of the unit will be. If your school's English program is based upon student-selected mini-courses, the catchy topic can be just that—catchy. One school includes in its list of English courses: "Where It's At: A Study of Popular Culture"; "Where It Was: Greek and Roman Mythology"; and "I Think, Therefore I Am: Existential Literature." In other schools with year-long English courses, a series of units can help break the year into manageable time frames: "Colonial Literature" and "American Literature before the Civil War," or "The Romantic Period," "The Victorians," and "Twentieth-Century British Literature." More importantly, selecting a topic also gets you started on selecting works to be read that concern that topic.

Knowing your students is extremely important if the unit is to be a success. What are their ages? Do you know their intellectual maturity? Their previous experiences with literature? What are their reading interests? Do they belong to different ethnic groups, or is the class monocultural? If multicultural, will their culturally determined learning styles determine what types of activity you will employ? Reading interest inventories will help you determine many things about your students. Both closed and open-ended inventories can be created, the open-ended variety also telling you about your students' abilities to communicate. See Reproduction Pages 27 and 28.

REPRODUCTION PAGE 27

READING INTEREST INVENTORY

1. Name one novel that you did not enjoy reading.

2. What was your favorite novel? Why?

3. What is your favorite nonfiction book? Why?

4. What magazines do you read regularly?

5. What is your favorite television program? Why?

6. What was your favorite movie? Why?

7. Do you have any hobbies? If so, what?

8. Do you work at a regular job? What?

9. If you could choose the career that you would have for the rest of your life, what would it be?

10. What do you enjoy most about English class?

11. What activity do you enjoy least in English class?

12. Name three living people that you admire most in the world.

    A.

    B.

    C.

13. If you could be like one historical person, who would that be?

14. What subject do you enjoy most in school?

15. What subject do you enjoy least in school?

16. If you had three wishes, what would they be?

17. If you ever wrote a book, what would its title be?

18. What would you like to change most about conditions in the world today?

19. Do you read any newspapers or magazines regularly? If so, what are they?

20. If there is anything special that you feel like writing about now, go ahead.

REPRODUCTION PAGE 28

READING INTEREST INVENTORY

Please put an X in the column that best describes how you feel about reading these books.

	1 Like	2 Like a little	3 Dislike	4 Dislike very much
1. Reading books	( )	( )	( )	( )
2. Reading books about real people	( )	( )	( )	( )
3. Reading books that are funny	( )	( )	( )	( )
4. Reading adventure books	( )	( )	( )	( )
5. Reading books about hobbies	( )	( )	( )	( )
6. Reading books about the same problems you have	( )	( )	( )	( )
7. Reading mystery books	( )	( )	( )	( )
8. Reading books about family life	( )	( )	( )	( )
9. Reading books about romance	( )	( )	( )	( )
10. Reading science-fiction books	( )	( )	( )	( )
11. Reading sports books	( )	( )	( )	( )
12. Reading books about teenage problems	( )	( )	( )	( )
13. Reading books about animals	( )	( )	( )	( )
14. Reading books about the past	( )	( )	( )	( )
15. Reading books about the present	( )	( )	( )	( )
16. Reading books about love	( )	( )	( )	( )
17. Reading books about religion	( )	( )	( )	( )
18. Reading books with a lot of violence	( )	( )	( )	( )
19. Reading books about social problems	( )	( )	( )	( )
20. Reading books about people like you	( )	( )	( )	( )
21. Reading books about different people	( )	( )	( )	( )
22. Reading books about people younger than you	( )	( )	( )	( )
23. Reading books about people older than you	( )	( )	( )	( )
24. Reading books about people near your age	( )	( )	( )	( )
25. Reading books about people in cities	( )	( )	( )	( )
26. Reading books about people in the country	( )	( )	( )	( )
27. Reading books about people in the suburbs	( )	( )	( )	( )
28. Reading books that seem real	( )	( )	( )	( )

29. What is your favorite magazine? _____

30. What is the best book you have ever read? _____

The time limits placed on the unit serve as a reminder for you and the students. Since most schools issue grade reports every six or nine weeks, units based on modules of three seem to work well. A nine-week grading period may have three units, two units (one three weeks and the other six), or one unit. The duration of the unit may also indicate what and how much can be read within the time limits.

Justifications or Rationale

On the surface, justifying your unit may appear unnecessary. If it is justified, though, problems may be avoided. Questions that may come from administrators, other teachers, parents, or community members may be answered by the justification. A good justification may reinforce your plea for new books, film rental money, or a field trip. Justifying the unit may also answer the perennial student question, "Why do we have to do this?" Finally, if you cannot justify it, should you be teaching it?

A long essay is not necessary to justify your unit. A paragraph may do. If your topic is even a bit controversial, justification is important. The parent who reads something in the unit plan or, worse, hears about it from a neighbor, discovering that the class is studying literature concerned with death or social protest, may be upset. The school board member who hears about a course being taught in "Speculative Fiction" may wonder whatever happened to *Ivanhoe*. Other teachers could be curious about why you are wasting time teaching rock poetry. The local school watchers may be more curious about your unit on boy-girl relationships. A simple statement justifying the topic may solve these problems before they start. (See also our recommendations for handling censorship later in this chapter and on Reproduction Pages 29 and 30.)

Teachers can think of exciting things to do with every unit they teach. A visit to a Shakespearean-style theater in Ontario, Canada; Connecticut; Utah; or California would certainly enhance a Shakespeare unit. Feature-length film versions of a novel one is teaching can develop the students' understandings of the book. Five or ten copies of the thirty or forty best science-fiction novels would liven up that class in speculative fiction. If a teacher justifies his unit and especially his monetary requests in relation to the justification, his chances of being able to conduct some of the more ideal activities can be greater. Faced with one request for a film because it would be fun and another with carefully worded reasons as to the value of the unit and the film's place in it, most administrators would choose the justified expenditure.

One of the most frustrating experiences for teachers is to have students constantly question why they have to study specific works or complete certain assignments. Actually, these are good questions. If teachers knew the reasons beforehand and explained the general steps in a unit while introducing it, then the students would not have to ask. One of the weakest reasons is "Because that's what we always do in an English class."

A written justification, then, accomplishes several goals. It can negate criticism of the unit by giving reasons for its importance. It can also serve as a plea for extra resources. It explains for the student the purposes for the selections and activities. And finally, it gives you an opportunity to justify the unit to yourself.

Resources

Resources include what is to be read, seen, heard, or used by students and teacher. Depending on the type of unit you are planning, a list of resources may range from one entry to many. It will certainly include what the students will read—one novel or several short stories, novels, and poems, for example. It might also include a bibliography of several novels, stories, or poems from which the student is required to select a specific number. Supplementary materials should also be listed. These might be guest speakers, games, films, slide programs, filmstrips, recordings, videotapes, film loops, field trips, or methods books and resources for the teacher only. Deciding on these materials before the unit is taught will not only help you block out the time spent on the unit but also allow you to schedule films, field trips, and speakers. It is not unusual for popular films to be booked six months in advance, and speakers deserve the courtesy of invitations well in advance of the invitational date. Deciding on your resources early not only lets the students know what they will be involved with but also gives you the flexibility to choose the best resources for your particular class from those that are available. A good unit plan is one that may be used and adapted year after year. List as many resources as you can—be a dreamer. While your school may not have the money to send the class on a particular field trip this year or purchase a special game, next year they might, and you would not want to forget the item then.

Objectives

To discuss the many arguments for and against behavioral objectives or the components of behavioral objectives is beyond the purpose of this book. Nevertheless, this is clear: By focusing upon objectives, the teacher can develop a plan that enables students to learn what is important. If the objectives specify what is to be done, then the teacher can select appropriate activities. If the objectives specify how students are to demonstrate their learnings, then the evaluation procedures follow naturally. If the objectives treat both the cognitive and the affective learning areas, then the teacher is able to concentrate upon both specific learnings and attitudes. Finally, more and more school districts require that their teachers write curricular objectives.

Skills

If there is anything basic about English, it is the learning of pragmatic and aesthetic skills. Regardless of what the literature component of a unit plan may be, certain skills must be learned by the students. If an English department has a sequential plan for teaching students communication skills, then they may be taught as part of literature units regardless of the specific content.

Skills lists may include writing skills, speaking skills, listening skills, reading skills, and thinking skills. Some argue quite well that these matter more than the literature studied, that literature study is only the means toward greater ends. Skills lists may also include lists of terms that are essential for students to learn, terms that relate to the focus of the unit or special vocabulary that the student will encounter in the readings.

Motivating Activities

Stating motivating activities lets us think through how we will introduce our unit. A good unit begins with activities that set the tone, act to stimulate students, and provide background knowledge if necessary. They are devices that prepare the students to study the topic.

The tone of a unit is set at the beginning. If the teacher begins a poetry unit by discussing various poetic devices, foot, meter, and form, students will realize that they are in for a somewhat pedantic close analysis of text. If the intention is to make poetry more accessible, the teacher will have to begin with some lighter activities.

Students in public schools may have to be there physically, but no one says they have to like it. Many new units require the teacher to do a "selling job" to motivate the students. Attractive bulletin-board displays, exciting films, thought-provoking discussions, creative drama exercises, and involving games can stimulate the students to want to begin the unit.

Often a unit, especially one taught as an elective, requires some background information. Students can read Shakespeare without any knowledge of the Elizabethan Age, but some acquaintance with the times may help a class understand his work. The play may be the thing, but the realization that the Globe Theatre was the Elizabethan equivalent of Broadway, rock concerts, or at least the local movie house puts perspective in the study.

The success of a unit can rest on how it is begun. An exciting beginning that sets the tone, provides motivation, and fills in background material is a solid base for the entire unit. Motivating activities may be compared to the cover of a paperback book or a preview of coming attractions.

Learning Activities

Learning activities are the heart of the unit. If you have written unit objectives, the selection of activities should follow naturally. The activities are more than objectives in that they are related to assignments, are more detailed than objectives, and spell out how you hope to achieve the objectives.

Learning activities constitute the core of this book. Select as many as possible to accomplish your objectives when you develop your unit plan. What works best for one class one year may be totally inappropriate for another class in another year. Vary the types of activity, choose those that involve the students with the content of the unit, and be alert for possible amendments and improvements suggested by students and other teachers or conceived by yourself. Some teachers wisely include a few blank pages at the end of their unit plans so that they can write evaluative comments about the resources and activities once they have finished the unit. Others simply type the unit plan leaving very wide margins for written notes. Using either method makes the format of the unit more flexible.

Evaluative Techniques

Here the teacher selects and plans the procedures for evaluating student work: essays, creative-writing assignments, tests, surveys, projects, oral reports, debates, and other methods of determining whether students have learned the skills, met the objectives, and changed their behaviors or attitudes appropriately. Samples of the evaluative devices may be included. Grading scales may be explained. If a contract system is employed in the class, a copy of the contract, complete with options, should be part of the unit plan.

Since your classes may change from year to year or even from period to period, the evaluative devices you create ought to be flexible and suggest options. No one essay question can determine whether all the students have learned all there is to know about a given novel, short story, play, poem, or nonfiction selection. No one project may elicit the best from all students. But your evaluative techniques ought to reflect your objectives. (See the March 1975 issue of *English Journal,* which is devoted to testing, assessment, and grading.)

Options

Options may be included as a separate section or as part of the activities-and-evaluation section. What will you do with the student whose ability precludes his understanding of Emerson or Coleridge or Saul Bellow? If a student's religion does not permit him to read *The Screwtape Letters* or *Diary of the Late Great God*, and you do want to focus on literature about religion, what will you do? If a parent objects to *Lord of the Flies* because it is too violent, or to a guest speaker from a planned-parenthood group because the group's values run counter to those of the family, or to a simulation game because the activity leads students to question community standards, you must be prepared to offer the student an optional activity. No one activity and no one reading selection is so important that it cannot be changed. And what about that student who reads everything assigned the first weekend into the unit? Or the one who, hearing you say that Joyce's *Ulysses* is difficult reading, checks the book out of the local library on Friday and wants to discuss it with you on Monday morning when you are trying to create an improvisation as a prereading activity for Shaw's *Pygmalion*? How can that student contribute to the class, satisfy an honest intellectual curiosity about Molly Bloom, and still not interfere with the progress of the class? Advanced, typical, or remedial students' needs for options will always arise. The following are two examples of unit plans, one for junior high school, *Animals in Literature*, and one for senior high school, based upon plans developed by Lynne M. Rand "New Eyes, New Worlds."[1] As examples, they illustrate the wide range of possibilities exhibited in unit plans.

UNIT PLAN: ANIMALS IN LITERATURE

Audience: Junior high or middle school, heterogeneous group.

Limitations: This language arts unit is designed to last three weeks. It is part of the regular English program.

Justification: Animals have been an appropriate subject for literature since the earliest fables. Animal stories have been written both anthropomorphically and literally. The high interest most students have in animals provides a pleasant topic for exploring several of the common themes in literature.

Key Words and Concepts:

character	fable	environment	instinct
nature	symbol	treatment	conflict

Resources:

    A. Books:

        Aesop, *Fables*

        Fred Gipson, *Old Yeller*

        Jack London, *The Call of the Wild*

        Jack London, *White Fang*

---

1. Lynne M. Rand, "New Eyes, New Worlds" (unpublished manuscript). From an unpublished manuscript with permission of Lynne Rand.

Navaho, *Coyote Tales*

James Thurber, *Fables for Our Times*

B. Short Stories and Poems:

Coffin, "The Spider"

Kipling, "Rikki-Tikki-Tavi"

Field, "Donkeys"

Roethke, "The Hippo"

Updike, "Seagulls"

Marquis, "pity the poor spiders"

Maier, "The Red Dog"

Markham, "Wise Child"

North, "The Great Dan Patch"

Paredes, "Los Animales"

Whitman, "A Noiseless, Patient Spider"

Salkey, "Anancy"

C. Films:

The Red Pony

Moby Dick

The Yearling

The Old Man and the Sea

Objectives:

A. Cognitive:

1. Students will analyze their novels, both orally and in writing, employing the following concepts:

   a. What kinds of conflict are present?

      (1) animal versus man

      (2) animal versus animal

      (3) animal versus nature

   b. What are the causes and results of the conflict?

   c. How does the animal react in the setting?

      (1) How does the animal react to threatening situations?

      (2) What characteristics of man enable him to adapt to many environments? How does this compare with animals' survival capabilities?

    d. How does the author treat the animal?

        (1) Is the animal given the position of the main character, a secondary character, or a symbol?

        (2) Does the author attribute human characteristics to the animal, or is the animal portrayed as a creature of instinct?

  2. The students will be able to identify the use of animals as symbols.

  3. The students will be able to write an original fable to be shared with the class.

  4. After reading the poems and short stories, students will be able to explain the way in which the authors treat animals as characters.

B. Affective:

  1. Students will have a better understanding of the interrelationship between, and interdependence of, man, animals, and nature.

  2. Students will volitionally read novels and short stories from the course bibliography.

Motivating Activities:

A. Through the use of readability formulas and cloze tests, the teacher will determine how to group students for reading the three novels.

B. An opening discussion on whether or not students like animals, what their favorite animals are, whether they have any pets, and so on.

C. Introduction to unit objectives and assignments.

Learning Activities:

A. Students will be grouped to read and analyze the novels: *The Call of the Wild* (best readers), *White Fang* (average readers), *Old Yeller* (slow readers). Possible ways to group for daily work would be:

Group I White Fang	Group II The Call of the Wild	Group III Old Yeller
1. silent reading	1. writing	1. oral discussion
2. oral discussion	2. silent reading	2. writing
3. writing	3. oral discussion	3. silent reading

B. Writing activities, both individual and group, may include:

  1. answering concept questions.

  2. rewriting a section of a book from another point of view.

  3. composition on student experience with animals.

C. Each student, either individually or in small groups, will do one of the following:

  1. build models of animals in scenes from the book.

2. draw maps of areas covered in the book.

3. view and write reports on television programs about animals.

D. Students will read selections from the Navaho Coyote tales, Aesop, and Thurber in class and compare or contrast them.

E. Students will read poems and short stories with class discussion centering on characterization.

Culminating Activities:

A. Students will write an original fable.

B. Students will select and read at least one outside novel each. They will write an essay employing terms from the unit concepts.

Evaluation:

A. Test on the novel read in class—25%

B. Quizzes and discussions on short stories and poems—25%

C. Outside reading essay—25%

D. Project—25%

UNIT PLAN: NEW EYES, NEW WORLDS

Parameters:

A. Length: six weeks

B. Class Characteristics: tenth grade, heterogeneous ability grouping, average motivation, predominantly white middle class.

Rationale:

Science fiction, a growing interest-grabber among adolescents, can be used to arouse new interest in "old" themes. The high-powered creativity of science fiction, exploring the fantastic, the future, and the unknown, compels readers to examine new possibilities and, as Bernard Hollister comments in his article "Grokking the Future," to "suggest serious questions for the future."[2]

Objectives:

1. Students will become more aware of the uses of language and elements of the American culture through assignments requiring observation, class discussions, and reading of science fiction.

2. Students will learn to function better in group-study situations.

3. Students will improve their writing skills while producing numerous short paragraphs and a project paper.

---

2. Bernard Hollister, "Grokking the Future," *Media and Methods* (December 1972).

4. Limiting, focusing, and organizational skills will be improved by the demand that they be exercised in determining the scope and nature of their individual projects.

5. Students will read three novels (or the equivalent) and three short stories for class.

6. Students will become more knowledgeable about point of view, setting, and atmosphere in literature.

7. Students will formulate a definition of science fiction based upon their experiences of reading the assigned books and short stories.

Resources:

1. Films:

   Andromeda Strain. Universal; color, 131 min.

   Evolution. Learning Corp. of America; color, 20 min.

   La Jette. Contemporary/McGraw-Hill; b/w, 29 min.

   Omega. Pyramid; color, 12 min.

   2001: A Space Odyssey. Metro-Goldwyn-Mayer; color, 141 min.

   Understanding Movies. Perspective Films; color, 13 min.

2. Short Stories:

   Isaac Asimov, "Nightfall"

   ___ , "Youth"

   Charles Beaumont, "Elegy"

   Fredric Brown, "Puppet Show"

   Frederik Pohl, "The Census Takers"

   Clifford D. Simak, "Desertion"

   Walter Tevis, "The Ifth of Oofth"

3. Books:

   A. Catastrophe

      Edwin Corley, *The Jesus Factor*

      Michael Crichton, *The Andromeda Strain*

      Pat Frank, *Alas, Babylon*

      D. F. Jones, *Implosion*

      Nevil Shute, *On the Beach*

      George R. Stewart, *Earth Abides*

   B. Colonization

      Ray Bradbury, *The Martian Chronicles*

Robert A. Heinlein, *Farmer in the Sky*

___, *Tunnel in the Sky*

Frank Herbert, *Dune*

C. Speculation Earth

Ben Bova, *The Weathermakers*

Ray Bradbury, *Fahrenheit 451*

Anthony Burgess, *A Clockwork Orange*

Karel Čapek, *War with the Newts*

Arthur C. Clarke, *Earthlight*

Walter M. Miller, Jr., *A Canticle for Leibowitz*

D. Aliens

Brian Aldiss, *The Long Afternoon of Earth*

Robert A. Heinlein, *Stranger in a Strange Land*

C. S. Lewis, *Out of the Silent Planet*

Clark Aston Smith, *Hyperborea*

H. G. Wells, *War of the Worlds*

E. Panoramic View of Civilization

Isaac Asimov, *The Foundation Trilogy*

___, *Pebble in the Sky*

Arthur C. Clarke, *2001: A Space Odyssey*

Clifford D. Simak, *City*

4. Anthologies:

Isaac Asimov, ed. *The Hugo Winners.* New York: Doubleday, 1962, vol. 2, 1971.

___, ed. *Nebula Award Stories Eight.* New York: Harper & Row, 1973.

Ed Farrel, Tom Gage, John Pfordresher, and Raymond Rodrigues, eds *Science Fact/Fiction.* Glenview, Ill.: Scott, Foresman, 1974.

Robert Silverberg, ed. *Tomorrow's World.* Hauppauge, N.Y.: Award Books, 1977.

Donald A. Wollheim, ed. *World's Best Science Fiction 1977 Annual.* New York: Daw Books, 1977.

5. Teacher Resources:

Ronald LaConte, *Teaching Tomorrow Today: A Guide to Futuristics.* New York: Bantam.

A fine, practical guide to futuristics. LaConte goes beyond science fiction to include nonfiction in the study of the future. Objectives, activities, and study guides to several works including: *The Martian Chronicles, The Terminal Man, WE, Future Shock,* and *Design for a Real World.* An excellent resource.

Doris M. Paine and Diana Martinez, *Guide to Science Fiction.* New York: Bantam.

Short, inexpensive guide to teaching science fiction. Contains units, activities, behavioral objectives, and bibliographies for teaching science fiction. Everything you need to develop several units. The only drawback is that only Bantam books are mentioned as possible sources.

Group Activities:

1. Groups created at random (five students each) to work on creating a "new world" in the classroom. After initial group discussions, areas for work will be formulated by the entire class and then assigned to groups to carry out. Suggested areas: music, class billboard, manners, new names, and a partial language. Groups will present their contributions to the class.

2. Groups based on similarity of projects will work on project days. The project is an individual assignment in most cases, but the group will provide additional aid and feedback for the students.

Individual Activities:

1. Watch television commercials in class. Write your reactions to three of the commercials from an alien's point of view.

2. Collect a list of words, phrases, and sentences that are frequently used but that would make little sense to someone not acquainted with U.S. culture. Consider how an alien might react to these.

3. In one paragraph, describe a typewriter to a person who communicates by mental telepathy. Or explain what snow is and what it does to a child who has always lived in the desert and has never seen snow.

4. Fill out a personality square (see Johari Window, Chapter 3, pp. 66–67) on Red from the short story "Youth."

Projects:

1. Read *Andromeda Strain* for your first required book. Write a paper responding to these questions: What is your interpretation of the book's ending? What are the possible future problems?

2. Create a game for one book that the entire class can join in playing. It may deal directly with the story (but please remember that some have not read the book) or be a takeoff on some elements in the novel.

3. Write a paper comparing three short stories dealing with a similar theme. Consider atmosphere, tone, and theme.

4. Develop a project on survival (e.g., short story, report on wilderness trekking, possible solutions to a hypothetical survival situation, etc.). Read an

article on survival if you wish to do this project. Discuss the article with the teacher and the class.

5. Write a short science-fiction story in the first-person point of view. Write it from the point of view of an alien.

6. Rewrite Arthur C. Clarke's "Before Eden" or Fredric Brown's "Puppet Show" as a radio play. Select other students and perform the play for the class as readers' theater.

7. Design book covers for two books and two short stories. Be prepared to explain your interpretation of the stories' settings, major characters, and themes as revealed in the designs.

8. Devise your own project with the approval of the teacher.

Evaluation:

1. In-class test on first book required from the categories of "Catastrophe" and "Colonization."

   A. Describe the novel's major character.

   B. Describe the major setting.

   C. Explain the relationship between the physical setting and the major character or characters.

   D. What are the main character's motivations for doing what he or she is doing and for being in that situation?

   E. Explain the major conflict or crisis of the book for the major group of characters. There are probably a number of conflicts, so be sure to limit yourself to one of the main ones.

   F. If you were there, what would you have done? How might you have felt? What would be your plans for next year?

2. Take-home test on second book required (one selection from the books in groups C, D, and E).

   A. How would you like living in this particular society? What would you find most distasteful about it? Most enjoyable?

   B. If you could change one thing about this society, what would it be and why?

   C. What poses the greatest threat to this society? Why?

   D. What importance does the major setting in the book have?

   E. What is the author's basic attitude toward man? Is man good? Bad? Trustful? Corrupt?

   F. (1) For books in group C:

   To what extent do you see the present-day United States in the story? What would have to specifically happen for the United

States (or the world) to become like the story? How might it be prevented?

(2) For books in group D:

Describe the social structure of the alien society. If you were an alien from this society, where might you fit in? (Consider whether the alien society has anything in common with human societies.)

(3) For books in group E:

Select your favorite "slice of time" and describe it. What do you like about it? What do you dislike? How does the author incorporate separate scenes or stories into the whole to develop the panoramic effect?

3. At the end of the unit, possibly have the students respond to Ray Bradbury's statement in the introduction to his *Martian Chronicles:* *"It is good to renew one's wonder,"* said the philosopher. *"Space travel has made children of us all."*

CENSORSHIP

For an English teacher, censorship may be one of the dirtiest words in the language, undermining the ability to think clearly and grinding down the gears of creative teaching. In fact, parents and community members do have a right to judge what is taught in the schools, but teachers may encounter judgments that are excessive and irrational or, worse yet, impinge upon the students' right to read.

As the American Library Association and others have advised, the question is not what to do when the censor arrives but what to do *before* the censor arrives. Although the ALA has suggested the following procedures for librarians, they make good sense for teachers:

1. Maintain a definite materials selection policy.

2. Maintain a clearly defined method for handling complaints.

3. Maintain lines of communication with civic, religious, educational, and political bodies of the community.

4. Maintain a vigorous public relations program on behalf of intellectual freedom.[3]

The ALA has prepared free materials relating to censorship and the Library Bill of Rights. Single copies may be requested by writing: Office of Intellectual Freedom, American Library Association, 50 East Huron Street, Chicago, Illinois 60611.

As you prepare your unit plans, you can consider potential censorship problems when writing your justifications. To be prepared for such problems, each teacher ought to prepare

---

3. Mary Duncan Carter, Wallace John Bank, and Rose Mary Magrill, *Building Library Collections* (Metuchen, N.J.: The Scarecrow Press, 1974), 335–336.

and each English department ought to maintain a file of rationales for materials taught in common or materials that are possibly censorable. Reproduction Page 29 is based upon a form prepared by Diane P. Shugert, Chair, New England Association of Teachers of English Committee on the Profession. She advises that such forms be filled out by individual teachers and that all teachers be familiar with the rationales written for materials they are teaching. (Reproduction Page 30 is an example of a form that citizens may fill out in censorship cases.)

REPRODUCTION PAGE 29

RATIONALE FOR LITERATURE SELECTION

School:
Teacher:
Title of selection:
Grade or course:

Approximate date(s) selection will be used:

This selection will be:
_____ studied by the entire class
_____ recommended to individual students
_____ optional reading

The selection is part of a larger study of:

Ways in which the selection is especially appropriate for students in this class:

Ways in which the selection is especially pertinent to the objectives of this course or unit:

Special problems that might arise in relation to the selection and some planned activities that handle each problem:

Some other appropriate selections an individual student might read in place of this one:

This form is based on an original prepared by Diane P. Shugert, Chair, NEATE Committee on the Profession.

REPRODUCTION PAGE 30

CITIZEN'S REQUEST FOR RECONSIDERATION OF A BOOK*

Author   Hardcover   Paperback
Title
Publisher (if known)

Request initiated by _____

Telephone _____ Address _____

City _____ Zone _____
Complainant represents

_____ himself

_____ (name organization) _____

_____ (identify other group)   _____

1. To what in the book do you object? (Please be specific: cite pages.)

   _____

   _____

2. What do you feel might be the result of reading this book?

   _____

   _____

3. For what age group would you recommend this book?

   _____

4. Is there anything good about this book?

   _____

   _____

5. Did you read the entire book? _____ What parts?

   _____

6. Are you aware of the judgment of this book by literary critics?

   _____

7. What do you believe is the theme of this book?

   _____

   _____

8. What would you like your school to do about this book?
   _____ do not assign it to my child
   _____ withdraw it from all students as well as from my child
   _____ send it back to the English department office for reevaluation

9. In its place, what book of equal literary quality would you recommend that would
   convey as valuable a picture and perspective of our civilization?

   _____

                                    _____
                                    Signature of Complainant

*National Council of Teachers of English
_____

   In addition, we can become aware of suggestions for handling censorship, such as those in Ken Donelson's "Censorship in the Schools." *English Journal* 63, February 1974, 47–51. Other valuable publications include:

Kenneth Donelson, ed. "Censorship and the Teaching of English," *Arizona English Bulletin* 17 (February 1975); *English Journal* 66 (February 1977).

___, ed. *The Students' Right to Read.* Urbana, Ill.: NCTE, 1972.

NEA. *Kanawha County, West Virginia: A Textbook Study in Cultural Conflict.* Washington, D.C.: National Education Association, 1975.

A bibliography, "Freedom of Speech: A Selected Annotated Basic Bibliography," is available from the Speech Communication Module, ERIC Clearinghouse on Reading and Communication Skills, Statler Hilton Hotel, New York, New York 10001.

   Any reading selection can be questioned, the possible areas where challenges may arise usually relating to community, family, personal values, and to specific language in the selection. In "Censorship and Arizona English Teaching, 1971–1974," Ken Donelson reports a survey that found the following selections most frequently attacked:[4]

Catcher in the Rye (22 attacks)	*The Pigman* (8)
Go Ask Alice (14)	*The Grapes of Wrath* (7)
Brave New World (12)	*The Lottery* (film version) (7)
Slaughterhouse Five (12)	*Mr. and Mrs. Bo Jo Jones* (7)
The Learning Tree (9)	*Soul on Ice* (7)
Of Mice and Men (9)	
Manchild in the Promised Land (8)	

In addition, the survey tallied the most frequently banned materials or those removed or placed on a closed shelf:

Catcher in the Rye (9)	*Mr. and Mrs. Bo Jo Jones* (4)
Brave New World (7)	*The Learning Tree* (3)
Slaughterhouse Five (6)	*Mad Magazine* (3)
Go Ask Alice (4)	*The Pigman* (3)
Manchild in the Promised Land (4)	*Soul on Ice* (3)

It is not enough to assume that your selections are "safe." Seemingly innocuous books, such as *Mrs. Mike*, may offend some people. *Mad Magazine* is philosophically conservative, attacking excesses both moral and personal, and yet, as the survey showed, it is vulnerable. Perhaps the best advice when attacked is that given by the ALA in their information sheet, "How Libraries Can Resist Censorship":

> Remain calm. Don't confuse noise with substance. Require deliberate handling of the complaint under previously established rules. Treat the group or individual who complains with dignity, courtesy, and good humor. Given the facts, most citizens will support the responsible exercise of professional freedom by teachers and librarians, and will insist on protecting their own freedom to read.[5]

LEARNING ACTIVITIES FOR THE LITERATURE TEACHER

Pick at least one of these each marking period and try it. Experiment more. Let others know the results of your experiments.

1. Buy a copy of Sylvia Spann and Mary Beth Culp's *Thematic Units in Teaching English and the Humanities.*[6] This is a collection of fifteen unit plans treating

4. Ken Donelson, ed., "Censorship and Arizona English Teaching 1971-1974, *Arizona English Bulletin* 17 (1975), 4.

5. Mary Duncan Carter, *Building Library Collections* (Metuchen, N.J.: The Scarecrow Press, 1974), 336.

6. Sylvia Spann and Mary Beth Culp, *Thematic Units in Teaching English and the Humanities* (Urbana, Ill.: NCTE, 1975).

topics such as family life, the occult, death, the literature of sports, rural culture and folklore, an introduction to filmmaking, media and the representation of life, utopias, growing old, and conscience versus established authority. Try one unit and evaluate it. Keep in mind that many anthologies are arranged in thematic units, such as the following:

Farrell, Ed, Gage, Tom, Pfordresher, John, and Rodrigues, Raymond J., eds. *Fantasy: Shapes of Things Unknown.* Glenview, Ill.: Scott, Foresman, 1974.

____ , *Myth, Mind, and Moment.* Glenview, Ill.: Scott, Foresman, 1976.

____ , *Reality in Conflict: Literature of Values in Opposition.* Glenview, Ill.: Scott, Foresman, 1976.

Stanford, Gene, Adler, Charles S., and Adler, Sheila M., eds. *We Are But a Moment's Sunlight: Understanding Death.* New York: Pocket Books, 1976.

Stanford, Gene, and Stanford, Barbara, eds. *Love Has Many Faces.* New York: Pocket Books, 1973.

____ , *Strangers to Themselves.* New York: Bantam Books, 1973.

2. Get together with another teacher and design a course using a humanities approach. For fine ideas, read Brooke Workman's *Teaching the Decades: A Humanities Approach to American Civilization.*[7] Among the approaches suggested are the collecting of oral history; viewing TV shows; studying art, music, dance, architecture, movies, and artifacts of the period; and, of course, reading literature. The three periods for which course outlines, handouts, and bibliographies are provided are the 1920s, 1930s, and 1945–60. When you finish these, ask your students to collect materials representing 1961 to the present or 1971 to the present.

3. Start a unit by telling your students that they will have to select the literature to be read. Pick a unit for which there are no anthologies. Ask your students to suggest topics. Send them to the library to gather materials. Develop evaluative criteria with the students. As a final exercise, have the class formalize the unit by writing it, including tests, for some future class.

4. Each time you teach one selection to several classes, vary the approach with each class: Use lecture with one, recitation with another, small-group discussions with yet another, individual reading and no discussion with another. Record the results after tests and/or essays. Ask students to evaluate each approach. Discuss the experiment with other teachers.

5. Teach one unit by assigning very specific readings for the class. Teach a unit on the same subject by giving your students an extensive bibliography of available readings and requiring them to read a specific number of selections, but not specific titles. Teach the unit to a third class, this time not requiring any specific number of readings or titles. Evaluate the results in several ways: Compare test results, qualities of discussions, content mentioned in essays, and voluntary readings by the students.

---

7. Brooke Workman, *Teaching the Decades: A Humanities Approach to American Civilization* (Urbana, Ill.: NCTE, 1975).

6. Prepare a list of activities to fill the last minutes of a class period. For good suggestions, read Sue Ellen Holt's "Fill 'er Up: Fourscore Language Arts Activities for the Last Ten Minutes of the Period" or the activities suggested in Ted Hipple's *Teaching English in Secondary Schools*.[8] Invite students to suggest brief, fun language and literature experiences.

7. In several different classes, evaluate student comprehension of one reading assignment in varying ways: an assigned essay in one class, an open topic essay in another, a choice of media projects in another, a short-answer essay test in another, an objective test in another, or an individual choice of any of those in yet another class. Which method produced the most satisfying results? Share those results with other teachers.

8. Plan a thematic unit using literature of only one genre. Plan the same theme study using any one of the other genres. Finally, create the thematic unit employing selections from a variety of units. Which do you feel most comfortable teaching? Which do your students prefer? Which produced the best results? Try this experiment with other themes. Do some themes lend themselves more to poetry than to fiction or to mixed genres?

9. Introduce a unit being taught to several different classes by employing different introductory techniques: improvisation; introductory lecture; simulation game; a multimedia event involving slides, music, film, sound effects, black lights, oscilloscope, and self-programmed typewriters. (Read Eliza Krekeler's "See the Light: An Electronic Happening.")[9] Then, teach the remainder of the unit in the same way to all classes. Can you determine whether the style of the introductory lesson influenced student behaviors and involvement throughout the rest of the unit? If you began with a multimedia event and did not include any media presentation later, did interest die off? Did the straight lecture introduction fail to involve students, or did the media event cause them to view the unit as frivolous? In addition to your gut-level reactions to student involvement, survey students in writing at the end of the unit to determine their perceptions.

10. Compare and contrast the effectiveness of specific literature selections in relation to the unit being studied. Which leads to the best discussions? Which prompts the most revealing dramatic improvisations? Which employs vocabulary or stylistic devices that defeat student comprehension and interest? For instance, if you are studying modern versions of traditional fables with junior high school students, which of these two poems seems best for your class: Marianne Moore's "The Grasshopper and the Ant" or John Ciardi's "John J. Plenty and Fiddler Dan"? Ask a senior high school teacher involved with a unit on fables to test the same problem. Compare notes.

11. Together with another teacher who has read this book, find two activities that you have differing opinions about—one that one of you thinks will fail but which the other teacher believes will succeed. Teach both of the activities in both of

---

8. Sue Ellen Holt, "Fill 'er Up: Fourscore Language Arts Activities for for the Last Ten Minutes of the Period," *English Journal* (September 1976), and Ted Hipple, *Teaching English in Secondary Schools* (New York: Macmillan, 1973).

9. Eliza Krekeler, "See the Light: An Electronic Happening," *English Journal* (March 1976), 57–59.

your classes, get together afterward, and come to some conclusions. Can a teacher's attitude toward an exercise have anything to do with its success or failure?

12. Survey past graduates of your classes or your school to determine the answers to the following questions: Which literature selections do you remember reading while you were in _____(school name)_____? Did you ever reread any of them? If so, which? Would you recommend that students today read any of them? If so, would you please explain which and why? Is there anything you have read since leaving _____(school name)_____ that you wish you had read when you were a student here? If so, supply the title and briefly tell why. As a teacher professional, you may want to know more about the person who answers the survey, such as age, education, and occupation. But be aware that many people may consider that information confidential and therefore may not respond to your survey. If you are mailing the survey, research indicates that people tend to respond more when they find a stamped, self-addressed envelope with the survey. Ask your principal for funds—school boards would appreciate information about the success of school programs and the increased community involvement in curriculum planning. (A captive audience for such a survey is a class reunion. Another captive audience consists of people attending a school board meeting, although few may be former graduates of the school. Or, you could send the survey home with your students.) Report the results to other English teachers in the school or write an article for your local newspaper. Use the results to help yourself plan.

13. To determine whether student involvement in planning leads to more learning, try the following experiment: Plan a unit entirely by yourself and teach it to one class. In another class, ask the students to plan the same unit. Provide them with the basic ingredients of a unit as specified earlier in this chapter. For ideas, read articles such as Paul Silverman's "Mini-Vue Today!: An Alternative Program for Student Involvement," Raymond J. Rodrigues's "Student-Created Games," and Bernarr Folta's "Seven Ways to Involve Students in Curriculum Planning," keeping in mind the advice of John L. Wright in "Learning Objectives and the Teaching of English."[10] Compare the results of the two units. If there are advantages to each, make use of them.

14. Whenever you conduct an experiment such as those suggested here, write up the results for a professional journal such as *English Journal, Media & Methods, Today's Education,* or a state English publication. Mary Butler and Lee H. Mountain provide suggestions for potential article markets in "To Be or Not-to Be a Writer: The How and Where of Publishing Language Arts Articles."[11]

15. When you plan a language arts unit, include multiethnic materials. Pluralize the content. You do not always have to point out to students that the selections were written by different ethnic-group members. Sources may be located among a

---

10. Paul Silverman, "Mini-View Today!: An Alternative Program for Student Involvement," *English Journal* 65 (October 1976), 57–59; Raymond J. Rodrigues, "Student-Created Games," *English Journal* 65 (May 1976), 70–72; Bernarr Folta, "Seven Ways to Involve Students in Curriculum Planning," *English Journal* 63 (April 1974), 42–45; and John L. Wright, "Learning Objectives and the Teaching of English," *English Journal* 65 (April 1976), 32–36.

11. Mary Butler and Lee H. Mountain, "To Be or Not to Be a Writer: The How and Where of Publishing Language Arts Articles," *English Journal* (January 1975).

number of excellent bibliographies and discussions published in *English Journal*, such as:

Baldwin, Lewis. "Chicano Literature in Paperback." May 1976.

Dybek, Caren. "Black Literature for Adolescents." January 1974.

Garcia, Ricardo. "An Overview of Chicano Folklore." February 1976.

Kakugawa, Frances. "Asian-American Literature." October 1974.

Mangione, Anthony Roy. "Dramatic Touchstones toward a New Cultural Pluralism." October 1976.

_____, "Literature on the White Ethnic Experience." January 1974.

Mersand, Joseph. "The Literary Impact of Jewish Culture." February 1975.

Perry, Jesse. "Notes toward a Multi-Cultured Curriculum." April 1975.

Povey, John. "African Literature in Paperback." April 1976.

Rodrigues, Raymond J. "A Few Directions in Chicano Literature." May 1973.

Stanford, Barbara Dodds. "Literature of the Human Race." February 1972.

Stensland, Anna Lee. "Traditional Poetry of the American Indian." September 1975.

Trevino, Albert D. "Mexican-American Short Fiction for the High School Program." May 1976.

The *English Journal* 66 (March 1977) is devoted primarily to multicultural literature resources.

Also check: Anne Troy's "Appalachia in Children's and Adolescents' Fiction" and Gene and Barbara Stanford's "Extending Our Planetary Vision: Oriental Literature."[12]

16. In selecting materials for your units, be sure women are fairly represented. As with multiethnic materials, there will be obvious gaps from periods when women were seldom published. Nevertheless, you can find good suggestions in the following selection of *English Journal* articles:

Beebe, Sandra. "Women in American Literature." September 1975.

Fowler, Lois Josephs. "Sirens & Seeresses: Women in Literature & the High School Curriculum." November 1973.

Nilsen, Alleen Pace. "Books for Young Adults: The Feminist Influence." April 1974.

Wells, Nancy. "Women in American Literature." November 1973.

Wilson, Norma. "A Liberated Glossary—Guide to Feminist Writings." September 1974.

Jeanne Betancourt has produced a catalogue reviewing feminist and nonsexist films: *Women in Focus.* Write to Pflaum/Standard, 38 West Fifth St., Dayton, Ohio 45402. In addition, the following books will start you on gathering literature and activities for women's studies:

Cade, Toni, ed. *The Black Woman: An Anthology.* New York: NAL, 1974.

Clapp, Ouida H., ed. *Responses to Sexism.* Champaign, Ill.: NCTE, 1976.

---

12. Anne Troy, "Appalachia in Children's and Adolescents' Fiction," *Language Arts* 54 (January 1977), and Gene and Barbara Stanford, "Extending Our Planetary Vision: Oriental Literature," *English Education* 5 (December–January 1974).

Ferguson, Mary Ann, ed. *Images of Women in Literature.* New York: Houghton Mifflin, 1976.

Goulianos, Joan, ed. *By a Woman Writt: Literature from Six Centuries by and about Women.* New York: Penguin, 1974.

McGrady, Mike. *The Kitchen Sink Papers.* New York: NAL, 1976.

Murray, Michele, ed. *A House of Good Proportion: Images of Women in Literature.* New York: Simon and Schuster, 1973.

Nilsen, Alleen Pace; Bosmajian, Haig; Gershuny, H. Lee; and Stanley, Julia P. *Sexism and Language.* Champaign, Ill.: NCTE, 1976.

Stanford, Barbara. *On Being Female.* New York: Pocket Books, 1974.

Stanford, Barbara and Stanford, Gene. *Roles and Relationships: A Practical Guide to Teaching about Masculinity and Feminity.* New York: Bantam, 1976.

Sullivan, Victoria and Hatch, John, eds. *Plays by and about Women.* New York: Random House, 1973.

17. When you develop a set of questions, whether to be answered in writing or orally, answer them yourself. Better yet, ask one of your colleagues to answer them to see whether you receive the answer that you expected.

18. To determine whether students understand or remember a selection, a rational strategy for developing questions is to begin with factual questions, move on to inference questions to determine if the students are able to grasp the implications or intent of the story, and then ask extension questions to develop the students' abilities to think beyond the selection and relate it to other aspects of literature and life. Finally, move into tangents and imaginative areas that develop out of the reading. But is this system applicable to all selections and all classes? Experiment. Mix up your questioning procedures purposefully. Then come to some conclusions about which procedures work best with which types of selections and classes.

19. With other English teachers, role-play what you would do if you received the following letter:

> Dear _____ :
>   My daughter brought home a book, _____, which she says you assigned. If you did I am *extremely* upset by your choice of books. If you have read the book you have used *very* poor professional judgment in assigning it, or you have, in fact, not read it.
>   There is *no* redeeming quality in "literature" that must resort to the type of dialogue found on p.___, line___ , p.___ lines ___ and ___, and p.___ line ___ . I find it intolerable that my children are "required" to read such trash. I demand that you cease teaching this book. I also would like to receive a bibliography of other books taught in your school.
>
>   Sincerely,
>
>   _____

As you role-play the situation, remember that this parent is sincere and that other parents may share these feelings. Continue the situation by role-playing what you will do when the parent arrives in school for a conference. Then, assume that you do not receive this letter. What will you say when the parent suddenly arrives at the door of your classroom with book in hand?

20. Experiment with various ways to grade students. Try a pseudo-contract system in which you specify exactly what the student must do to acquire a specific grade. In another class, develop a real contract system after negotiating with the students individually. In another class, let the students assess and grade themselves. In another class, grade students as you always have if different from the above methods. Finally, evaluate the development of students in all the classes. Has the grading system (which is not the same thing as evaluation) influenced student performances? Share the results with others.

21. Try role playing, improvisations, and oral readings with other teachers. How do you feel doing them? Discuss what this may mean for students in the classes.

22. Write to editors of anthologies you use. Talk about what you like and dislike in their books. Show the responses to other English teachers.

23. Get together with a colleague you can work with, one who teaches at least one class that you teach at the same time that you teach. For specified units, vary the number of students between your classes. One of you teach only ten students while the other has all the rest. Switch these arrangements. Come to some conclusions.

APPENDIX A

Addresses of Producers of Resources

Addison Wesley Publishing Company
Reading, Massachusetts 01867

Allyn and Bacon, Inc.
470 Atlantic Avenue
Boston, Massachusetts 02210

Amsco School Publications
315 Hudson Street
New York, New York 10013

Applause Productions
85 Longview Road
Port Washington, New York 11050

Arco Publishing Company
219 Park Avenue South
New York, New York 10003

Argus Communications
7440 Natchez Avenue
Niles, Illinois 60648

Bantam Books
666 Fifth Avenue
New York, New York 10019

Barnes and Noble
Division of Harper and Row, Publishers
10 East 53rd Street
New York, New York 10022

Barron's Education Series
113 Crossways Park Drive
Woodbury, New York 11797

Channing L. Bete Company
45 Federal Street
Greenfield, Massachusetts 01301

Cambridge Book Company
488 Madison Avenue
New York, New York 10022

CEBCO/Standard Publishing
104 Fifth Avenue
New York, New York 10011

Center for the Humanities
Two Holland Avenue
White Plains, New York 10603

Citation Press
906 Sylvan Avenue
Englewood Cliffs, New Jersey 07632

Clarke, Irwin and Company, Ltd.
791 St. Claire Avenue, W.
Toronto, Ontario M6C 1B8 Canada

College Entrance Publications
104 Fifth Avenue
New York, New York 10011

Eaton Paper Company
Pittsfield, Massachusetts 01201

Educational Research Associates
Box 767
Amherst, Massachusetts 01002

Educators Publishing Service, Inc.
75 Moulton Street
Cambridge, Massachusetts 02138

Encyclopaedia Britannica Educational Corp.
425 N. Michigan Avenue
Chicago, Illinois 60611

Everett/Edwards, Inc.
Post Office Box 1060
Deland, Flordia 32720

Eye-Gate
146-01 Archer Avenue
Jamaica, New York 11435

Filmstrip House
6633 West Howard Street
Niles, Illinois 60648

Folkways Records
701 Seventh Avenue
New York, New York 10036

Follett Publishing Co.
1010 W. Washington Blvd.
Chicago, Illinois 60607

Frederick Muller Ltd.
Victoria Works, Edgware Road
London NW 2, 6 LE, England

Glencoe Press
8701 Wilshire Blvd.
Beverly Hills, California 90211

Globe Book Company
175 Fifth Avenue
New York, New York 10010

Greystone Films Inc.
Box 303, Kingsbridge Station
Riverdale, New York 10463

Guidance Associates
757 Third Avenue
New York, New York 10017

Harcourt Brace Jovanovich
757 Third Avenue
New York, New York 10017

Hart Publishing Company
15 West Fourth Street
New York, New York 10012

Hayden Book Co., Inc.
50 Essex Street
Rochelle Park, New Jersey 07662

D.C. Heath and Company
125 Spring Street
Lexington, Massachusetts 02173

Holt, Rinehart & Winston
383 Madison Avenue
New York, New York 10017

Houghton Mifflin Co.
2 Park Street
Boston, Massachusetts 02107

Independent School Press
51 River Street
Wellesley Hills, Massachusetts 02181

Interact
P.O. Box 262
Lakeside, California 92040

Thomas Klise Company
P.O. Box 3418
Peoria, Illinois 61614

Laidlaw Brothers
Thatcher & Madison
River Forest, Illinois 60305

J.B. Lippincott Company
East Washington Square
Philadelphia, Pennsylvania 19105

Littlefield, Adams, & Co.
81 Adams Drive
Totowa, New Jersey 07512

London Association for the Teaching of English
Blackie & Son, Ltd.
5 Fitzhardinge Street
London, W.I., England

Loyola University Press
3441 North Ashland Avenue
Chicago, Illinois 60657

Macmillan Publishing Co., Inc.
866 Third Avenue
New York, New York 10022

McDougal, Littell & Co.
P.O. Box 1667
Evanston, Illinois 60204

Mentor Book Company
1301 Avenue of the Americas
New York, New York 10019

National Council of Teachers of English
1111 Kenyon Road
Urbana, Illinois 61801

New York State English Council
Alan Nelson, Executive Secretary
Union College Humanities Center
Schenectady, New York 12308

Oxford University Press
200 Madison Avenue
New York, New York 10016

Pendulum Press, Inc.
The Academic Building
Saw Mill Road
West Haven, Connecticut 06516

Prentice-Hall, Inc.
Educational Book Division
Englewood Cliffs, New Jersey 07632

Prentice-Hall Media
150 White Plains Road, Box 186
Tarrytown, New York 10591

Random House, Inc.
201 E. 50th Street
New York, New York 10022

The Reading Lab, Inc.
55 Day Street
South Norwalk, Connecticut 06854

RMI Educational Films, Inc.
701 Westport Road
Kansas City, Missouri 64111

S-L Film Productions
P. O. Box 41108
Los Angeles, California 90041

Scholastic Book Services
904 Sylvan Avenue
Englewood Cliffs, New Jersey 07632

Scholastic Records
906 Sylvan Avenue
Englewood Cliffs, New Jersey 07632

Scott Education Division
104 Lower Westfield Road
Holyoke, Massachusetts 01040

Silver Burdett Company
Morristown, New Jersey 07960

Teachers College Press
1234 Amsterdam Avenue
New York, New York 10027

Teachers & Writers Collaborative
490 Hudson Street
New York, New York 10014

The University of Chicago Press
5801 Ellis Avenue
Chicago, Illinois 60637

J. Weston Walch, Publisher
Portland, Maine 04104

Westwood Educational Production
701 Westport Road
Kansas City, Missouri 64111

John Wiley & Sons, Inc.
605 3rd Avenue
New York, New York 10016

H. W. Wilson Co.
950 University Avenue
Bronx, New York 10452

Xerox Educational Publications
Education Center
1250 Fairwood Avenue
Columbus, Ohio 43216

University Film Rental Libraries

University of Arizona
Bureau of Audiovisual Services
Tucson, AZ 85721

Arizona State University
Audio-Visual Center
Tempe, AZ 85281

Boston University
Abraham Krasker Memorial Film Library
School of Education, 765 Commonwealth Avenue
Boston, MA 02215

Buffalo State College
Film Rental Library
1300 Elmwood Avenue
Buffalo, NY 14222

University of Colorado
Bureau of Audiovisual Instruction
University Extension Division
Boulder, CO 80302

Florida State University
Educational Media Center
Tallahassee, FL 32306

University of South Florida
Film Library
4202 Fowler Avenue
Tampa, FL 33620

University of Georgia
Center for Continuing Education
Athens, Ga 30601

University of Illinois
Visual Aids Service
1325 S. Oak Street
Champaign, IL 61820

Indiana University
Audio-Visual Center
Bloomington, IN 47401

University of Iowa
Audiovisual Center
Iowa City, IO 52240

Kent State University
Audio-Visual Services
221 Education Bldg.
Kent, OH 44240

University of Maine
Film Rental Library
Shibles Hall
Orono, ME 04473

University of Michigan
Audio-Visual Educational Center
416 S. 4th Street
Arbor, MI 48103

University of Minnesota
Audio-Visual Extension Service
General Extension Division
2037 University Avenue S.E.
Minneapolis, MN 55455

University of Mississippi
Audio-Visual Education
School of Education
University, MS 38677

University of Missouri
University Extension Division
119 Whitten Hall
Columbia, MO 65201

Eastern New Mexico University
Film Library
Portales, NM 88130

Northern Illinois University
Audio-Visual Center
DeKalb, IL 60115

University of Oklahoma
Extension Division
Educational Materials Services
Audio-Visual Education
Norma, OK 73069

Oklahoma State University
Audio-Visual Center
Stillwater, OK 74074

Oregon State University
Audiovisual Services
Corvallis, OR 97331

Pennsylvania State University
Audio-Visual Aids Library
University Park, PA 16802

University of South Carolina
College of General Studies and Extension
Audio-Visual Division
Columbia, SC 29208

Southern Illinois University
Learning Resources Service
Carbondale, IL 62901

Syracuse University
Film Library
Collendale Campus
1455 E. Colvin Street
Syracuse, NY 13210

University of Texas
Visual Instruction Bureau
Division of Extension
Austin, TX 78712

University of Utah
Educational Media, 207 Milton Bennion Hall
Salt Lake City, UT 84112

University of Washington
Audio-Visual Center
Seattle, WA 09195

University of Wisconsin
Bureau of Audio-Visual Instruction
137 University Avenue
Madison, WI 53701

APPENDIX C

Reproduction Pages

The pages that follow have been provided to facilitate the reproducing of exercises, sample compositions, and materials needed for activities suggested in the preceding pages. Each page is perforated to make removal from this book easier. Once removed, a page can be used in several ways:

1. *For projection with an opaque projector.* No further preparation is necessary if the page is to be used with an opaque projector. Simply insert it in the projector and the page can be viewed by the entire class.
2. *For projection with an overhead projector.* The Reproduction Page must be converted to a transparency for use on an overhead projector. Overlay the Reproduction Page with a blank transparency and run both of them through a copying machine.
3. *For duplication with a spirit duplicator.* A master can be made from the Reproduction Page by overlaying it with a special heat-sensitive spirit master and running both through a copying machine. The spirit master can then be used to reproduce 50 to 100 copies on paper.

ABSURD DRAMA EXERCISE

STAND UP, CLAP YOUR HANDS SLOWLY, AND, EVERY TIME YOU HEAR SOMEONE SAY, "OH, HOW I HATE STUDENTS," SHOUT, "I WAS A STUDENT ONCE!"

COUNT SLOWLY, USING THE NUMBERS *1* THROUGH *10*, BUT MIXING THEM UP, OVER AND OVER.

EVERY TIME YOU HEAR THE NUMBER 5, SHOUT, "OH, HOW I HATE STUDENTS!"

WHENEVER YOU HEAR SOMETHING NEGATIVE SAID, SAY, "OH, THAT'S AWFUL!" GO TO THE PERSON NEAREST YOU AND PAT THAT PERSON ON THE SHOULDER.

IF YOU SEE SOMEONE TOUCH SOMEONE ELSE, SHOUT FOR THE POLICE.

WALK AROUND THE ROOM RECITING ANY POEM THAT YOU CAN REMEMBER. IF YOU CANNOT REMEMBER ONE, MAKE ONE UP.

PRETEND THAT YOU ARE A LARGE CLOCK. WHENEVER YOU HEAR SOMEONE CALL THE POLICE, STRIKE WHATEVER HOUR YOU FEEL LIKE STRIKING.

THERE IS A PERSON SQUATTING IN THE MIDDLE OF THE ROOM. TRY TO SELL THAT PERSON A USED CAR.

YOU ARE A SHOE INSPECTOR. INSPECT THE SHOES OF EVERYONE IN THE ROOM.

YOU ARE TRAPPED IN A HAUNTED HOUSE. TRY TO FIND THE SECRET PASSAGEWAY OUT OF THIS ROOM.

STRIKE UP A CONVERSATION WITH AN EMPTY CHAIR. IF THE CHAIR BORES YOU, MOVE ON TO ANOTHER.

IF YOU SEE SOMEONE TALKING TO A CHAIR, GO SIT IN IT. IF HE STARTS TALKING TO ANOTHER CHAIR, PICK IT UP AND CARRY IT AWAY. IF HE TALKS TO ANOTHER CHAIR, CARRY IT TO THE PERSON WHO IS RECITING A POEM AND ASK THAT PERSON TO RECITE THE POEM TO THE CHAIR. CONTINUE THIS CYCLE AS NECESSARY.

SQUAT IN THE MIDDLE OF THE ROOM. IGNORE ANYTHING THAT IS SAID TO YOU.

YOU ARE A USED CAR. DRIVE AROUND THE ROOM AND FIND THE PERSON WHO IS TRYING TO SELL YOU. TRY TO CONVINCE THE POTENTIAL BUYER THAT YOU REALLY DO NOT WANT TO BE SOLD.

YOU ARE A POLICEMAN. IF SOMEONE CALLS YOU, GO TO THAT PERSON AND FIND OUT WHAT THE PROBLEM IS. TREAT THE PROBLEM IN THE WAY YOU THINK A POLICEMAN WOULD.

TERMS EMPLOYED BY TELEVISION WRITERS

ANGLE—The angle or relationship of the camera to the subject. High Angle would be a bird's-eye view. Other angles include Wide Angle and Low Angle.

CLOSE-UP—A very close view of the subject, perhaps of the head only; sometimes this is a view of only the lips or the hands.

CRANE SHOT—A view taken from a moving platform.

CUT TO—Switching from one scene to another without any transition; as opposed to Dissolve or Fade.

DISSOLVE TO—The gradual fading out of one picture while another picture gradually appears.

DOLLY IN or BACK—Physically moving the camera closer to, or farther from, the subject.

ESTABLISHING SHOT—A large view with no particular focus. Used to set a scene usually.

FADE IN or OUT—To go from a completely blacked out picture to a full picture or vice versa.

FREEZE FRAME—Stop action; the picture is "frozen."

FULL SHOT—A complete view of the subject.

LONG SHOT—A distant view of the subject; sometimes Extremely or Medium Long Shot.

MONTAGE—A quick sequence of shots to indicate time passing rapidly or for emotional impact of some sort.

PAN TO—Remaining stationary, the camera moves horizontally from one side of the scene to another.

REAR PROJECTION—A film shown behind the subject. Television newsmen are sometimes superimposed over scenes of the news.

SLOW MOTION—All the action is artificially slowed down; extremely popular in playbacks of sporting events.

SPLIT SCREEN—The picture is separated into two or more scenes occurring at the same time

STOCK SHOT—Film of something stored in the film library for use whenever a director may want, such as a view of stars for use in space programs.

SUPERIMPOSE OVER—The placing of one scene over another; often titles are superimposed over scenes.

ZOOM IN—To rapidly move in on a particular close shot; often used for sudden, dramatic effect.

Worth noting: Television writers do not give directions for every camera shot to be made. They usually include the directions that they believe are absolutely necessary to communicate their scenes best. Variations are usually left up to the director of the show.

THE WELL-WROUGHT LINE

Directions: *The following famous lines are from well-known plays. You are to select one of these lines from a play you have not read or seen. Put the line into some dramatic situation. Then write the situation, including that line somewhere. You may write a play, a poem, a short story, or an essay. When you finish, find the line in the original play. Does it mean something different from your interpretation?*

A. She speaks, yet she says nothing. (Shakespeare, *Romeo and Juliet*)

B. Life . . . is a tale
Told by an idiot, full of sound and fury,
Signifying nothing. (Shakespeare, *Macbeth*)

C. Cowards die many times before their deaths;
The valiant never taste of death but once. (Shakespeare, *Julius Caesar*)

D. Though this be madness, yet there is method in it. (Shakespeare, *Hamlet*)

E. Excess of wealth is cause of covetousness. (Marlowe, *The Jew of Malta*)

F. He's a wonderful talker, who has the art of telling you nothing in a great harangue. (Molière, *Le Misanthrope*)

G. Though a man be wise,
It is no shame for him to live and learn. (Sophocles, *Antigone*)

H. I have to live for others and not for myself; that's middle class morality. (Shaw, *Pygmalion*)

I. . . . the strongest man in the world is the man who stands alone. (Ibsen, *An Enemy of the People*)

J. You see, we neither love nor hate in my world. We simply have hobbies. (Gore Vidal, *Visit to a Small Planet*)

BE YOUR OWN REVIEWER!

Have you seen a television show or film lately that you would like to tell others about? Maybe it was an excellent production and you would like to recommend it to others. Or perhaps it was terrible and you want to warn them not to waste their time or money. The questions below are intended to be a guide to give you ideas to write about. You do not have to answer all the questions. Pick those that apply only to the work you are reviewing. Then write the review honestly from your own viewpoint. Remember, in order to convince people, you have to explain what you mean.

1. What is the name of this production?

2. If you know them, who are the main actors?

3. What was the main point of the production supposed to be?

4. Did it accomplish its purpose well or not?

5. Was the character portrayal good? Were the characters believable in that situation? Could other actors have done a better job? Who? Why?

6. Was the language believable? Did the characters speak as you would expect people to speak in a similar situation?

7. Was the action believable? Would people behave that way in real life?

8. Did you ever see a similar production that did a better job? A worse job?

9. Would you recommend this production to others? Who? Why?

A GLOSSARY OF DRAMA TERMS

ALLEGORY—A play (or story or poem) in which the characters and events have meanings other than the obvious surface meanings. For example, in the play *Everyman*, we encounter characters such as Good Deeds, Death, and Knowledge. They are portrayed as people, but they represent more. Yet they are also more than merely symbols, having both human character and qualities. For that reason, Ossie Davis's *Purlie Victorious* is an allegorical comedy.

ANTICLIMAX—The substitution of an unexpected, usually unimportant, event when one expects a play to build toward a climax. Used on purpose, it creates humor; used accidentally, it weakens the structure of the play.

ASIDE—A comment by a character onstage that is intended to be heard by the audience but not by the other characters.

CATHARSIS—Either (1) when the audience learns through the mistakes and behaviors of a character in a play how to avoid those wrong behaviors; or (2) when the audience is, according to Aristotle, purged or made psychologically whole by sharing the emotions of the main character but not the actual punishments.

CLIMAX—The point of greatest dramatic importance. Usually found near the end of a work, climax has been called the turning point of the action, when what has been going well suddenly turns against the main character (as in tragedy), or vice versa.

COMEDY—As opposed to tragedy; a type of drama that results in a pleasant ending. Comedy may be funny or not. Generally, in comedy the world is viewed as ultimately a good place. Humorous comedy results from incongruous speech and behaviors.

CONVENTION—The willing acceptance by both author and audience of certain procedures that are not realistic. Examples are: when an actor pretends to be dead, when days pass in seconds, when we accept artificial scenery and pretend it is real. It is also a convention, or an accepted practice, to applaud at the end of a production (assuming that we have enjoyed it).

DENOUEMENT—The final resolution or revealing of events in a play. In comedy, events fall together. In tragedy, events fall apart.

DRAMA—Either (1) any representation of life on a stage employing dialogue and conventions; or (2) a serious play but not necessarily a tragedy.

EXPOSITION—The point or points in a play in which the playwright provides needed information about characters or past events. Usually, but not always, it occurs at the beginning of the play.

FORESHADOWING—Hints to the audience of what will happen later. Characters typically provide foreshadowing without knowing they are doing so.

MELODRAMA—A funny tragedy in which the characters are stereotypes, having little motivation for their actions, and in which the plot is all-important, circumstances being more important than carefully structured actions.

MIME or PANTOMIME—In this form, the characters act through gestures, facial expressions, and other actions, but without talk.

MOTIVATION—The cause or reason for a character's behavior. By knowing the motivation of a character, we understand the character better.

SOLILOQUY—A relatively long speech in which the character talks to the audience or to no one in particular, expressing the character's innermost thoughts or providing background information for the audience. It is not common in modern plays.

TRAGEDY—A form of serious drama in which the main characters must commit themselves to specific courses of action in order to accomplish their goals, whether the goals are evil or good. Inevitably, the main character fails. In classic tragedy, this failure is the result of a *tragic flaw*, or important character weakness, which leads to the character's downfall.

THE SHORT STORY

I. Characteristics of the Short Story

II. History of the Short Story

III. Types of Short Stories

    A. The Plot Story

    B. The Action Story

    C. The Plotless Story

    D. The Episodic Story

E. The Character Story

F. The Thematic Story

G. The Psychological Story

THEME

Directions: *Read the following questions after you have read a story.*

A.   Does the story say anything about life (the theme), or is the story simply a description of a character or tale of a series of events?

B.   What does the story say about life?

C.   How does the author reveal the theme? Does one of the characters state it? Does the author tell you? Do you have to realize it yourself?

D.   Do you agree with the theme of the story, if there is one?

E.   Is the theme an important theme for people to think about, or is it a very minor theme, appropriate to only a few people or for people in a limited period of time, or is the theme hardly worth considering?

F.   Is the author trying to convince you of his point of view through his development of the theme, or is the theme something that many people can agree with?

G.   Is the theme related very closely to the setting, to the plot, or to the characters? Explain your answers.

SETTING

Directions: *Setting may tell us something about a story that we may not have noticed. After you finish reading a story, answer the following questions:*

A. When and where did the story happen?

B. Could the story have happened somewhere else? At another time?

C. How long a period of time is encompassed by the events of the story?

D. Would it have changed the story any if the author had shortened or lengthened the time period?

E. Does the author follow one time line from beginning to end or jump back and forth in time (flashbacks)?

F. If the author does jump around in time, would the story have been different if the story were rewritten with time moving chronologically from beginning to end?

G. Is the setting important to the story? Why or why not?

H. Does the setting influence the plot or the characters in any way?

I. Is the setting believable?

J. Does the setting help create a particular mood? Is that mood essential to the story?

K. How much time does the author spend describing the setting? At what points in the story? Is this done on purpose?

SETTING

Directions: *Read the selection below from D. H. Lawrence's "Tickets, Please." Then answer the questions that follow and be prepared to discuss your answers.*

There is in the Midlands a single-line tramway system which boldly leaves the county town and plunges off into the black, industrial country-side, up hill and down dale, through the long ugly villages of workmen's houses, over canals and railways, past churches perched high and nobly over the smoke and shadows, through stark, grimy cold little market-places, tilting away in a rush past cinemas and shops down to the hollow where the collieries are, then up again, past a little rural church, under the ash trees, on in a rush to the terminus, the last little ugly place of industry, the cold little town that shivers on the edge of the wild, gloomy country beyond. There the green and creamy coloured tramcar seems to pause and purr with curious satisfaction. But in a few minutes—the clock on the turret of the Co-operative Wholesale Society's shops gives the time—away it starts once more on the adventure. Again there are the reckless swoops downhill, bouncing the loops: again the chilly wait in the hill-top market-place: again the breathless slithering round the precipitous drop under the church: again the patient halts at the loops, waiting for the outcoming car: so on and on, for two long hours, till at last the city looms beyond the fat gasworks, the narrow factories draw near, we are in the sordid streets of the great town, once more we sidle to a standstill at our terminus, abashed by the great crimson and cream-coloured city cars, but still perky, jaunty, somewhat dare-devil, green as a jaunty sprig of parsley out of a black colliery garden.

A. Notice (perhaps list on paper) the adjectives the author employs. What sort of mood is he creating? And in this case, do the adjectives change in feeling anywhere? Why does the author include both categories of adjectives? Which indicates what the story might be like? How do you know?

B. List all the adverbs. What do they indicate to us?

C. List all the things (objects, people, animals, machines, etc.) that the author includes. Do they have anything in common? If not, are they placed there for contrast? Why does the author choose to talk about those things and only those things?

CHARACTER

Directions: *Pick one of the characters from a short story you have just read Where the questions below say CHARACTER, substitute the name of the character you have picked. Then answer the questions.*

A. CHARACTER has just been given a ticket for speeding. How will CHARACTER respond?

B. In a contest sponsored by a commercial company, CHARACTER has won $100,000. Describe what CHARACTER will do with the money.

C. CHARACTER is thinking about getting married (after a divorce, after the death of the spouse, etc.). What characteristics will CHARACTER look for in a marriage partner? How do you know?

D. CHARACTER wants to buy a new house. What type of home will CHARACTER look for? Where will it be located? How much will it cost? What kind of landscaping will it have?

E. You offer to give CHARACTER a ticket to any type of sporting event CHARACTER would enjoy seeing. What type of sporting event will CHARACTER choose? Why?

F. You are the director of a movie based upon the short story which you have just read. Whom will you cast in the role of CHARACTER? Why?

G. CHARACTER has just entered a restaurant that serves every type of food in the world. The waiter asks CHARACTER, "What would you like?" CHARACTER replies: _____ . Explain the choice.

CHARACTERIZATION QUALITIES

Directions: *Pick a character from a short story you have just read and answer the following questions. Be prepared to discuss your answers.*

Is CHARACTER more like:

A. May or December?

B. A Subaru or a Mercedes Benz?

C. Brown or blue?

D. A snowstorm or a rainy day?

E. The letter *A*, the letter *M*, or the letter *Z*?

F. Vanilla ice cream or charlotte russe?

G. New York, San Francisco, Salt Lake City, or New Orleans?

H. A hammer or a nail?

I. A short story or a poem?

J. White, rye, or pumpernickel bread?

K. A TV quiz show or a news report?

L. Soap or dirt?

M. Fire, water, earth, or air?

N. A cathedral, a pup tent, or a log cabin?

O. Africa, Asia, Australia, Europe, or South America?

P. A horse show, a hockey match, or a track-and-field event?

Q. A filing cabinet or a garbage pail?

R. A lock or a key?

S. A forest fire or a mountain stream?

T. The comics, the sports section, the business report, or the editorial page?

U. A wood lathe or a kitchen stove?

QUALITIES OF A CHARACTER

Directions: *Either check the words below that describe a character in a story you have just read or use the most appropriate ones in your written character description:*

Mental Qualities

intelligent	unintelligent
educated	unschooled
smart	dumb
wise	ignorant
gifted	simple
clever	puerile
ingenious	obtuse
brilliant	vacuous
learned	narrow-minded
scholarly	shallow
astute	dull
competent	incompetent
sensible	unreasonable
talented	incapable
intellectual	bigoted
precocious	ignorant
rational	irrational

Moral Qualities

moral	immoral
kind	cruel
considerate	inconsiderate
idealistic	unprincipled
innocent	corrupt
righteous	vile
upstanding	deceitful
truthful	lying
honest	unscrupulous
honorable	dishonorable
loyal	untrustworthy
helpful	self-centered
virtuous	dissolute
pure	vulgar
puritanical	degenerate
austere	sensual
polite	insulting
respectable	base

Physical Qualities

strong	weak
healthy	sickly
handsome	hideous
beautiful	ugly
pretty	graceless
cute	emaciated
robust	clumsy
hardy	awkward
dainty	grotesque
delicate	odious
charming	coarse
ravishing	repulsive
adroit	ungainly
skillful	unkempt
lively	decrepit

Social Qualities

cooperative	contentious
hospitable	inhospitable
congenial	impolite
cheerful	sullen
supportive	antagonistic
urbane	boorish
worldly	provincial
debonair	brusque
suave	obsequious
elegant	unpolished
courteous	petulant
tactful	crude
cordial	crabby
convivial	critical
encouraging	caustic
merry	grumpy

UNDERSTANDING CHARACTERS

Directions: *Use the following questions whenever you have to analyze and understand characters:*

A. Who are the characters in the story?

B. What are these characters like?

C. Is there a common problem that all of the characters must face?

D. Do the characters fall into particular groups? Are these groups against one another?

E. Is one of the characters the main character, or are there several main characters?

F. Do the characters change or grow as individuals, or are they alike throughout the story?

G. If the characters change, is there a good reason for their change? If so, what is it?

H. If there are any minor characters, what is their purpose in the story? To help move the plot along? To provide a change of pace in the story? To balance one character against another, or to provide a contrast to a main character? To help explain the motivations of the main character or characters?

I. Are the characters realistic? Stereotyped? Unbelievable? Romantic?

J. Are all the characters necessary to the story, or could the author have left some of them out?

K. Does the author let you know a great deal about the characters, or does the author tell you about one main characteristic only?

L. How important is our knowing more about the characters, or do we appreciate the story without knowing much about the characters? Does this factor indicate something about the author's purpose in writing the story?

JOHARI WINDOW

	Self Blind	Self Aware
Other blind	Character or others in story not aware of these aspects of the character; an omniscient author would be.	Character is aware, but does not let other characters know about these aspects of character.
Other aware	Other characters realize this about the character, but the character does not.	Both the character and others in the story are aware of these characteristics.

	Self blind	Self aware
Other blind		
Other aware		

COAT OF ARMS

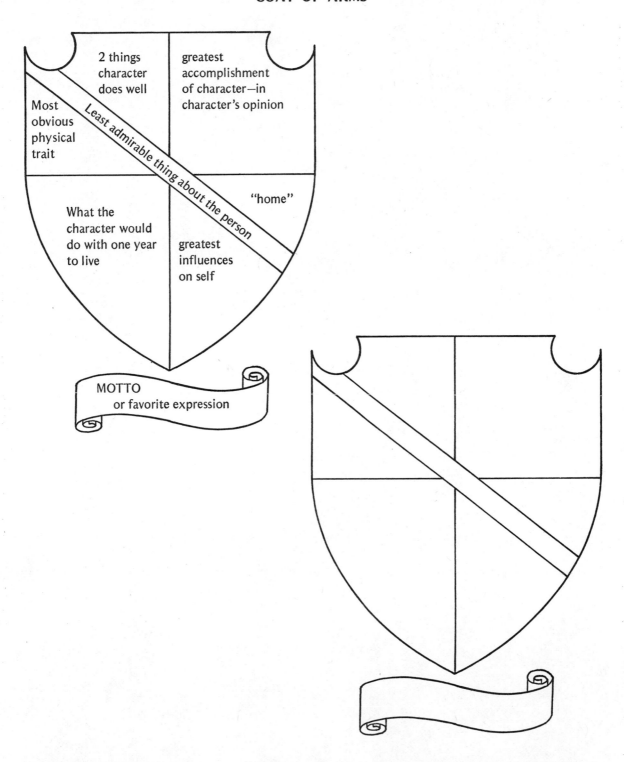

CONFLICT

Directions: *Answer the following questions and discuss your answers in class:*

Is the conflict significant or trivial?

Consider the following examples for discussion:

A. Your alarm clock goes off in the morning. Should you get up or not?

B. You see a classmate cheating on an exam. Should you report him or not?

C. You want money from your parents to buy a new record or tape. You know they consider that an unnecessary purchase. You could tell them that the money is for school supplies. Should you? Suppose you know that your parents cheat on their income tax report every year?

D. You believe in saving the environment. Every demand for new electricity justifies more strip-mining and power-plant pollution. Yet, you would really like to have a stereo component outfit or a radial arm saw.

E. If you move away from your family, you can get a better job and move up in the world. Yet, by moving you are leaving your parents and other members of your family.

F. You know that stealing is wrong, but if you do not steal a little food from the food stand, you may starve to death.

Is the conflict worth writing about?

Consider the following examples for discussion:

A. Football team A is leading football team B by a score of 62–0 in the last quarter.

B. Football team A is leading football team B by a score of 14–13 in the last quarter.

C. A heavy snowstorm has just covered the tulips, which are blooming. One of the tulips struggles to keep its stalk from breaking.

D. The army of Napoleon has just met the army of Wellington.

E. George Washington does not consider Gen. Charles Lee to be a good officer. Gen. Charles Lee is very popular with the Continental Congress.

Is the conflict believable?

Consider the following examples for discussion:

A. The beautiful belle of the ball has to leave her prince charming at the dance or else her fine carriage will turn into a pumpkin, her prancing horses into mice, and she into a scullery maid.

B. Having lost all his money in a bad investment, the businessman is considering committing suicide.

C. The teenage girl has just met a new boy in school. Should she tell him that she has fallen in love with him?

D. An ant has found the largest bread crumb he has ever seen. Should he struggle to bring it in by himself, or should he get help and lose some of the glory for the find?

E. The spaceman must disentangle himself from the clutches of the mile-high space monster.

F. The president of the United States has just asked you to accompany him to Russia on a diplomatic visit as his key adviser. Should you accept?

TONE AND CHARACTER

Directions: *Answer the following questions about a story you have just read:*

A. Would the author be sorry to see this character die?

B. Would the author invite any of the characters in the story to a party at the author's house?

C. If the character is the opposite sex from the author, is the character the type of person the author would be likely to marry, assuming author and character to be capable of doing so?

D. Would the author trust the character with the author's life?

E. Would the author want the character to handle the author's money?

F. If the author knew the character, would the author want to help the character?

G. Do you believe the author would ever consider the character a friend?

H. If this short story were made into a movie or TV show and if the author could choose the person to play this character, whom would the author choose?

I. How does the author feel about the situation this character is in?

J. Does the situation relate in some way to the central problem (or problems) of the story?

K. How does the author feel about the character's behavior in the story?

L. What is the author's attitude toward this character?

EVALUATING LITERATURE

Directions: *Use the following questions to help you evaluate literature you have read:*

A. Theme

1. What is the theme of each short story?

2. Which theme means more to you as a human being? Why?

3. Which theme has more meaning for mankind in general? Explain.

4. If you were asked to argue against one of the themes, which would you choose to argue against and why? What would you say?

5. State whether you believe the following elements of each story were chosen by the author in order to illustrate the theme well: (a) the characters; (b) the setting; (c) the plot.

6. In general, which author develops the theme better?

B. Plot

1. Summarize the plot of each short story.

2. Which plot is more true to life? Why?

3. Which plot is more interesting? Why?

4. Is there anything unbelievable about either plot?

5. Do you believe that the characters involved in each plot would have behaved the same way if the events had happened in real life?

6. Is the plot of each story likely to happen in the setting the author chooses? Why or why not?

7. Is the plot predictable? If so, when did you first realize how it would turn out? Did you enjoy the story less because of that? If the plot was not predictable, was the ending a complete surprise? If so, was the surprise justified, or did the author end the story just to get it over with?

8. In general, which plot is developed better?

C. Setting

1. Describe the setting used in each story.

2. Is the setting essential in each story, or could any setting be used?

3. If the setting is essential, why? Does the setting enable the plot to develop? Does the setting influence the behavior or personalities of the characters? Is the setting related to the theme?

4. Is the setting believable? Is it realistic? After answering the first two questions, consider whether your answers reveal anything about the author's purpose in writing the story.

5. In general, which story makes the better use of setting?

D. Characterization

1. Describe the main characters in each short story.

2. Did you find each of those characters to be believable? Explain.

3. If any of those characters were not realistic, was there a reason for that lack of realism?

4. Explain why each of the characters was essential to the plot. If any were not essential, explain why not.

5. Was each character fully developed or shallow, round or flat, or stereotyped or realistic? Did the author develop them that way on purpose, or was his portrayal of the characters weak?

6. Did any of the characters relate in some way to the theme? If so, how?

7. Did the setting have any influence upon any of the characters? If so, how?

8. In general, which author makes the better use of the characters?

E. Summary Evaluation

1. If you had to decide which of the two stories was the better, what would your decision be, and why? In order to help yourself answer this question, reread your answers to the last questions in sections A, B, C, and D.

TYPES OF POEMS

I. Lyric—an imaginative, melodic poem that conveys subjective feelings
   A. Songs
   B. Sonnets
   C. Elegies and epitaphs
   D. Epigrams
   E. Dramatic poems

II. Narrative—a poem that tells a story
   A. Epics
   B. Ballads
   C. Fables
   D. Metrical romances

POETRY TERMS

Alliteration— the repetition of sounds in words that are close to each other (usually initial sounds).
ex.: "*M*any a *momm*y has clothing to *m*end."

Assonance—the repetition of vowel sounds.
ex.: "The b*a*d c*a*t stole my h*a*t and r*a*n."

Consonance—the repetition of consonant sounds.
ex.: "The *s*nake hi*ss*ed and *s*lithered *s*lowly through the gra*ss*."

Cliché—a word or phrase that has been used so many times that it has lost its original impact and is now stereotyped and too familiar.
ex.: red as a rose, tried and true, happy as a lark

Figure of speech—a changing of the word order or meaning of words in order to gain greater impact upon the meaning. Some figures of speech are similes, metaphors, metonymies, personifications, and synechdoches.

Imagery—the use of words to represent sensations. Images may be literal ("The sun was hot-yellow") or imaginary ("The sun's stare turned me into jello").

Lyric—the use of words so that the sounds are melodic, or "sing."

Metaphor—an implied comparison; one item may be given the characteristics of another or may be described in terms of the other.
ex.: "My car is my friend—he takes me where I want."

Metonymy—a figure of speech in which an object is referred to by a term closely associated with it.
ex.: "We are waiting to hear from the White House." *White House* is a metonymy for the president or his associates.

Onomatopoeia—the suggestion of a particular sound by means of a word.
ex.: the bee *buzzed*, her dress *swishes*, the saw *whined*

Personification—giving an inanimate object the characteristics of an animate object.
ex.: "The door complained when I opened it."

Refrain—lines that are repeated at the ends of different stanzas.

Rhyme—the repetition of like sounds in different words, especially in the last syllables and when the words are physically near one another.

Simile—a direct comparison using the words *like* or *as*.
    ex.: "He is as constant as the tide."
       "Her hair is like coarse wire."

Stanza—a group of lines repeated in similar groups throughout a poem.

Symbol—an object, person, or event that stands for something in addition to itself.
    ex.: The American flag stands for the United States.
       A handshake is symbolic of friendship.

Synechdoche—a figure of speech in which part of an object is used to represent the entire object.
    ex.: "hired hands" "set the table"

Verse—a single line of poetry; or poetry in general, usually poetry that has rhythm and rhyme.

POETIC TECHNIQUES IN PROSE

Directions: *Edgar Allan Poe began his short story, "The Fall of the House of Usher," with a paragraph that is very poetic. Read this paragraph and answer the questions below it. As you read, pay particular attention to the sounds the words make, to the comparisons the author makes, and to places where Poe tells you how he feels.*

During the whole of a dull, dark, and soundless day in the autumn of the year, when the clouds hung oppressively low in the heavens, I had been passing alone, on horseback, through a singularly dreary tract of country; and at length I found myself, as the shades of evening drew on, within view of the melancholy House of Usher. I know not how it was—but, with the first glimpse of the building, a sense of insufferable gloom pervaded my spirit. I say insufferable; for the feeling was unrelieved by any of that half-pleasurable, because poetic, sentiment, with which the mind usually receives even the sternest natural images of the desolate or terrible. I looked upon scene before me—upon the mere house, and the simple landscape features of the domain—upon a few rank sedges—and upon a few white trunks of decayed trees—with an utter depression of soul which I can compare to no earthly sensation more properly than to the after-dream of the reveler upon opium—the bitter lapse into everyday life—the hideous dropping off of the veil. There was an iciness, a sinking, a sickening of the heart—an unredeemed dreariness of thought which no goading of the imagination could torture into aught of the sublime. What was it—I paused to think—what was it that so unnerved me in the contemplation of the House of Usher? It was a mystery all insoluble; nor could I grapple with the shadowy fancies that crowded upon me as I pondered. I was forced to fall back upon the unsatisfactory conclusion that while, beyond doubt, there are combinations of very simple natural objects which have the power of thus affecting us, still the analysis of this power lies among considerations beyond our depth. It was possible, I reflected, that a mere different arrangement of the particulars of the scene, of the details of the picture, would be sufficient to modify, or perhaps to annihilate, its capacity for sorrowful impression; and, acting upon this idea, I reined my horse to the precipitous brink of a black and lurid tarn that lay in unruffled lustre by the dwelling, and gazed down—but with a shudder even more thrilling than before—upon the remodeled and inverted images of the gray sedge, and the ghastly tree-stems, and the vacant and eye-like windows.

1. List all the examples of alliteration that you can find in this selection. What types of sound are they? How do they make you feel?

2. List all the metaphors that Poe employs. What is the purpose of each metaphor?

3. Underline all the places where Poe tells you how he feels rather than where he describes the scene to let you determine how he feels. Now circle all places where Poe describes rather than tells. Which occurs more often? Do you think this is good or bad? Why?

4. What aspects of the house has Poe selected to describe or tell about? What other things could he have talked about? What does this indicate about his purpose in writing this passage?

5. Look at the sentence beginning with "There was an iciness. . . ." Does Poe repeat the idea of iciness with other words or images? Or does he change from iciness to some other image? What is his purpose?

6. What colors does Poe talk about? Why did he select those particular colors? Could he have used any other colors to convey the same mood?

7. Try to arrange this selection into the form of a poem. You may have to leave some words out, but try to use as much of the original version as possible. Which version do you think conveys the mood better, yours or Poe's?

MELVILLE AS A POET

Directions: *The following is Herman Melville's description of a whale's head. As you read it, note how he compares an object (the head) that you may never have seen with objects that may be familiar to you. Underline these comparisons. Then list the poetic techniques that the author uses. How well does he use those techniques? Do they make his description clearer or more confusing? Explain.*

Crossing the deck, let us now have a good long look at the Right Whale's head.

As in general shape the noble Sperm Whale's head may be compared to a Roman war-chariot (especially the front, where it is so broadly rounded); so at a broad view, the Right Whale's head bears a rather inelegant resemblance to a gigantic galliot-toed shoe. Two hundred years ago an old Dutch voyager likened its shape to that of a shoemaker's last. And in this same last or shoe, that old woman of the nursery tale, with the swarming brood, might very comfortably be lodged, she and all her progeny.

But as you come nearer to this great head it begins to assume different aspects, according to your point of view. If you stand on its summit and look at these two *f*-shaped spout-holes, you would take the whole head for an enormous bass-viol, and the spiracles, the apertures in its sounding-board. Then, again, if you fix your eye upon this strange, crested, comb-like incrustation of the top of the mass—this green, barnacled thing, which the Greenlanders call the "crown," and the Southern fishers the "bonnet" of the Right Whale; fixing your eyes solely on this, you would take the head for the trunk of some huge oak, with a bird's nest in its crotch. At any rate, when you watch those live crabs that nestle here on this bonnet, such an idea will be almost sure to occur to you; unless, indeed, your fancy has been fixed by the technical term "crown" also bestowed upon it; in which case you will take great interest in thinking how this mighty monster is actually a diademed king of the sea, whose green crown has been put together for him in this marvelous manner. But if this whale be a king, he is a very sulky looking fellow to grace a diadem. Look at that hanging lower lip! what a huge sulk and pout is there! a sulk and pout, by carpenter's measurement, about twenty feet long and five feet deep; a sulk and pout that will yield you some 500 gallons of oil and more.

Herman Melville
Moby-Dick: or, *The Whale*

EMILY DICKINSON'S USE OF WORDS

Directions: *Read Emily Dickinson's poem. Read it again. Think about the specific words she uses to describe her subject. Then answer the questions that follow.*

A narrow Fellow in the Grass
Occasionally rides—
You may have met Him—did you not
His notice sudden is—

The Grass divides as with a Comb—
A spotted shaft is seen—
And then it closes at your feet
And opens further on—

He likes a Boggy Acre
A Floor too cool for Corn—
Yet when a Boy, and Barefoot—
I more than once at Noon
Have passed, I thought, a Whip lash
Unbraiding in the Sun
When stooping to secure it
It wrinkled, and was gone—

Several of Nature's People
I know, and they know me—
I feel for them a transport
Of cordiality

But never met this Fellow
Attended, or alone
Without a tighter breathing
And Zero at the Bone—

Explain why you think Dickinson chose the following metaphors:

1. Why *narrow* (1.1)? Why not *thin*? Or *skinny*?

2. Why *rides* (1.2)? Why not *travels*? Or *slithers*? Or *slinks*?

3. Explain the image of the grass dividing "as with a Comb—" (1.5). Is that what happens when a snake moves through grass?

4. Why *shaft* (1.6)? Why not *rope*? How does a snake move?

5. Draw or explain "a Whip lash/Unbraiding in the Sun." What is the snake doing here?

6. Why does Dickinson use the word *wrinkled* (1.16)? Are there more accurate metaphors possible, such as *unwound*?

7. What is another way of saying "Zero at the Bone—"? What is a cliché that many people use to mean the same thing as "Zero at the Bone—"? (List as many responses as possible on the board and then ask if any are better—some may be. Substitute them at the end of this poem and determine with the class whether these other versions are better or not and why.)

EVALUATING IMAGES

Directions: *Consider the following images that are intended to describe women. Which is the best image? Which is the worst? Why? If you were a woman being described this way, how would you feel? If you were a man whose wife was being described this way, how would you feel? Why? If you think the way you would feel depends upon the situation, explain what the possible situations might be and then answer the questions above.*

    A. She was a phantom of delight

    B. O my luve is like a red, red rose

    C.   the youthful hue
       Sits on thy skin like morning dew

    D. She walks in beauty, like the night

    E. O Helen fair, beyond compare!

    F. Her face is like the milky way i' the sky

G. Was ever book containing such vile matter
    So fairly bound?

H. 36-24-36

SOME LOGICAL FALLACIES

"Logical Fallacies" are attempts, purposefully or accidentally, to persuade through incorrect thinking. They may be used on purpose to twist or cloud or hide the truth. If not used purposefully, they are examples of weak thinking.

ARGUMENT TO THE MAN (AD HOMINEM): Arguing against the person rather than the person's ideas: "How can you believe a convict?"

BANDWAGON: Arguing that something is right because it is popular: "Most people do this—they can't all be wrong."

BEGGING THE QUESTION: Assuming something is true before proven true: "High school students can't write because they watch too much television." (Is it true that they cannot write?) "You wouldn't want to hire a man who was arrested, would you?"

FALSE COMPARISON (FALSE ANALOGY): Comparing things that are not truly comparable: "If Abraham Lincoln became president of the United States, so can you."

EITHER/OR FALLACY (FALSE DILEMMA): Providing only two choices when many more may exist: "If you don't support me, then I'll know you're my enemy." "Work hard or you will never be happy."

HASTY GENERALIZATION: Coming to a conclusion without enough information: "These students did poorly on their first essays—their teachers didn't teach them anything." "I just failed the test—teachers sure are hard here!"

NON SEQUITUR: A conclusion that does not follow from the evidence: "Many lambs did not survive the winter—the coyote population must be increasing."

SYNTACTIC ANALYSIS SHEET

Speaker or author's name:
Title of selection analyzed:
Additional data to identify source:

A. no. of sentences analyzed _____

B. average sentence length (no. of words), or average t-unit length (main clause with all subordinate elements) _____

C. average no. of subordinate clauses per sentence _____

D. av. no. subordinate clauses beginning sentence _____

E. av. no. prepositional phrases _____

F. av. no. prepositional phrases at beginning _____

G. av. no. of adjectives _____

H. av. no. of parallel single words _____

I. av. no. of parallel phrases _____

J. av. no. of parallel clauses _____

K. av. no. of transitional words or phrases _____

L. av. no. of similies or metaphors _____

M. av. no. of letters per word _____

N. av. no. of words with Latin or Greek roots _____

O. memorable word choices: maxims, metaphors, etc. _____

READING INTEREST INVENTORY

1. Name one novel that you did not enjoy reading.

2. What was your favorite novel? Why?

3. What is your favorite nonfiction book? Why?

4. What magazines do you read regularly?

5. What is your favorite television program? Why?

6. What was your favorite movie? Why?

7. Do you have any hobbies? If so, what?

8. Do you work at a regular job? What?

9. If you could choose the career that you would have for the rest of your life, what would it be?

10. What do you enjoy most about English class?

11. What activity do you enjoy least in English class?

12. Name three living people that you admire most in the world.

A.

B.

C.

13. If you could be like one historical person, who would that be?

14. What subject do you enjoy most in school?

15. What subject do you enjoy least in school?

16. If you had three wishes, what would they be?

17. If you ever wrote a book, what would its title be?

18. What would you like to change most about conditions in the world today?

19. Do you read any newspapers or magazines regularly? If so, what are they?

20. If there is anything special that you feel like writing about now, go ahead.

READING INTEREST INVENTORY

Please put an X in the column that best describes how you feel about reading these books.

	1 Like	2 Like a little	3 Dislike	4 Dislike very much
1. Reading books	( )	( )	( )	( )
2. Reading books about real people	( )	( )	( )	( )
3. Reading books that are funny	( )	( )	( )	( )
4. Reading adventure books	( )	( )	( )	( )
5. Reading books about hobbies	( )	( )	( )	( )
6. Reading books about the same problems you have	( )	( )	( )	( )
7. Reading mystery books	( )	( )	( )	( )
8. Reading books about family life	( )	( )	( )	( )
9. Reading books about romance	( )	( )	( )	( )
10. Reading science-fiction books	( )	( )	( )	( )
11. Reading sports books	( )	( )	( )	( )
12. Reading books about teenage problems	( )	( )	( )	( )
13. Reading books about animals	( )	( )	( )	( )
14. Reading books about the past	( )	( )	( )	( )
15. Reading books about the present	( )	( )	( )	( )
16. Reading books about love	( )	( )	( )	( )
17. Reading books about religion	( )	( )	( )	( )
18. Reading books with a lot of violence	( )	( )	( )	( )
19. Reading books about social problems	( )	( )	( )	( )
20. Reading books about people like you	( )	( )	( )	( )
21. Reading books about different people	( )	( )	( )	( )
22. Reading books about people younger than you	( )	( )	( )	( )
23. Reading books about people older than you	( )	( )	( )	( )
24. Reading books about people near your age	( )	( )	( )	( )
25. Reading books about people in cities	( )	( )	( )	( )
26. Reading books about people in the country	( )	( )	( )	( )
27. Reading books about people in the suburbs	( )	( )	( )	( )
28. Reading books that seem real	( )	( )	( )	( )

29. What is your favorite magazine? _____

30. What is the best book you have ever read? _____

RATIONALE FOR LITERATURE SELECTION

School:

Teacher:

Title of selection:

Grade or course:

Approximate date(s) selection will be used:

This selection will be:

_____ studied by the entire class

_____ recommended to individual students

_____ optional reading

The selection is part of a larger study of:

Ways in which the selection is especially appropriate for students in this class:

Ways in which the selection is especially pertinent to the objectives of this course or unit:

Special problems that might arise in relation to the selection and some planned activities that handle each problem:

Some other appropriate selections an individual student might read in place of this one:

This form is based on an original prepared by Diane P. Shugert, Chair, NEATE Committee on the Profession.

CITIZEN'S REQUEST FOR RECONSIDERATION OF A BOOK*

Author   Hardcover   Paperback

Title

Publisher (if known)

Request initiated by _____

Telephone _____   Address _____

City _____   Zone _____

Complainant represents

     _____ himself

     _____ (name organization) _____

     _____ (identify other group) _____

1. To what in the book do you object? (Please be specific: cite pages.)

   _____

   _____

2. What do you feel might be the result of reading this book?

   _____

   _____

3. For what age group would you recommend this book?

   _____

4. Is there anything good about this book?

   _____

   _____

*National Council of Teachers of English

5. Did you read the entire book? _____ What parts?

   _____

6. Are you aware of the judgment of this book by literary critics?

   _____

7. What do you believe is the theme of this book?

   _____

   _____

8. What would you like your school to do about this book?
   _____ do not assign it to my child
   _____ withdraw it from all students as well as from my child
   _____ send it back to the English department office for reevaluation

9. In its place, what book of equal literary quality would you recommend that would convey as valuable a picture and perspective of our civilization?

   _____ _____

                                             _____
                                             Signature of Complainant

Feedback Form

Your comments about this book will be very helpful to us in making revisions in *A Guidebook for Teaching Literature*. Please tear out the form that appears on the following page and use it to let us know your reactions to *A Guidebook for Teaching Literature*. The authors promise a personal reply. Mail the form to:

Dr. Raymond J. Rodrigues and
Dr. Dennis Badaczewski
c/o Longwood Division
Allyn and Bacon, Inc.
470 Atlantic Avenue
Boston, Massachusetts 02210

Your school: _____

Address: _____

City and state: _____

Date: _____

Dr. Raymond J. Rodrigues and
Dr. Dennis Badaczewski
c/o Longwood Division
Allyn and Bacon, Inc.
470 Atlantic Avenue
Boston, Massachusetts 02210

Dear Ray and Dennis:

My name is _____ and I wanted to tell you what I thought of your book *A Guidebook for Teaching Literature.* I liked certain things about the book, including:

I do, however, feel that the book could be improved in the following ways:

There were some other things that I wish the book had included, such as:

Here is something that happened in my class when I used an idea from your book:

Sincerely,